THE
COMMITMENT

ALSO BY DAN SAVAGE

Skipping Towards Gomorrah
The Kid
Savage Love

THE
COMMITMENT
Love, Sex, Marriage, and My Family

DAN SAVAGE

DUTTON

DUTTON
Published by Penguin Group (USA) Inc.
375 Hudson Street, New York, New York 10014, U.S.A.
Penguin Group (Canada), 90 Eglinton Avenue East, Suite 700, Toronto, Ontario, Canada M4P 2Y3
(a division of Pearson Penguin Canada Inc.); Penguin Books Ltd., 80 Strand, London WC2R 0RL,
England; Penguin Ireland, 25 St Stephen's Green, Dublin 2, Ireland (a division of Penguin Books
Ltd); Penguin Group (Australia), 250 Camberwell Road, Camberwell, Victoria 3124, Australia (a divi-
sion of Pearson Australia Group Pty Ltd); Penguin Books India Pvt Ltd, 11 Community Centre,
Panchsheel Park, New Delhi – 110 017, India; Penguin Books (NZ), cnr Airborne and Rosedale
Roads, Albany, Auckland 1310, New Zealand (a division of Pearson New Zealand Ltd); Penguin Books
(South Africa) (Pty) Ltd, 24 Sturdee Avenue, Rosebank, Johannesburg 2196, South Africa

Penguin Books Ltd, Registered Offices: 80 Strand, London WC2R 0RL, England

Published by Dutton, a member of Penguin Group (USA) Inc.

 REGISTERED TRADEMARK—MARCA REGISTRADA

ISBN 0-525-94907-0

Printed in the United States of America
Set in Galliard
Designed by Leonard Telesca

For my mother

Contents

THE
COMMITMENT

PART I

Proposals

—1—
Road Trip

I can't shake the feeling that I've lived this moment before.

Maybe that's because, like Jennifer Lopez walking into divorce court, I *have* lived this moment before—over and over, again and again, for close to ten years now. Consequently, a sense of dread creeps over me when I'm about to get into a car with my boyfriend, Terry. For I know that just as soon as I buckle my seat belt, he will inflict the same headache on me that he's inflicted on me hundreds of times before. It's a pounding headache that prevents me from reading or sleeping or doing anything at all—anything, that is, except for fantasizing about the elaborate murder/suicide that presents the only hope of ending this misery.

For I know that just as soon as I get into the passenger seat, the car's resident disc jockey—that would be Terry, who operated a pile-driver in a previous life or will in a subsequent one—will begin blasting loud, monotonous dance "music" through speakers inches from my ears. Lately I've been treated to worse than dance music, which, as much as I may hate it, I have some sort of genetic affinity for as a gay man. It is, after all, the music of my people. That is decidedly not the case with the White Stripes, the Faint, or Grand Theft Auto, noisy rock bands that we've been listening to lately, groups that leave me longing for the days when Björk, the Icelandic lunatic, was the most offensive thing I had to listen to in the car.

Terry isn't all that into the White Stripes, the Faint, or Grand Theft Auto, so he claims to feel something close to my pain. It's the budding music snob strapped into the car seat behind us who requires rock. Our six-year-old son, D.J., has rather sophisticated tastes—and it's not just new bands he likes. After hearing one of their songs on the soundtrack of a skateboarding DVD when he was four—four!—D.J. asked Santa to bring him Black Sabbath's *We Sold Our Soul for Rock 'n Roll* for Christmas. Santa came through, and Black Sabbath has been on regular rotation ever since, always played at top volume.

In the car.

Inches.

From.

My.

Ears.

I blame myself for D.J. turning out this way. I had to be the go-to-work parent, the one who just ached to pay the bills, the one on the receiving end of all those mortifying cat's-in-the-cradle moments. ("He's *walking*?") My boyfriend, home alone with our impressionable son, drove him to preschool, playdates, and the grocery store while blasting selections from his enormous CD collection. I did my best on nights and weekends to undo the damage Terry was doing, bringing home the DVDs of *Mary Poppins*, *Chitty Chitty Bang Bang*, and, naturally, *The Wizard of Oz*. But my musicals were a quiet drop of water in Terry's terrifyingly loud ocean. It became clear that all was lost when, two months shy of his fourth birthday, D.J. refused to be buckled into his car seat until Terry went back into the house and got a Daft Punk CD—and not just any ol' Daft Punk CD, mind you, but *Discovery,* the French dance band's retro-disco/techno-beats CD. You know that Daft Punk CD, right? Yeah, me neither.

I'm as despondent about by my son's taste in music as my father was about mine. When D.J. was five, I walked into his room and caught him playing air guitar and jumping up and down on his bed to Black Sabbath's "Iron Man." I made the exact same face that my father did when he walked in on me high-kicking around my bedroom to the original Broadway cast recording of *Cabaret* when I was thirteen: a look of horror, quickly followed by a look of resignation. My son is what he is, my father and I both concluded at those terrible moments, and there wasn't a damn thing either of us could do about it.

You might think that someone so phobic about getting into a car with his musically challenged boyfriend and son would never agree to go on a cross-country road trip. But the summer after D.J. turned six, Terry somehow managed to talk me into driving about 1,500 miles from the artsy-fartsy island where we live in Puget Sound to Saugatuck, Michigan, an artsy-fartsy resort town on Lake Michigan. We spent a week in Saugatuck the previous summer, renting a house and inviting my mother and stepfather to join us, and had such a good time that we decided to make it an annual event.

Getting to Michigan and back in our car would "only" mean spending twelve days on the road, Terry said when he informed me we were driving to Michigan instead of flying. We were having one of our frequent just-the-two-of-us nights out, one of the secrets to our success as parents, I'm convinced. Unlike some of the other adults we'd met since crossing over into Parent World, we can't brag that we haven't been to dinner or a movie alone since we became parents. We realized relatively quickly that the only time we remembered why we liked each other well enough to want to have kids together in the first place was when we were alone together. (You may need to read that last sentence twice.) So contrary to the popular belief that parents should never leave their child's side, we've been making time for dinners, movies, and the occasional weekend away ever since.

Sitting in one of Seattle's post–Internet bust restaurants (fewer truffles, more realism) six weeks before we were going to leave for Michigan, Terry broached the subject of driving. It would "just" mean spending about nine hours a day in the car for twelve days, Terry assured me. We had booked a summer rental for two weeks in Saugatuck this year, and driving there instead of flying would "only" double the amount of time I would have to take off work. Being the stay-at-home parent for five years has left Terry with a rather warped sense of vacation time. Informing my boss, the publisher of *The Stranger*, the Seattle weekly newspaper I edit, that I would "only" have to take two extra weeks off to get to and from the place I was planning to spend my two weeks' summer vacation was, in Terry's mind, not that big a deal. Two weeks off, four weeks off—what's the difference? When you've spent the last 250 weeks off, it doesn't seem like a lot to ask. As for spending "just" nine hours a day in the car— or 100 plays in a row of Black Sabbath's "We Sold Our Souls for Rock 'n Roll" (running time: 74:00 minutes)—Terry felt that I didn't have a right to bitch about that. He would be doing all the driving, for starters, since I never learned how to drive, and he wasn't bitching about spending two weeks—336 hours in a row—in Michigan with my family, was he?

"Yes, you are," I said. "You're bitching about it by claiming that you're *not* bitching about it. The implication is that being with my family is something you *could* bitch about if you weren't choosing *not* to bitch about it. That's bank-shot bitching, Terry, but it's still bitching."

He gave me a look—head tilted to one side, corners of his mouth pulled down, eyes narrowed—that could only be construed as non-verbal bitching. I let it slide. If I'd learned anything after being in a relationship for nearly ten years, it's the importance of letting your boyfriend win one every once in a while. And this was one that Terry badly wanted to win: His family spent their vacations on the road. They drove to Yellowstone, Mount Rushmore, Glacier National Park. If we were going to spend our summer vacations in Saugatuck every year with my family doing what my family enjoys doing during the summer—eating and drinking, which is pretty much what we like to do in the winter, spring, and fall, too—then, by God, we were going to drive.

End of discussion.

And besides, driving meant we could take the dog.

The dog—oh, wait. D.J.'s chocolate toy poodle does have a name. The dog actually went through a few different names on the Christmas morning that he jumped out of a box under the tree and ran straight to D.J., including—and I swear to God that I am not making this up—*Pierre*. It sounds unbelievable, I realize, an easy reach for an easy joke, but it's the truth. There's a Maurice Sendak short story about a snotty little boy named Pierre and D.J. loved this story, so . . . why not name his new dog Pierre? Terry and I exchanged panicked looks. Homos for dads and a poodle named Pierre? We might as well send him to school in a little pink dress.

"I don't know," Terry said, "Pierre sounds too much like his name is pee. Do you want your friends to think you named your dog after pee-pee?"

D.J. did not. I couldn't resist pointing out, quietly and only to Terry, that if D.J. is worried about what his friends are going to think, we probably shouldn't have gotten him a poodle at all, regardless of its name. Terry told me, loud enough for my mother, stepfather, and D.J. to hear, to shut up about the poodle already. It's not like we imposed the poodle on D.J.; he selected the breed. His best friend had a toy poodle, so D.J. decided he wanted one too. He had no idea that he was asking for a gay dog.

Sitting cross-legged on the floor with D.J. after knocking down Pierre, Terry said, "Let's think of another name for the little stinker."

D.J. smiled.

And that's how the dog's name came to be Stinker. Stinker, the six-hundred-dollar chocolate toy poodle that "Santa" brought us. Stinks, for short. Stinks, the poodle that makes me anxious about what other people must think.

But love your kid, love his pet.

I brought a cat home from Arfa's, a bakery down the alley from the apartment where I grew up in Chicago, when I was five years old. I named him Morris after the finicky cat in the television commercials. My dad hated Morris at first but he gave in—his sensitive son loved the cat, he loved his sensitive son, so eventually he came to love the cat. That's been my arc with Stinker. First, I hated him for being a dog; I'm allergic to dogs, and a lifetime of canine-induced asthma attacks can instill a powerful aversion in a person. I also hated him for being a poodle, as I feared what people were going to say about us for getting our son a poodle. But my son loves his dog, and I love my son, and so now I love his dog. Oh, I may get jealous sometimes. Terry drags Stinker around on a leash, takes him to obedience classes, and sometimes makes him wear a collar that administers a little a shock whenever he barks. Terry's never done any of those things for me. But my jealousy fades when I hear D.J. whispering to Stinker in his room at night, or when I check on D.J. at night and find Stinker curled up next to him in bed. And the day D.J. announced, out of the blue, that Stinker's full name was Stinker Farmer Brown Pierce, and that he was Stinker's dad, well, how cute is that?

* * *

Where was I?

Oh, yes: Terry and I were arguing about driving to Michigan. I was hoping we could discuss it like adults and, more importantly, that I would get my own way. Alas, it was not to be. Just when I was about to tick off several dozen reasons why it was a bad idea, Terry said we were driving and that was that.

"End of discussion?" I asked, knowing the answer.

"End," he said.

So I agreed to the road trip—but it was a strategic, insincere agreement. Two weeks before we were supposed to leave, I played my trump card: Driving to Michigan and back would mean driving through—not to mention sleeping, eating, and going to the bathroom in—some of the least welcoming places for gays and lesbians in the country: the reddest of the dreaded Red States.

"Gay couples driving across Montana or South Dakota aren't on a road trip, Terry," I said. "They're on a suicide mission." There was still time to buy plane tickets and fly to Michigan. "Wouldn't you rather wave at the bigots from 30,000 feet up than make small talk with them in truck stop restrooms?"

"You can be such an unbelievable pussy sometimes," Terry said.

He was right. I can be a pussy, and the thought of driving through Montana had me spitting up hairballs. Not so Terry. He's from Spokane, a strange, depressing city in eastern Washington near the Idaho border. He spent a great deal of time in rural areas as a kid, so Terry doesn't fear places like South Dakota the same way I do. I grew up in the big city, and as an adult I can't relax anyplace the *New York Times* isn't delivered; as far as Terry's concerned, it's not a vacation unless he's surrounded by folks who don't know who David Brooks is and don't care how much he admires them and their "values."

And, yes, I'll admit that my fear of South Dakota reveals a deep streak of pussyhood, although in my defense I will point out that I'm not afraid of a lot of "big city" things that apparently scare the shit out of the people of South Dakota, things like subways, sodomites, and sit-ups. Still, whenever we venture out of our urban bubble, I'm put to shame by Terry's comfort level in rural areas. Once, while driving through rural Oregon, we stumbled onto a lumberjack contest at a county fair. Terry insisted we stay and watch. Many of the contestants in the "lumberjackoff," as I insisted on calling it, were straight out of the gay man's fantasy handbook—sweaty, muscular, bare-chested guys in work jeans cutting down trees, leaping over logs, running relay races with chain saws in their hands—but I couldn't enjoy the scenery. I have a hard time relaxing around extremely good-looking, muscular guys holding chain saws. But Terry? A tall, willowy blond who wears his T-shirts tight and his hair long? He was in his element. While I was checking to make sure we had a clear getaway if we had to dash for the car, Terry was leaning back in the bleachers, eating deep-fried candy bars and cheering for his favorite lumberjack.

We were about halfway to Saugatuck, dog and all, when Terry pulled off in Billings, Montana, a town I would never have visited of my own accord. We checked into a hotel with a lovely view of empty storefronts and collapsing warehouses—Billings has perhaps the most depressing downtown west of Gary, Indiana. Shortly after plopping down in bed, D.J. was fast asleep. Terry was already under the covers when the dog started scratching at the door, the signal that he needs to go, and Terry turned his pleading eyes to me. Walking the dog, I reminded Terry, was one of the jobs I wasn't supposed to be asked to do if I agreed to get one. Again, a lifetime of dog-induced asthma attacks is an effective form of aversion therapy, and, as a result, I loathed dogs, all of them, even innocent little hair-not-fur poodles, the one breed that had never done me any harm.

"Please?" said Terry. "I've been driving all day. I'm tired. Just this once."

At home we just open the back door and let the dog out in the yard, where he does his business under cover of darkness. It crossed my mind that we might be able to do something similar at the Billings Sheraton, which we appeared to have all to ourselves. The hallway was deserted and dark . . . we could just open the door to our room and let . . . but no.

The dog was ready to burst at this point, and Terry played his trump card: He'd been driving all day—*walking the dog was the least I could do.*

You haven't really gambled with your life until you've walked a chocolate-brown toy poodle in downtown Billings, Montana, at 11:30 at night. There isn't much to see in downtown Billings 'cept for drunks, bums, and thugs, so a nervous gay guy walking his son's poodle around the Sheraton tends to draw the locals' attention. Stinker didn't feel menaced by the hoodlums in Billings, probably because he could barely see them and couldn't hear them at all. You see, Stinker has only one eye. And he's deaf. And brain damaged.

It's a long story but, hey, you bought the book:

One sunny day the previous summer, Terry was driving home and Stinker was leaning out of the car window, his ears flapping in the wind, when he suddenly toppled out. He landed on his little poodle face and—sensitive readers may want to skip the rest of this paragraph—shattered his skull. He was bleeding from his ears, mouth, and nose when Terry scooped him up. One of his eyes had been knocked out of its socket.

Three heaven-sent hippie chicks driving by saw Terry jump out of the car and scoop up the dog. They bundled Terry and Stinker into their van, and sped off to the island's veterinary clinic, which was only a few hundred feet away. The vet advised Terry to go home and wait by the phone, and the hippie chicks—God bless them—could see that Terry was too distraught to drive and so they drove him home in our car.

Once home, the hippie chicks offered to get Terry high. He declined, which may have been a mistake. When he called me at work he was so hysterical that, at first, I thought something had happened to D.J. I was already out the door, cell phone still pressed to my ear, by the time I realized that the dog was hurt, not the kid.

Terry and D.J. had been going through a rough patch—some normal, if aggravating, five-year-old crap. D.J. alternates between combating and worshipping Terry—such is the burden of the stay-at-home parent. Terry has to do most of the correcting, hectoring, and disciplining, so when D.J. pushes the boundaries he's ususally pushing against Terry. But D.J. also worships Terry—he even looks like Terry. D.J. favors tight T-shirts, just like his dad, and he wears his dirty-blond hair long, just like his dad. But they had been having a rough time of things during the week leading up to the accident; D.J. had been telling Terry that he hated him. "—And now I've killed his dog!" Terry sobbed into the phone. "He's going to hate me forever!"

Knowing that Terry wasn't in any shape to get a call from the vet informing him that D.J.'s dog was dead, I called the vet and asked the receptionist how the dog was doing. The vet's receptionist curtly informed me that they couldn't release a patient's confidential medical information to someone who wasn't a family member.

There was a long pause as I picked the pieces of my brain up off the sidewalk.

"Excuse me?" I finally said.

Terry's was the only name listed on the dog's medical records. Unless I was a member of the immediate family—you know, a husband or a wife—releasing information to me would violate their confidentiality policy.

"You have got to be kidding me," I said, doing my best not to explode. For years I worried that I would one day be denied the right to make medical decisions for Terry in the case of an emergency. It never occurred to me that, as a gay couple, we would face discrimination during our *poodle's* medical emergency. "Lady, it's a dog—and the hysterical fag who brought the dog in? That's my boyfriend. And the dog isn't even technically his dog. It's my son's dog. And I paid for that dog. And you know what? You have my permission to release my dog's confidential medical information to anyone on earth who expresses the least bit of interest in it. Christ!"

The receptionist didn't budge. Who knew that one of the rights that married people enjoy is the ability to find out about the medical conditions of their sons' poodles?

"Okay, fine. Don't tell me," I said. "Just promise me you won't call my home and tell my boyfriend his dog is dead before I get home. He's hysterical, and if you call and tell him the dog is dead when he's alone, he'll hang himself. So promise me you won't call—can you do that?"

That they could do.

When I got home to my hysterical boyfriend, the dog was still hanging in there. Stinker needed overnight care, however, and that meant we had to get him to an animal hospital sixty miles away. We arranged for a playdate for D.J. and headed to the vet's to pick up the dog. The vet explained to us—excuse me, to *Terry*—that the dog would have to be held during the trip to the animal hospital. His head had to be elevated at all times to prevent blood from sloshing back into his brain. His eye was back in the socket, held in place by a bandage, but he was still bleeding from his ears. And drooling—continuous drooling, non-stop drooling, a mighty stream of poodle drool. Dog drool mixed with dog blood.

So off we went to the animal hospital, Terry sobbing and driving while I, the non-driving dog hater, held Stinker in my lap, holding his head upright and pressed against my chest, a pool of bloody poodle drool slowly spreading over my shirt. Stinker stared up at me with his one good eye. Only a complete asshole wouldn't melt under the circumstances and, incomplete asshole that I am, I spoke softly to the dog, asking him not to die. I don't think my Grinch heart grew three sizes that day, but it did grow enough for my son's tiny toy poodle to squeeze in. I told Stinker that we loved him, and that D.J. needed him to pull through, and that we would do whatever it took to keep him alive.

It took $3,000.

Five days after we dropped a very sick dog off at the animal hospital, we picked up D.J.'s one-eyed (the damaged eye had to be removed), deaf (due to the trauma), and slightly brain-damaged toy poodle. We were worried that D.J. might reject the now facially asymmetrical Stinker that we brought home from the animal hospital. But D.J., going through a pirate phase, was only too delighted to be the owner of a one-eyed dog. Stinker can't hear us when we call him, and he runs into walls now and then, and if you approach him on his blind side he jumps, but he's my kid's dog, and I love my kid, so I love his dog.

On that night in Billings, however, I took an objective view of the situation: a gay man walking a deranged and deformed toy poodle near midnight in a redneck part of a redneck town in a redneck state—my chances for survival looked bleak. Oh, I like to think I'm not all that gay looking. I like to think that I can pass for straight when I must. Passing is something all gay men need to do from time to time. However out you are, however over it your mom is, there are times when even the biggest fag doesn't want his homosexuality to be an issue.

Restaurants in truck stops, for instance, or your first day in the Marine Corps, or any time you find yourself in downtown Billings, Montana. But no man can look straight while walking a toy poodle.

Not that I didn't make a good-faith effort to pass. Looking annoyed at having to walk the poodle struck me as perhaps the best, if not the only, available disguise. Plus it came easy—after all, I was annoyed at having to walk the poodle who, sensing how tense I was, decided to take his sweet time. I hoped that anyone tempted to kick my ass after seeing the poodle would change his mind once he saw the theatrically annoyed look on my face. "This isn't my poodle," I wanted the look to say to all the drunks, bums, and thugs I passed on the street. "It's my wife's poodle, guys, and just between us straight guys, straight guys, I am one unhappy straight guy!" The disguise worked pretty well—I lived to type the tale—but I got overconfident. Outside what appeared to be biker bar about two blocks from the hotel—the dog was still searching for that one perfect spot in all of Montana to take a crap—I caught the eye of a rough-looking man. I attempted an annoyed little shrug. "You do what you gotta do to get yourself a little pussy," I meant for the shrug to say. "You've probably done similar stuff for a piece of ass—female ass—right, my fellow straight guy?" My fellow straight guy wasn't buying it. While I meant for the shrug to make me look annoyed-but-seeing-the-humor-in-my-predicament-and-anxious-to-get-home-and-get-some-pussy, I only succeeded in looking constipated—and what is constipation but a ten-dollar word for packed fudge? If the dog hadn't pooped right then, right there in front of the biker bar, allowing me to turn tail and hurry my gay, poodle-walking ass back to the hotel, I would probably be dead now.

However narrow my escape, I survived Billings, Montana, and by the time we got back on the road the next morning, I began to relax. Oh, there were other nervous stretches of road—particularly in Wyoming and South Dakota—when I felt like we were on an African safari: safe so long as we stayed in the car. But just as Terry predicted, we weren't harmed by any of the locals—unless you count the food they served us. Farms, farms everywhere and not a goddamned vegetable to eat.

Despite all of my dire predictions, the family vacation—if I may be so bold as to use the word "family" to describe the three of us (a conservative Christian group disputed my right to use the word after I applied it to the three of us in an op-ed piece in the *New York Times*)—was off to a good start. It seemed that a boy, his two dads, and his blind, deaf, brain-damaged poodle could take a road trip across America unmolested after all. I started to feel like any other family on the road. Until we stopped at a skate park in the middle of South Dakota so D.J. could stretch his legs.

Terry had been taking D.J. to skate parks on Vashon Island and in Seattle for almost a year and the kid was getting good. As D.J. sailed around the concrete bowls, out-skating the teenage boys in the park, Terry and I sat on top of a picnic table in the only bit of late-afternoon shade for a mile in either direction. There was a church directly across the street from the skate park and, as we waited for D.J. to wear himself out in the sun, the doors opened and a wedding party poured out. No rice was thrown, no joy was apparent. The bride and groom did not get into a waiting limo and speed off. As we sat in the shade and watched, a heavyset photographer began arranging the wedding party on the steps of the church in an infinite number of groupings. As is the case with most modern weddings, documenting the event was taking precedence over actually experiencing it. First some photos of the Bride and Groom. Then the Bride and Groom and Best Man and Maid of Honor. Then the Bride and Groom and Mothers and Fathers. Then the Bride alone. Then the Bride and her Attendants. Then Groom and his Groomsmen. The Bride and the

Flower Girl. The Groom and the Ring Bearer.

We were in the shade, but the wedding party was not. The wedding party looked miserable and the photographer was beginning to lose his patience with some of the less cooperative members of the wedding. After they had been dismissed, a handful of the groomsmen and bridesmaids crossed the street and stood in the shade with us, smoking cigarettes and bitching about the heat. They were anxious to get to the reception already. The photographer had dismissed the wedding party prematurely, however, and he shouted for the bridesmaids and groomsmen to come back—back to the church steps, back into the sun, back for one more round of pictures. The young men and women in the sweat-soaked tuxes and synthetic-fiber dresses groaned, stubbed out their cigarettes, and trudged back across the street.

"Thank God we never have to go through that shit," Terry said. D.J. rolled up on his skateboard, kicked it up, and caught it with his right hand.

"Can we go now?" D.J. asked.

"You bet," Terry said.

—2—

The Big Stink

Two days later, in a water park in Sioux Falls, South Dakota, I came to a couple of realizations: First, anyone who denies the existence of the obesity epidemic in the United States hasn't been to a water park in Sioux Falls, South Dakota. (The owners of water parks in the U.S. must be saving a fortune on water and chlorine bills; floating in the deep end of the wave pool with D.J., Terry observed that there was an awful lot of water being displaced. If the South Dakotans floating around us all got out of the pool at the same time, the water level would most likely have dropped six feet.) The second thing I realized was that we weren't going to escape the gay marriage debate on this vacation, not even in a water park.

As Terry and D.J. paddled around in their matching father/son Speedos, the rock radio station that was blasting over the park's sound system cut away for a newsbreak. Suddenly we heard Senator Rick Santorum's voice oozing over the water slides. Debating the anti–gay marriage amendment to the U.S. Constitution in the Senate, Pennsylvania's junior senator compared gay marriage to terrorism. "Isn't that the ultimate homeland security," Santorum said, "standing up and defending marriage?" As D.J. splashed his way through the park, his masochistic dads wandered closer to a loud-speaker.

"I would argue that the future of our country hangs in the bal-ance," said the senator who famously compared gay people to dog-fuckers, "because the future of marriage hangs in the balance."

Soooooooooo . . .

Same-sex couples that wish to marry, in Santorum's opinion, are the moral equivalent of terrorists who hijack airplanes and fly them into office buildings. I wondered in the water park that day if Sena-tor Santorum was aware that there were gay people on those planes and in those office buildings on 9/11—all three of the buildings that were hit, including the Pentagon. Daniel Brandhorst and Ronald Gamboaa, a gay couple, and their three-year-old adopted son, David, were on American Airlines Flight 11, the plane the terrorists flew into the north tower of the World Trade Center. They were the only en-tire family to perish in the 9/11 attacks. Sheila Hein, a civilian army management analyst, died at her desk in the Pentagon—she was wearing a gold band on her finger when she died, a ring given to her by Peggy Neff, her partner of eighteen years. Mark Bingham, a gay man, was one of the heroes of American Airlines Flight 96, the hi-jacked plane that crashed in a field in rural Pennsylvania when the passengers attempted to storm the cockpit. Flight 96 may have been headed to the U.S. Capitol building. If Santorum had appeared in the water park at the moment I heard him, I would've drowned him in the Lazy River with my bare hands.

Like a lot of gay Americans, I was naive enough to believe that nothing would be the same after 9/11. Among the many lessons our country learned that morning, from a pressing need to secure cock-pit doors to the realization that the Saudis might not be our best friends in the world, was that the full integration of gays and lesbians into our civic life could no longer be denied. There were gay people on all three planes; there were gay people in both of the Twin Towers; there were open lesbians hard at work at their desks in the freaking *Pentagon*. Gay employees of Cantor Fitzgerald perished along with gay employees of Windows on the World. One of the things that Islamo-fascist terrorists hate about the "decadent" West is its tolerance of homosexuality. On September 12, 2001, I assumed that the deaths of so many gay and lesbian Americans on September 11, 2001, would open the eyes of Americans like Rick Santorum to the fact that we weren't a threat. If nothing else, being the enemy of our enemies would have to redound to our benefit.

No such luck. When it comes to gays and lesbians, Christian conservatives and their standard-bearers in Washington, D.C., march in lock-step with Osama bin Laden and his Islamo-fascist buddies.

Hearing Rick Santorum's voice in that water park made me tense up again. I wasn't feeling much love in the heartland, not with all the Bush/Cheney signs attached to barbed wire fences, but the more time we spent on the road, the less conspicuous I felt. We didn't fit in, but we weren't sticking out either. I didn't feel judged and scrutinized by the South Dakotans in the water park because I was too busy judging and scrutinizing them myself. I had never seen so many morbidly obese people in one place in my life—and I've been to "fat acceptance" conventions. But my relatively panic-free state of mind was shattered when I heard Rick Santorum's voice. We weren't going to able to escape the gay marriage debate on our family vacation, not even while we were in South Dakota. Especially in South Dakota.

We probably couldn't have escaped it anywhere in America that summer, the summer of 2004, the year same-sex marriage hit the fan. In the spring, the mayor of San Francisco invited same-sex couples to come down to City Hall and get married; soon renegade public officials were marrying same-sex couples in Oregon, New York, and Nevada. Days before we left for Saugatuck, same-sex couples began to get legally married in Massachusetts. At the same time lawsuits were being filed to win gay couples the right to marry in New York, California, and Washington, conservatives were filing initiatives to ban gay marriage in eleven other states. Everything in Iraq was going swimmingly that summer (if you don't count the looting, the beheadings, the roadside bombs, the missing explosives, and on and on), so George W. Bush carved out some time to promote a Federal Marriage Amendment that would not only ban gay marriage, but any recognition of same-sex relationships whatsoever—no civil unions, no domestic partnerships, no nothing. The language of the Federal Marriage Amendment was so vague that some legal scholars weren't sure same-sex couples would be able to get dinner reservations if it was approved.

While we, like most homos, enjoyed being the center of attention in the spring of 2004, we were ready for the gay marriage debate to end by the beginning of the summer. For months it had been impossible to turn on the radio in the morning without hearing gay relationships described in less-than-flattering terms—and we listen to NP fuckin' R. There's only so much you can take, only so long you can laugh off the insults, only so many jokes you can make about Gary Bauer's appearance, only so many times you can listen to the Democratic presidential candidate to whom you've sent large checks categorically state his opposition to gay marriage before you reach your limit.

You reach your limit more quickly when your kid is sitting at the kitchen table in his Incredible Hulk pj's, eating his breakfast, pausing now and again to wiggle one of his loose baby teeth, all the while listening to his parents' relationship described as a threat to all things decent and good. Somewhere around June 15, we stopped paying attention. If we were in the car and NPR was interviewing people "on both sides of this contentious issue," Terry would pop in a Black

Sabbath or Scissors Sisters CD without any complaints from me. Eventually I couldn't bring myself even to read the op-eds about gay marriage in the papers—not even the ones I was writing. Heading out on our summer vacation, I was looking forward to a few weeks without having to hear one goddamn thing about gay marriage.

I'm not sure why the debate over gay marriage affected me so deeply—it's not as if Terry and I even wanted to get married. We would like to have access to all the legal benefits of marriage—we would like to be the other's next of kin; in a crisis we would like to be able to make medical decisions for each other, or even for our dog. Terry, the stay-at-home parent, would also love to have my Social Security benefits were I to drop dead. But somehow we can't picture ourselves exchanging vows. We're not against marriage for ideological reasons; we don't believe, like some hard-left homos, that other gay and lesbian couples should be denied the right to marry because we don't approve of the institution of marriage; nor do we believe that gay people were put on earth to subvert the traditional family. Gay sex is a lot of (wonderful) things, but it is not, as many sex radicals assert, The Revolution.

Besides, Terry and I are fans of the traditional family—our family is more traditional than most. With the exception of all the homosexual sodomy, most of what goes down under our roof is a social conservative's wet dream. Thanks to Terry's willingness to forgo contact with adult human beings for days on end, our son has never seen the inside of a day care center. Normally this would please social conservatives, as they despise day care, but D.J. spent most of the time he wasn't in day care hanging out with an avowed homosexual, which kind of spoils things for Reverend Falwell.

Even so, Rev. F., we do hew to some pretty strictly defined roles in our house, roles that pretty neatly parallel the male/female roles you would like to see mandated by law. My boyfriend cooks and

cleans (He likes it! I'm not oppressing him!); I mow lawns and remove dead, stinking rat carcasses from the crawl space under our
house (I hate it! He's oppressing me!). I don't have to do my laundry and Terry doesn't have to pay his Visa bills. We lead a far more
traditional lifestyle than a certain unmarried, childless, withered,
aging right-wing attack hag that I would name if I weren't so damn
polite. (Oh, fuck it: Ann Coulter.) But while we enjoy our traditional
family structure, and while we would like to have the legal benefits
of marriage, we weren't planning on flouncing down the aisle in
matching tuxes anytime soon. We believe gay marriage should be
legal, not mandatory.

D.J. was exhausted when we left South Dakota's largest water park;
he was fast asleep before we finished strapping him into his car seat.
As we drove over the Missouri River, passing from Sioux Falls, South
Dakota, into Sioux City, Iowa, Terry and I fell into a conversation
about marriage. We agreed that the idea of pissing off huge assholes
like Senator Rick Santorum, tiny assholes like Gary Bauer, and dan-
gerously powerful assholes like Dr. James Dobson made marriage
tempting, but . . . *still*. Pissing off right-wing assholes is a terrible reason to do anything. And we're already homos—it's not like we have
to go to any extra effort to piss off Rick Santorum. We annoy Santorum a half dozen different ways every morning before breakfast. I
wake up in bed next to my boyfriend (1) and give him a kiss (2) before I head downstairs to read the *New York Times* (3). When my kid
(4) wakes up I make him breakfast and then I head to work, where I
write about sex (5) and occasionally update a Web site about what an
asshole Rick Santorum is (6). Annoy Santorum? Mission accom-
plished without marriage.

But just as attempts at censorship only create more demand for
whatever it is that you're being told you shouldn't view or read or

hear, the hysteria of the right wing as it attempts to ban gay marriage is making marriage more attractive to homos. Being told we can't is making a lot of homos wanna.

A lot of homos, just not the homo I'm with. As we sped through Iowa with D.J. sound asleep in the backseat, Terry emphasized that even if it made Rick Santorum's head explode, he couldn't see himself getting married. But he did want to mark our upcoming tenth anniversary somehow. Perhaps it was time to do something symbolic, something low-key, as a sign of our commitment to each other.

"There's always the tattoos," Terry said.

Early in our relationship we joked about getting "Property of Terry Miller" tattooed on my upper arm and "Property of Dan Savage" tattooed on his. Neither of us had any tattoos when we met—something of a miracle, considering that we were young, foolish, and frequently inebriated in Seattle in the early 1990s. Very few of the young and the foolish made it out of Seattle in the '90s without at least one, and sometimes several, regrettable tattoos.

On the upside, Terry said, we could get matching "Property of . . ." tattoos without having to invite our friends and family to the tattoo shop to watch, sparing Terry the public spectacle that he hates.

"On the downside," I said, "tattoos are even jinxier than wedding vows."

How can two gay guys be in favor of legal same-sex marriage and huge fans of the traditional family without wanting to marry? My boyfriend, rather hilariously, says he doesn't want to get married because—and I quote—"I don't want to act like straight people." I believe the first time he made this comment he was folding my laundry, balancing our baby on his hip, and stirring a pot of grits on the stove.

My excuse is a bit more reasoned: Making a big, public stink about your big, beautiful relationship seems to be the kiss of death—and not just for straight couples (think of all those divorce lawyers out there), but for gay couples as well. Way, way back in the early 1990s, a pair of hunky bodybuilders, Bob Paris and Rod Jackson, got "married," hyphenated their last names, and made a pile of money posing for coffee table "art" books. They cowrote a memoir about their big, beautiful gay "marriage," which included these memorable lines from the invitation to Bob and Rod's big gay wedding ceremony:

> *Let this be our destiny,*
> *To love, to live,*
> *To begin each day together,*
> *To share our lives forever.*

The "married" gay bodybuilders eventually got "divorced," of course.

And who can forget Ellen DeGeneres and Anne Heche on *Oprah*, blathering on about being each other's "wives" after they'd been together for, what, four days? Or Melisssa Etheridge and Julie Cypher on Larry King talking up their eternal love (and David Crosby's fast-acting spunk) shortly before they split? More recent casualties: gay actor B. D. Wong wrote a book about having a child with his partner, Richie Jackson, and then promptly broke up with Jackson after the book tour. Gay comic Bob Smith closed his memoir, *Openly Bob*, with the uplifting story of how he finally met Mr. Right. His next book was about breaking up with Mr. Right. Chip and Dale, the impossibly good-looking gay couple on one season of *The Amazing Race*, insisted that they be identified as a married couple. They broke up eleven seconds after they cashed their check.

There isn't room in this or any other book to list all the high-profile straight couples who split up after making a huge public stink about their relationships, but in the interest of being fair and balanced, here are a few off the top of my head: Billy Bob Thornton and Angelina Jolie; Brad Pitt and Jennifer Aniston; Henry VIII and Catherine of Aragon; Lisa Marie Presley and Michael Jackson; Charles Windsor and his distant cousin Lady Diana Spencer; Ronald Reagan and his first wife; Bob Dole and his first wife; Newt Gingrich and his first two wives; former Republican Congressman Bob Barr and his first three wives; Rush Limbaugh and his first four wives; Jennifer Lopez and a cast of thousands; Martha Stewart and her husband; Tom Cruise and his first wife, whose name is lost to history; Tom Cruise and second wife, Nicole Kidman; Tom Cruise and his next wife.

And who can forget the national tragedy that was Liza Minnelli and David Gest?

> DAVID GEST: We're never away from each other. We hate to be away from each other. And it's such a wonderful, wonderful romance. I love her nose. I think she's got the cutest nose in the world.
> LIZA MINNELLI: David!
> DAVID GEST: We're totally in love. And people that know us and were at the wedding really saw what we have between us.

That was Liza and David on *Larry King Live* on May 17, 2002. Minnelli filed for divorce on October 22, 2003.

On some level, I'm not sure we would marry even if it were legal for men to marry men. I'm too superstitious and, except on the dance floor, Terry refuses to make a spectacle of himself. That, I believe, is his real reason for not wanting to get married—it's certainly not that he "doesn't want to act like straight people." We're straighter than most of the straight people we know. It's the idea of exchanging vows in front of everyone he knows that unnerves Terry; for me it's the idea of promising to stay together forever, in the presence of whatever God we decided to invoke (the Roman God Antinous would be my choice), that presents the problem. It's just so . . . jinxy. It's whistling past a very large, very crowded graveyard—I mean, there isn't a busier graveyard than the one where divorced straight couples go to bury their wedding albums. Whistling past the graveyard? No, getting married is like standing on a flatbed truck tricked out with strobe lights, a DJ blasting tunes, a dozen humpy go-go dancers grinding away, and whistling into a bullhorn as you drive back and forth past a mass grave.

Hell, I'm bad luck at *other* people's weddings. The very first one I was invited to as an adult ended in divorce in less than a year; the last wedding I attended ended in divorce less than six months later. Terry and I attended a same-sex commitment ceremony in Seattle and they broke up—and they were lesbians, and lesbians never break up! There's something jinxy about my presence when other people are making promises to each other about the future. I can't imagine my luck would be any better if I were the one making the promises.

"We are *not* going to break up," Terry said firmly.

We were killing time in a large, empty parking lot waiting to board the car ferry that crosses Lake Michigan twice a day between Mani-towoc, Wisconsin, and Ludington, Michigan. While D.J. cruised around on his skateboard, Terry and I sat talking on a curb in the shade. Terry had brought up the idea of getting matching tattoos again. They worked for him, I said, because they were private, but they didn't work for me because, although private, they were still jinxy.

"Do you think we're going to break up?" he asked.

"No, of course not," I said. "But no couple thinks they're

going to. My parents didn't think they were going to. It just feels jinxy to me."

"Well, what about my feelings?" Terry said as he tossed his arm over my shoulder. " 'Property of Terry Miller' is how I feel about you."

"Property of . . ." does capture the true spirit of marriage. "My husband . . ." "My wife . . ." Isn't it all about possession? Claiming ownership? Back in The Bad Olde Days, a woman was her father's property until he handed her off to another man, at which point she became her husband's property. Women are no longer the property of their husbands—not in the West, anyway—but the idea that your spouse is your personal property lives on in our culture, albeit in a slightly more egalitarian form. Socially and sexually, wives own their husbands, husbands own their wives. Instead of being given away by their families, modern brides and grooms give themselves to each other, ceding all expectations of autonomy.

"Tattoos seem extreme," I said.

"Yes," Terry said, "extremely hot."

Yes, yes, I conceded. At the right moment, that kind of "I own you" talk can be terribly, terribly sexy. That the institution of marriage establishes ownership is often cited as one strike against it by some lefties, but isn't it nice to be wanted? Isn't sex all about being wanted?

"Wouldn't it be nice to know you were wanted every time you saw your arm?" Terry said.

"But when we have a fight," I pointed out, "we're going to want to cut our arms off."

"But we won't cut our arms off," Terry said, "just like we won't break up. Come on. Don't be such a pussy. Let's get tattoos."

"I think that would be a bad idea," I said.

My aversion to marriage and tattoos was of a piece: If you value X and you know or suspect that doing Y imperils X, it's sensible to avoid doing Y. Well, X is our relationship and Y could be marriage or its slightly less perilous, less terrifying alternative, tattoos. If same-sex marriage were legal where we live, I might be willing to bite the bullet and get married; I might even wear a suit and mumble some vows if it could secure us marriage's sexy benefits. But I can't see going to Canada or Massachusetts to marry Terry when all we're going to get for our trouble is the jinx and a scrap of paper that would be worthless in the state where we live. And what would tattoos get us? All the jinx and no scrap of paper—my God, what would the point be?

—3—

The Enemy Within

And then there's the small matter of a certain member of the family who is adamantly opposed to gay marriage.

For a couple of guys who aren't sure they even want to get married, Terry and I have poured an awful lot of time into convincing this extraordinarily stubborn person that, yes, men *can* marry men, and women *can* marry women. Even my mother has spoken to him. But he refuses to budge. Boys don't marry boys, he insists, and girls don't marry girls. He's also made it clear that if Terry and I ever married, he would refuse to attend the ceremony.

Who is this stubborn relative? My father, the family's sole Republican? Terry's born-again Christian brother? My sister's Texan boyfriend?

Try D.J.

One of the ironies of being gay parents is that your children, raised in your non-gender-conforming home, go out into the world where gender roles are rigidly enforced by other children during "play." Our earliest taste of the soft bigotry of gender expectations came when D.J. announced from the backseat of the car that Terry and I didn't really love each other. Why not, we asked. "Because you're not married," D.J. explained calmly. "People who don't love each other don't get married, and since you're not married and can't get married, that means you can't love each other. Not really."

This childish circular logic came tumbling out of his mouth when D.J. was four. We traced it back to its source: a five-year-old girl, a charming little demon seed destined to be either the senator from Washington state or a professional dominatrix when she grows up. When her parents divorced, they told their only daughter they couldn't stay married because they weren't in love anymore. These words bounced around the little rock tumbler that is her mind until an opportunity to wound another child presented itself. Her parents weren't in love anymore and couldn't stay married, she told D.J. And since his parents can't get married, they can't love each other.

We've done our best to root this notion out, explaining to D.J. and that while most men marry women, and most women marry men, men can marry men and women can marry women. We've made a point of showing him same-sex wedding announcements in the "Sunday Styles" section of the *New York Times*. Before we instituted the gay marriage blackout, we watched some same-sex weddings on the evening news.

Now, D.J. concedes that we could get married, but he nevertheless insists that we shouldn't. If we do get married, he insists that he's not coming to the wedding. He'll come to the party after the wedding—provided there's cake—but there's no way he's going to the ceremony. He agrees that we can love each other, but he insists that boys don't marry boys and no gay wedding announcements in the *New York Times* are going to change his mind. It's odd to reflect that my sixty-four-year-old Catholic mom, raised to view marriage as a sacrament, believes marriage is about love and commitment, not about genitals, but my six-year-old son—raised by a gay couple, and not having seen the inside of a church since the day he was baptized—somehow came to believe that marriage is about matched sets of boys and girls.

How'd that happen?

D.J.'s traditional position on gender is not something he learned at home. While he was always into all the traditional boy things—cars, trucks, rockets—once upon a time he didn't perceive his toy preferences as a gender thing. While he's never met a sandwich he couldn't nibble into the shape of a gun, until he was four, the boy things he liked were just the things he happened to like. He liked guns because he liked guns, not because boys were supposed to like guns. Before he was four, he never talked about the way boys or girls were supposed to act, or what they were supposed to wear, or who boys were supposed to marry. He had playmates that were girls, and playmates that were boys. Gender didn't make any difference to him.

Then one day we packed D.J. off to preschool (which is not to be confused with day care) where he got a crash course in sex roles. It wasn't the teachers who poured this poison into his ears; we sent him to a progressive Montessori school on our left-leaning island, not some Southern Baptist preschool in a church basement. His teachers would sooner feed children tacks than force boys to do boy things and girls to do girl things. No, it was the other children who indoctrinated D.J. into the world of gender expectations. Along with the words to "Jingle Bells/Batman Smells," the children taught D.J. to think of boys and girls as two warring camps. From day one it was the boys vs. the girls, and there wasn't much the adults could do about it. When the children weren't engaged in Talmudic discussions about which toys or activities were male or female, the boys were chasing the girls around the yard during recess. When the boys got bored and went off to play with their boy toys, the girls would tease them until the chase started up again. Add fifteen years, some pubic hair, and a keg of beer, and it would be difficult to tell the difference between recess at Starbreak Montessori and Friday night at a frat house.

And what did D.J. learn from other children about marriage? It was a boy-and-girl thing, his classmates all agreed, and it wasn't an agreeable thing to the boys. Marriage was a weapon, something the girls would threaten to do to the boys if they ever actually caught them. To turn the tables during a game of chase, the girls only had to say the "m" word. Marriage was nuclear cooties. Once the threat was issued, the boys would turn tail and run, the girls chasing after them, like a bunch of magnetized pinballs whose charge had suddenly reversed.

So to D.J., it didn't make any sense that his two dads, both boys, would contemplate marrying each other. Boys weren't supposed to be interested in marriage any more than they were supposed to be interested in dolls or dresses or fairy tales about princesses. Marriage was a girl thing. And since there weren't any girls in our family, why was the subject even coming up?

Opponents of gay adoption argue that children raised by same-sex couples will grow up to be confused about gender. Only by observing the day-to-day interactions of one man married to one woman can a child learn how men and women relate to each other. If you believe that sex roles are taught, not innate, this objection might have some merit. Since children raised by gay or lesbian parents are no more likely to be gay or lesbian when they grow up than children raised by heterosexual parents, upwards of 90 percent of our children will wind up in heterosexual relationships as adults. If gender roles are all about nurture, and have nothing to do with nature, then straight children raised by homosexuals will be at a competitive disadvantage when they reach adulthood.

But do social conservatives really believe that sex roles are learned?

In the 1970s, feminists argued that gender was a social construct. If parents would just give trucks to girls and dolls to boys, we could stop the war in Vietnam and end apartheid and save the whales. There was no difference between the sexes, feminists argued, except for the myriad ways in which women were naturally superior. (More compassionate, less domineering, more empathetic, less controlling, more consensus-driven, less aggressive, etc.) Conservatives scoffed— gender was not, they sniffed, a social construct. Gender was innate, nature not nurture, and men and women were different. Attacking sex roles was yet another leftist plot to destroy the American family.

Liberal-minded and progressive parents sided with the feminists— the feminists had been right about so much else, after all, so they deserved the benefit of the doubt—and gave dolls to their sons and trucks to their daughters. But little boys went right on playing with trucks and little girls went right on playing with dolls. As it turned out, there *was* something innate about sex roles. Gender wasn't a conspiracy hatched by the patriarchy to enslave girls and traumatize boys. Most boys seemed to instinctively want traditional "boy" toys, and most girls instinctively want traditional "girl" toys. If you didn't give boys guns, they would make them out of sticks; if you didn't give girls dolls, they would put dresses on their toy trucks.

Ironically, the same social conservatives who today argue that children raised by lesbian or gay couples will be confused about gender are the ones who argued most loudly in the 1970s—and, again, were 100 percent correct—that gender was innate. You would think these same conservatives would be confident that the innate sense of gender identity that thwarted a generation of feminist moms and sensitive dads would overcome whatever confusion a child raised by same-sex parents might have about his gender. But no. Conservatives insist that a boy given a doll by his feminist parents will rip its legs off and point them at people and say "Bang!", but a grown man raised by two gay men won't know what to do with a grown woman's actual legs.

Opponents of same-sex couples adopting children have it exactly backward. D.J. isn't confused about gender—I wish that he were! If he weren't so acutely aware of gender, he might be a little less rigid about enforcing gender expectations. He might be willing to come to our wedding, if we were going to get married. Which we're not, but still.

Wait a minute. There *is* a girl in our family, as D.J. was quick to remind me when I asked him whether he was getting excited about seeing his whole family in Saugatuck. "My 'whole family' isn't coming," D.J. said. "Remember my mom?"

Of course we remembered his mom, I told him. How could we ever forget her?

Melissa was seven months pregnant by accident when she selected me and my boyfriend from our adoption agency's pool of pre-screened parent wannabes. Melissa was a nineteen-year-old street kid with long brown hair, a lip piercing, and a half dozen tattoos. We were her second choice; the first couple she chose, a straight couple, didn't want to do an open adoption with a homeless teenager who admitted to drinking during the early stages of her pregnancy. Six weeks after we met her on a gray afternoon in Portland, Oregon, the three of us sat in a recovery room at the hospital taking turns holding our son, a tiny infant who would quickly grow into a charismatic, blond-haired, blue-eyed skateboarder.

Some adoptive parents abuse pronouns (*"our* son," *"my* child") to establish possession; it's as if they're saying, *"our* child now, not *her* child anymore." But doing an open adoption means embracing the most plural definition of every plural pronoun, at least where your kid is concerned. When I say "our" son, Melissa is included. We may be D.J.'s full-time parents, but Melissa is his parent, too, and stealth-hostile pronouns can't change that.

There was one parent missing that day in the hospital, though. Melissa had hooked up with Bacchus for a few weeks the summer before D.J. was born. By the time Melissa realized she was pregnant, Bacchus was gone. When we adopted D.J., Bacchus didn't know he was a father or that a gay couple had adopted his son. So we were tense when Bacchus surfaced in New Orleans, appropriately enough considering his street name, shortly before D.J.'s first birthday. But in the end, Bacchus only wanted what we had agreed to give Melissa: pictures a few times a year, and the occasional visit. D.J. met his biological father, whose real name is Jacob, in a hotel off Bourbon Street a few weeks after he first got in touch with us. When Jacob's own dad, a retired truck driver living in Texas, called to thank us for taking "good care of my grandson," we started sending him pictures, too. The gay thing didn't appear to be an issue with Jacob or his father. It never came up.

There was no guarantee that doing an open adoption would get us a baby any faster than doing a closed or foreign adoption. In fact, our agency warned us that, as a gay male couple, we might be in for a long wait. That point was driven home when both birth mothers who spoke at the two-day open adoption seminar we were required to attend said that finding "good, Christian homes" for their babies was their top priority. But we decided to try to do an open adoption anyway. If we became parents, we wanted our child's biological parents to be a part of his life.

As it turns out, we didn't have to wait long. A few weeks after our paperwork was done, we got a call from the agency. The day we met Melissa, the agency suggested all three of us go out for lunch—all four of us if you count Wish, Melissa's German shepherd. Five if you count the baby she was carrying. We were bursting with touchy-feely questions—which we soon realized was a problem. Stoic and wary, Melissa was only interested in the facts: She was pregnant, she couldn't have a baby on the streets, and so she was doing an adoption. Melissa hated talking about her feelings, but she was willing to jump through the agency's hoops—which included weekly counseling sessions and a few meetings with us—because she wanted to do an open adoption, too. She wanted, she said, to be a part of her kid's life.

We were lucky enough to be with Melissa the day D.J. was born. And we were in her hospital room two days later when it was time for her to give him up. Before we could take D.J. home, before we could become a family, we literally had to take him from his mother's arms as she sat sobbing in her bed.

It was the hardest thing I've ever done in my life.

I was thirty-three years old when we adopted D.J., and I thought I knew what a broken heart was: how it felt, what it looked like. I didn't know a damn thing. You know what a broken heart looks like? Like a sobbing teenager in a hospital bed giving a two-day-old infant she knows she can't take care of to a couple she hopes can.

Like most homeless street kids, Melissa works a circuit. Portland and Seattle in the summer; Denver, Minneapolis, Chicago, and New York in the late summer and early fall; New Orleans, Phoenix, Las Vegas, or Los Angeles in the winter and spring. Then she heads back up to Portland, where she's from, and starts all over again. For the first few years after we adopted D.J., Melissa made a point of coming up to Seattle during the summer so we could get together. When she wasn't in Seattle, she kept in touch by phone. Her calls were usually short. She would ask how we're doing, we would ask how she's doing, then put D.J. on the phone. She didn't say much, and he didn't know what to say, but it was important to D.J. that his mother call, even if it was just so he could share a moment of silent connection.

About the time that D.J. was three, Melissa stopped calling regularly and stopped making it up to Seattle. When she did call, it was usually with disturbing news. One time she called the day after a boyfriend died of alcohol poisoning. They were sleeping on a sidewalk in New Orleans and he was dead when she woke up. She called after another boyfriend started using heroin again. Soon the calls stopped altogether. After six months without a call, I started phoning hospitals. Then morgues. When the clerk at the county morgue in New Orleans asked me to describe Melissa, without thinking, I started to say, "Well, she's kinda quiet—" The morgue attendant laughed.

"All my Jane Does fit that description," he said.

Melissa's absence started to become an issue when D.J. was nearing his fourth birthday. I was doing the "dad" thing, tearing down the wallpaper in an extra bedroom at home one night, when D.J. dragged a chair into the room. His friend Haven had just been picked up by his mother after a sleepover. I pulled wallpaper down in strips as D.J. sat quietly. "Haven has a mommy," he said softly, "and I have a mommy." D.J. was going through a phase where he was making statements of fact that were really questions; he liked us to confirm these statements for him. It was as if he were testing himself, making sure his take on reality jibed with our own. "That's right," I responded. "You have a mommy, too, just like Haven." He went on. "My mommy's name is Melissa. I came out of Melissa's tummy. I play with my mommy in the park." Then he looked at me and asked a question. "When do I get to see Mommy again?"

"This summer," I said, hoping it wasn't a lie.

We didn't see her in the summer. Or that fall, or the following spring.

All adopted kids eventually want to know why they were adopted, and sooner or later they start asking questions. "Why didn't my biological parents keep me?" "Didn't they love me?" "Why did they throw me away?" When kids who were adopted in closed adoptions start asking those questions, there's not a lot their parents can tell them. Fact is, they don't know the answers. We did an open adoption in part because we wanted to be able to answer those questions for D.J. We didn't want his mother to be a mystery. But instead of a mystery, his mother was becoming a mass of sometimes very distressing specifics. And instead of processing information about his birth mother at, say, eighteen or twenty-one, like most adopted children, D.J. had to do it at three and four. The last time she visited, D.J. wanted to know why his mother smelled. Melissa doesn't bathe or wash her clothes often; it's one of the ways she holds the world at bay. When we started to explain that she was homeless—she didn't have a bathroom to take showers in or a washing machine to do her laundry—D.J. got upset. How could we be so stupid? What could be more terrifying to a child than the idea of not having a home? For months D.J. insisted that his mother was going to come and live with us. She could sleep in the guest bedroom. When Grandma came to visit, Melissa could sleep in his bed and he would sleep on the floor.

We did eventually hear from Melissa again. She wasn't dead, just thoughtless. She lost track of time, she said, and didn't make it up to Seattle before it got too cold and wet; and whenever she thought about calling, it was either too late or she was too drunk. When she told me that she'd reached the point where she got sick when she didn't drink, I suggested that maybe it was time to get off the streets and stop drinking and using drugs. I could hear her shaking her head. One of the reasons she'd chosen us over all the straight couples she could've chosen for D.J. was that we didn't remind her of her parents. Most straight couples doing adoptions were older, many having gone through years of unsuccessful fertility treatments before deciding to adopt at forty or forty-five or fifty. We were thirty-two and twenty-five, close enough in age to be Melissa's siblings. She didn't want us to start acting like her parents now. She would get off the streets when she was ready, she said. She didn't raise her voice. She just wanted to make sure we understood each other.

For a long time, not much changed. D.J.'s mother made the awkward transition from street kid to homeless person. But besides aging—and living on the streets ages you fast—the details Melissa shared with us about her life were always the same. She would wake up, ask people for spare change, buy food for her dog, alcohol for herself and her friends, hang out, avoid the cops, get arrested for loitering every now and then, and move on. Boyfriends died, other homeless kids disappeared or got off the streets. Her dog Wish was the one constant. She lived for Wish and Wish lived for her. Having a large dog complicates hitchhiking and hopping trains, which is how she got around, but Melissa is a small woman and her dog offers her some protection—and the dog doesn't question or judge her.

I've heard people say that living on the streets is a kind of slow-motion suicide. Having known Melissa for six years now, I'd say that's pretty accurate. For D.J.'s sake, we desperately wanted Melissa to survive her long suicide attempt. The last time we talked, I got the impression that Melissa might be stepping back from the ledge. She is living in an apartment with some friends in Virginia, and she has a job making sandwiches at a fast-food place. I listened as Melissa talked about her life on the streets in the past tense and allowed myself to hope. Maybe one day she'll be able to join us in Saugatuck for a couple of weeks in the summer, so D.J.'s whole family can finally get together.

* * *

Although I grew up in Chicago, just a two-hour drive from Saugatuck, I'd never been to the popular summer resort as a child—I hadn't been to any summer resorts as a child, actually. My family was Catholic, and therefore large, and hence broke. When we wanted to go to a beach on Lake Michigan during the summer, we walked our pasty white asses half a mile east to one of Chicago's beaches, beaches that were named after the city streets that dead-ended in them—Albion or Pratt or Hollywood. In college, I spent most of my vacations in Chicago, waiting tables and going to the beach; after I graduated, I spent my vacations in big cities bar- and boy-hopping. It was only after D.J. turned five years old that I found my way to sleepy little Saugatuck for the first time. And it was my son's idea, or rather his needs, that landed us there.

I'm not going to sugarcoat this: Kids with gay parents—just like kids with mixed-race parents, divorced parents, disabled parents, turban-wearing parents, etc.—one day realize that their families are different, and that realization can be traumatic. And that, as they say, is okay. Or it should be. Couples whose children are all but assured of being traumatized by prejudice—minority couples or mixed-race couples—are not told to remain childless or urged to adopt white children in order to protect their children from racism; Jews are not told that they can protect their children from anti-Semitism by having them baptized. Instead, the prejudice that traumatizes children is regarded as the problem, and minority parents prepare themselves and their children for the inevitabilities of: 1) their children realizing they're different, and 2) encounters with prejudice.

The political right, however, wants to enforce a double standard when it comes to same-sex parents. Gay parents are told—most infamously by Kathleen Parker, a conservative columnist who discovered a "right" for a child to have a family that looks just like everyone else's—that it is the existence of gay parents, not anti-gay prejudice, that's the problem. Since we know our kids will suffer some teasing, Parker wonders, how could we be so selfish as to have kids in the first place? But every child suffers, as Parker must know (at one time she was a struggling single mother), and every child is disgruntled about some aspect of his or her childhood. I was traumatized by my parents' Catholicism, yet I would never argue that a young Catholic couple should refrain from having children in order to spare their offspring the agonies of midnight mass. At some point in their lives, or at several points, all kids have issues with the things that make their families different—but that's when parents parent, if I may use the noun and verb forms of the word one right after the other. You can't kid kids—shit, did it again!—so when your kid gets upset, you can't dodge the issue. You have to swing into action.

Which is precisely what we did when D.J. had a meltdown one day, a meltdown that ultimately took us all the way to Saugatuck. It was a meltdown that we should have seen coming, a meltdown we could have prevented, a meltdown that I sit up nights hating myself for allowing to happen. Shortly before his fifth birthday, D.J. asked how come he was the only kid in the whole wide world with two dads. We were eating D.J.'s favorite breakfast for cold winter mornings—bacon and toast—and he was looking angelic in his new Spider-Man pj's. He didn't sound upset; he sounded like his usual matter-of-fact self, a trait he got from his mother. Terry reassured D.J. that there were lots of other kids out there with two dads, that there were lots of other families like his. D.J. began to eat another slice of bacon and that, we thought, was that.

"Where are they?" D.J. quietly asked.

"Where are who?" I said.

"Where are the other kids with two dads?" he asked.

Terry shot me a "Say something!" look. I shot him a "*You* say something!" look.

"Where are they?" D.J. asked again. He had stopped eating.

"Well, honey, they're—" I said, but D.J., sensing that I was stalling, cut me off.

"WHERE ARE THEY?"

He was wailing now.

"WHERE ARE THEY? WHERE ARE THEY?"

We were so busted.

After we became parents, Terry and I were invited to join a support group for gay parents in Seattle. We declined. We've never really been *joiners*. We don't belong to clubs, we don't have hobbies. I'm bad at small talk, Terry is worse. Before we adopted, we made it to just one meeting of the support group our adoption agency hosts for couples waiting to adopt. From the sports we enjoy (biking, swimming), to the careers we've chosen (writing, pottery), to the stuff we enjoy doing in our free time (reading, reading), we're both contentedly solitary people. Which is part of what makes us so good together: We know when and how to leave each other alone.

Knowing that we were bad on the whole human-contact front, we went out of our way to make ourselves useful to other parents on the island. We volunteered to baby-sit; we had kids for overnights; we hosted playdates. As D.J.'s small circle of friends came together, he got to know other adopted kids, kids with divorced parents, and kids of other races. But somehow we never met other gay parents. There were other gay parents on the island—Terry's mentor, an island potter, is a lesbian and a parent, but her kid was in high school, and the kids of the gay male parents we met were all so much younger than D.J. that we didn't spend much time with them.

Like I said, we screwed up. We should have gone out of our way to meet other gay parents. We should have joined that support group. We should have hung out with gay dads, however old their kids were. Instead we coasted along, figuring we would eventually

meet other gay dads with kids D.J.'s age, so why force it? This strategy led directly to D.J.'s meltdown. So later that same night, after
D.J. went to bed, Terry and I sat down at the computer and typed
"gay family organizations" into a search engine. Eight seconds later
we were reading about COLAGE, or Children of Lesbians and Gays
Everywhere, which sponsors gay family weeks in two different resort
towns every year. One takes place in Provincetown, Massachusetts,
and attracts hundreds of families; the other take places in Saugatuck,
Michigan, and attracts dozens. Provincetown is a big gay mecca, and
we have friends who live there. But Saugatuck won because big gay
meccas often feel like open-air gay bars, and I don't much like gay
bars. I regard gay bars the same way most American Jews regard Is-
rael: I'm happy to have a homeland, but I'm not all that anxious to
live there.

It was my mother's lungs, however, that clinched Saugatuck
for us.

Six months after D.J. had his meltdown, my mother finally got a
diagnosis for a collection of symptoms that began during her prior
visit to Seattle. She had a bad cough she couldn't shake, was suffering from shortness of breath, and was having what appeared to be
asthma attacks. The symptoms began the Christmas we got Stinker,
and for a while my mother thought she was having an allergic reaction to D.J.'s dog. But when the symptoms continued for months
after she got home, she saw a number of doctors and specialists. Ultimately she had to undergo an open-lung biopsy, after which my
mother was diagnosed with idiopathic pulmonary fibrosis. It sounds
scary because it is scary. There's no cure, and until recently there
were no effective treatments. Most people diagnosed with idiopathic
pulmonary fibrosis survive only five years. My mother was diagnosed
early, however, and put on an experimental drug regimen. While the
disease isn't a cancer, the treatment is a course of chemotherapy. The

drugs only slow the disease's progression, they aren't a cure, so my mother will be on them for the rest of her life.

For the first few months after she got her diagnosis, my mother didn't feel comfortable flying—all the dirty air in plane cabins couldn't be good for her. I knew that if we opted for Saugatuck, my mother and stepdad could drive up and spend the week with us. Since it was clear now that my mother was mortal, and that she might not always be around, Terry and I decided that getting D.J. together was his grandmother was just as important as getting him together with other kids with gay dads.

So how were all the other gay dads? Pretty scarce. Apparently gay family week in Provincetown attracts more gay dads than gay family week in Saugatuck, which attracts mostly lesbian moms from small towns in Michigan. And the program couldn't have been structured in a worse way for us: All the events—the beach parties, the pizza parties, the ice cream socials—were informal. No name tags, no introductions, no forced interactions. Unless you were gregarious and outgoing—something Terry and I are not—it was hard to meet people, so we spent most of our time at the family camp visiting with my mom and stepdad. Other campers would occasionally approach us to say they thought it was wonderful that my parents came along, but that was the extent of most of our conversations. Still, D.J. got to see other same-sex parents with his very own eyes—including two male couples with sons, one too old for D.J. to play with, the other too young.

What was truly wonderful about Saugatuck, though, what brought us back for a second year, wasn't really gay family camp. It was the prospect of an expanded Savage Family Camp. We enjoyed spending time with family at Saugatuck the first year, and I figured that more time and more family could only mean more wonderful. So for year two we rented a *bigger* house for *two* weeks and invited not only my mother and stepfather to join us in Michigan, but all three of my siblings, and their partners and children. My eldest brother, Billy, and his girlfriend, Kelly, would be coming, along with older brother, Eddie, his wife, Mikki, their infant son, Delsin, and Thor, Eddie's fifteen-year-old son from his first marriage. My younger sister, Laura, her live-in boyfriend, Joe, and their two-year-old son, Cody, would also be joining us. To accommodate everyone we rented a big Victorian house "on the hill" in Saugatuck, walking distance from the town's little main street with its cafés, restaurants, and bars.

Inviting the whole extended family to Saugatuck had an extra benefit besides a simple family reunion. This year's week in Michigan would not only expose D.J. to other families with gay and lesbian parents but to all the family-structure options that would be open to him one day as the adult heterosexual he was likely to grow up to be. For two weeks we would be turning that house in Saugatuck into a living diorama of the many ways in which straight Americans structure their relationships: There would be one middle-aged second marriage (Mom & Jerry); one family blended by a second marriage (Eddie & Mikki); one non-married, non-cohabitating, childless heterosexual couple (Billy & Kelly); and one non-married, cohabitating heterosexual couple with one biological child (Laura & Joe).

When I was six years old I hadn't heard of divorce, much less cohabitation, blended families, or out-of-wedlock births. I hadn't heard of same-sex couples either, for that matter. I wondered what D.J. would make of it all.

—4—

One Roof

"Tattoos?"

My mom and stepdad arrived at the summer rental half a day before we did. By the time we drove up to the sprawling Victorian, they had already called the rental agency to complain about the chilly hot tub, the filthy kitchen, and the broken air conditioner. The house was big—five bedrooms, two baths—albeit run-down, but it would comfortably house my entire extended family for two weeks, which was the point. The first night, however, was reserved for D.J., his parents, and his grandparents. And thanks to Grandpa Jerry, my mom's second husband and the only handy person who has ever married into our family, D.J. was splashing around in a rapidly warming hot tub moments after we arrived. This allowed me and Terry to focus on more important things—like unpacking our bags, checking out the bedrooms, and making margaritas.

Terry was still slicing up the inaugural lime when my mom asked when we were going to get married. She was joking—sort of. Terry tossed out his standard response, one my mother had heard before: "We're not getting married, Judy. I don't want to act like straight people." Soon Mom and Terry were lobbing their well-rehearsed lines at each other from opposite sides of the kitchen counter like a couple of tennis pros casually knocking a ball back and forth across the net. Smiling sweetly, my mom reminded Terry that straight people have been having children for a lot longer than they've been getting married.

"We've been having babies since we were monkeys in trees, my dear," she said. "This marriage business is a comparatively recent development."

"Then our sweet monkey love is even more traditional than we thought," Terry replied, handing my mother a margarita. In a transparent attempt to change the subject, Terry started to complain about how pricey margarita mix is in Michigan. The two bottles of margarita mix we picked up on the way into town cost thirty dollars. In Seattle, a bottle of margarita mix costs four bucks.

"They must know people are coming here for summer vacation," Terry said, "and they figure they'll gouge you on drink mix."

I should have gone with the flow and made an observation about the price of beer or steered the conversation toward less contentious subjects like, say, assisted suicide or stem cell research or the fact that my heterosexual sister still isn't married to the man she lives with, the father of her two-year-old son. But I was tired after the drive and still suffering from post-traumatic stress induced by taking a poodle for a walk in Billings, Montana. That's the best excuse I can come up with for telling my mom we were thinking about getting tattoos to mark our upcoming tenth anniversary.

"Tattoos?" she said. "Tattoos of what? Tattoos where?"

"We're thinking 'Property of Dan Savage' on Terry's arm, 'Property of Terry Miller' on mine."

I smiled.

My mother nodded.

Terry kicked me, but my mother didn't witness this act of domestic violence from her side of the counter. She continued to nod slowly, a half-grimace/half-smile frozen in place on her face. It's a look that she's employed strategically ever since her children became adults. She can't tell us what to do anymore, but this look allows her to maintain some semblance of control—or the illusion of control.

"Tattoos are a wonderful idea," she said, taking a quick sip of her margarita. "Your brother's tattoo worked out so well."

Game, set, match.

I'm the only one of my mother's three sons who made it into his thirties without getting a tattoo. My oldest brother, Billy, had the Chicago Cubs' logo tattooed on his left shoulder (closer to his heart than his right arm, he says); my other brother, Eddie, has five tattoos— and counting. But I knew the particular brother and the specific tattoo to which my mother was referring. Shortly before Eddie joined the Air Force, shortly before he met and married a girl named Tina, Eddie had the name Jenny tattooed on his arm. Jenny was, as the song goes, only sixteen and too young to fall in love. Eddie was twenty-one at the time, but Jenny's parents approved of their relationship because, unlike their daughter's previous boyfriends, Eddie wasn't in a street gang. Eddie was from a nice Catholic family, his father used to be a cop, and he didn't have a record. But the tattoo— a rose and a heart with her name on a scroll—turned out to be an ill-timed, ill-advised show of devotion. While Eddie was in boot camp, a letter arrived from Jenny. She was seeing someone else.

My mother, calmly sipping her margarita, knew exactly what she was doing when she brought up Eddie's "Jenny" tattoo. We share the jinx gene, my mother and I, although in her case it's more explicitly Catholic. When your life is going along nicely, when things are looking good, the correct posture to assume is one of gratitude, absent of any hint that you expect your good fortune to last. It's kind of a defensive crouch. Good Catholics don't *presume*. The moment you start to expect things to continue going along nicely for you—the moment you begin to believe you're worthy of the good things in your life—God gets all Old Testament on your ass and does something vicious, something insane, something totally uncalled for. He gives you lupus or He allows Satan to slaughter your children and cattle or He delivers Ohio to George W. Bush.

A good, liberal Catholic, my mother wants to live long enough to celebrate the ordination of female priests. She doesn't go in for that dark, brooding, Italian brand of Catholicism. She somehow manages to stay sunny and upbeat while expecting the worst and praying for the best. And so far it's worked: She's got four kids and we're all still alive, she believes because she spends a great deal of time obsessing about the many, many ways in which we could all die. She doesn't presume we'll live, and she encourages us to make the same assumption. She tells her two kids who believe in God to expect the worst and pray for the best; she tells her kids who don't believe in God to expect the worst and hope for best. But she doesn't, and we shouldn't, *presume*. It might piss off the Supreme Sociopath.

So for my mother, matching tattoos commemorating our Big Gay Love would be presumptuous in the extreme, just as Eddie's "Jenny" tattoo had been. Billy's Cubs tattoo was acceptable, since Billy would always be a Cubs fan, even if that fact alone will prevent the Cubs from ever winning the World Series. Eddie has the name of his son from his first marriage—Thor—tattooed on his arm, and that's acceptable, since Eddie will always be Thor's father. There are some things even a vengeful God can't change. But getting your boyfriend's name—or your girlfriend's name—tattooed on your arm? God can and will do something about that. He won't be able to resist. And just as God stepped in and fucked up Eddie and Jenny, God would step in and fuck up Dan and Terry if we were so presumptuous as to get matching tattoos.

My mother, the great communicator, communicated all of this to us with a couple of waves of her margarita glass as she crossed to the sofa in the family room.

I quickly ran through all the reasons why getting married seemed more presumptuous than getting a tattoo—think of all the failed gay relationships, I said, think of all the high-profile gay couples whose relationships tanked after they made a big deal about their Big Gay Loves. And think of all those heterosexual couples that have divorced! Think of Eddie's first marriage, I told my mother, to say nothing of her current husband's first marriage. Or her own.

"Think of all that," I said, "and then tell me that marriage itself isn't presumptuous, isn't risky. It's riskier than tattoos."

"Yes, Danny, marriage is risky," my mother replied, "but unlike a tattoo, a wedding band can be removed. It *shouldn't* be removed, of course, but it *can* be. And while removing a wedding band may leave emotional scars, removing or covering up a tattoo leaves a visible scar, my dear, a permanent reminder of your failed relationship. An ex-husband can be out of sight, out of mind. But a tattoo is visible evidence of your stupidity. Ask your brother."

"But we're not going to break up," I said pathetically. "Why shouldn't we get tattoos?"

"Why shouldn't you act like grown-ups and think of your son?" Mom said, reaching for her purse. She pulled out an envelope and removed a newspaper clipping. My mother reads newspapers with scissors in hand, snipping out stories that might interest, involve, or frighten her children, clippings she mails to us in envelopes with just the "The Mad Clipper" as the return address.

"Did you see this?" she asked. Without waiting for an answer, she began to read. " 'In this case, we are confronted with an entire, size-able class of *parents raising children* who have absolutely *no access* to civil marriage *and its protection*.' " The words were from the Supreme Court of Massachusetts; the emphasis was my mother's.

"It sure sounds like they're talking about you two!" my mother said, gleefully waving the clipping at us.

I would like to pause here to mention my mom's car: Symbolically speaking, her car is a whole lot gayer than ours. There's a rainbow sticker on the rear windshield and a Parents and Friends of Lesbians and Gays (PFLAG) sticker on her bumper. My mother is determined to do her part for gay visibility in the part of unincorporated McHenry County, Illinois, where she lives with my stepfather. The previous summer a couple of rubes in a pickup truck mistook my sixty-something mom and stepdad for a gay couple and tried to run them off the road while screaming "Faggots!" My mom figures after that experience, she's earned the right to cry at our wedding.

Terry picked up the margarita pitcher and widened his eyes as he crossed behind my mother. "Gee, your mom seems unusually emphatic for this early in a visit," the look said. And he was right: Mom typically saves direct orders for a late-night game of Hearts. This visit, apparently, was going to be different. My mother had an agenda.

" 'It cannot be *rational* under our laws,' " my mother continued to read, " 'and indeed it is not *permitted*, to *penalize children* by *depriving them* of State benefits because the State disapproves of their *parents' sexual orientation*.' "

"God save that court," Terry said.

"You two shouldn't 'penalize' D.J. because you're uncomfortable with the idea of marriage," Mom said. "Even though your father and I ultimately divorced after twenty-three years of marriage, Daniel, you enjoyed State benefits and the emotional security of marriage when you were children."

"We don't live in a state where we have any rights," Terry

pointed out. "So even if we got married, Judy, our child would still be penalized."

"Just the jinx, Mom," I added. "All we would get out of marriage is the jinx, and not a single one of the benefits."

"Then maybe you should move to a state that doesn't discriminate," Mom said, "or stay where you are and help change things for the better by marrying, even if it's only a symbolic act for now. And D.J. still benefits from the emotional security."

I was about to bring up the fact that D.J. was emphatically opposed to us marrying, but just then Jerry and D.J. came in from the deck. Terry got up and went to the counter to mix up a fresh pitcher of margaritas. In another attempt to change the subject, Terry began to complain again about how expensive margarita mix is in Michigan. Now, normally, Terry doesn't mind running up our credit card bill, but he was desperately searching for a new topic. We were already on our second fifteen-dollar bottle; at this rate, Terry pointed out, margarita mix would wind up being our single largest vacation expense. As Terry poured my mother another drink, D.J., wrapped in a towel, curled up next to his grandma. As he listened to Terry complain about the pricey drink mix, my stepfather picked the empty bottle of mix out of the trash. Examining the label over the top of his glasses, Jerry quickly solved the mystery.

"This isn't a bottle of margarita mix," Jerry said, cackling. "It's a bottle of margaritas, Terry. It's already got tequila in it."

Terry snatched the bottle away from Jerry and read the label. His jaw dropped. No wonder Mom was so emphatic. Terry had been serving her doubles—or quadruples, more likely, considering how Terry makes drinks.

"Oh my God, Judy, I'm so sorry," said Terry, turning to face my mother, a bottle in one hand, his other hand pressed against his chest.

My mother, a light drinker, laughed and shook her head. She raised her glass—her third quad of the afternoon—and offered a toast: "Good-bye," she said.

"Two interesting things happened before you arrived," my mother announced as her children and grandchildren passed around platters of brats and corn on the cob. "First, Terry decided to get your dear old mother falling-down drunk yesterday. And second, Danny and Terry informed me that they're thinking of getting their names tattooed on each other."

"Where?" Laura asked as she cut up a bratwurst for her son, Cody.

"On our arms," I said. " 'Property of Dan Savage' on Terry's arm, 'Property of Terry Miller' on mine."

"That's a relief," Billy said. "Mom makes it sound like you're getting them on your foreheads."

"Don't do it," said Eddie, pointing to his old Jenny tattoo. He had had Jenny's name covered up with a string of black hearts years ago, but you could still read her name.

"We want to mark our tenth anniversary," Terry offered. "So we figured, why not get the tattoos?"

"Why not get married?" It wasn't my mother pushing a marriage on us this time, but Eddie, the only one of my siblings with any experience with marriage.

"I look at it this way," Eddie said. "So long as you've got a shovel and a place to dig, you can get rid of a spouse. But a tattoo is forever."

Mikki tore off a piece of a hot dog bun and tossed it at her husband's head.

"Dig deep," said Kelly, Billy's girlfriend. "Haste makes for shallow graves. And it's the shallow ones that dogs dig up, hikers step through, or a bloated corpse just pops right out of." Kelly had been an editor at a daily newspaper in Iowa before she moved to Chicago, and she learned a thing or two about the disposal of spouses while she lived in the heartland.

"Any other tips?" Eddie asked.

"Any hit man you meet in a bar is a cop," Kelly said.

"Why shouldn't they get the tattoos?" Billy asked my mother. "It'll make men out of them both."

"It didn't work for you two," Laura said, pointing at Billy and Eddie with her fork.

"Property of? It's sick," my mother said. "Danny doesn't own Terry, and Terry doesn't own Danny. They're not each other's slaves."

"Not even sometimes?" asked Billy, looking over at me.

Fifteen-year-old Thor snickered into his slaw.

"William," my mother said, glaring.

"Jerry Falwell has to live vicariously through somebody," Billy said. "Who's going to meet his needs if all the gays settle down and stop having kinky sex?"

"Could we please save this discussion for a time when there aren't children and teenagers at the table?" my mother said. Mom quickly walked everyone through our objections to marriage. Eddie and Laura could appreciate my objection, the jinx factor, but Billy hooted when my mother brought up Terry's objection.

"I've never wanted to act like 'straight people' either," Billy said to Terry, "and here's the secret to my success: I don't act like 'straight people.' You know, don't have kids, don't live together, don't take on traditional sex roles."

Terry smiled and ate while my family debated our marital and dermatological statuses. I couldn't tell if he was angry. In Terry's family, personal decisions are not hashed over by a committee of the whole during a meal. Jokes are certainly not made at the dinner table about people's sex lives, siblings don't casually insult each other, wives don't throw hot dog buns at their husbands. I kept an eye on Terry as he ate his corn on the cob—something he eats with a precision so perverse that it makes his other perversions seem wholesome; he eats the corn one tiny row of kernels at a time, methodically picking the cob clean—but he just stared at a point over my head somewhere.

"You okay?" I asked, touching his arm.

Suddenly the room got quiet. Everyone turned and looked at Terry. Had the Savages finally gone too far?

"I've been coming to this circus for ten years," Terry said. "I'm used to it. It's Mikki you should all feel sorry for."

I used to have a hard time with the circus.

Growing up in Chicago, I couldn't go anywhere without running into someone I was related to by blood or marriage. It's fun now, sort of, to walk around a big city like Chicago and everywhere I go run into people who share my DNA. But it was a different story when I was a teenager. At fifteen I knew I was gay, but I wasn't ready to come out to my family. I was ready, however, to hang out in the gay parts of town. But the sheer number of Savages—and Schneiders, Hollahans, Hirths—on the ground was a problem. If I walked around the gay neighborhood, one of my siblings might see me from a bus; if I snuck into a gay bar, one of my uncles might see me sneaking back out; if I stood in the gay section of a bookstore, a grandparent or a cousin or an aunt or a nephew or an uncle or—worst of all!—a parent might see me. The only way I would ever feel free enough to be gay, my frustrated and hormone-pickled brain concluded, was if I got as far away from my family as humanly possible.

All fifteen-year-olds feel this way, of course, but I would argue that my feelings were particularly intense. Coming out to my large Catholic family didn't seem to be an option at the time. I was convinced I would be pummeled with fists, not hot dog buns, and disowned. My urge to flee was entirely rational, not an adolescent overreaction. I had to run away. And I think the fact that I actually fled, unlike so many straight kids who only threaten to, underscores how dire my situation seemed to me at the time. All three of my siblings went to college in Chicago, but I went to college in downstate Illinois, hundreds of miles from home. Then I fled to Kentucky, Virginia, England, Germany, Wisconsin, and ultimately Seattle. Only by living far away from my family was I able to give myself permission to go places (bars, clubs, parties) and do things (dudes, drugs, drag) that I couldn't bring myself to do in a city crawling with my relatives.

Ironically, I came out to my family before I left for college and they became, after one rocky summer, aggressively supportive. So I didn't need to flee; I could have done all the dudes, drugs, and drag I liked in Chicago. But while the need to flee was gone, the urge remained. The years I spent in the closet—roughly age twelve to age eighteen—conditioned me to associate the physical presence of my parents, siblings, grandparents, aunts, uncles, and cousins with a debilitating fear of discovery and rejection. I believed for so long that I could be free only once I got the hell out of town that it became a self-fulfilling prophecy. Even after I got away, these feelings persisted. For most of my adult life, whenever I came home for a visit, I would get antsy after a day or two, anxious to get back to the life I'd made for myself in Berlin or Madison or Seattle.

Then one day the urge to flee was gone.

It was the summer D.J. was eighteen months old. We were staying at my sister's apartment for a week, and I was in her bathroom sitting on her toilet, when I noticed a framed poster on the wall opposite. ALL I NEED TO KNOW ABOUT LIFE I LEARNED FROM MY GUARDIAN ANGEL, it read. "Whenever you feel lonely, a special angel drops in for tea." "Leave space in your relationships so the angels have room to play." "After all, we are all angels in training." The cherub on the poster wasn't the only angel hanging out with me in the can—I was surrounded by winged pests. Ceramic angels, molded soap angels, needlepoint angels, stained-glass angels, angel night-lights, an angel tissue box, and on and on. Sitting there, I developed a crippling case of performance anxiety. It wasn't easy taking a dump in front of this heavenly host.

It was right after I stepped out of my sister's bathroom that I noticed the old urge was gone. Hmm. . . .

Between the ages of twelve and thirty-three, confronting angels in my sister's bathroom, being subjected to so much cheap sentiment and Hallmark spirituality while I was trying to take a crap, would've had me sprinting to the airport. "I'm not like them," the teenage closet case in my head would've screamed. "Get me out of here!" But when I got into the car and headed off to the airport a few days later, I told Terry I wanted to spend more time in Chicago with my family. I even wondered if a time might come when I could return to Chicago for good. My family no longer seemed like a threat and their quirks had become charming, not off-putting.

Terry smiled and patted my leg.

"That isn't going to happen, honey," he said. "Chicago for summer vacations, fine. Chicago winters? I didn't sign up for that."

Over the two weeks in Saugatuck, as I watched D.J. shift from playing adored grandson to adoring nephew, from worshipful younger cousin to wise older cousin, a familiar feeling crept over me: guilt. By inviting my siblings to join us in Saugatuck, I had recreated for D.J. at age six what "family life" looked like for me at the same age. Three generations of his family were all under one roof, all of us in the same house, all fourteen of us sharing two bathrooms.

What struck me most as we crowded around the dining room table every night wasn't so much the gorgeous mosaic laid out before D.J.—every relationship option represented save polygamy—but the size of the crowd. At home on Vashon Island, there are only three of us around the dinner table at night. In Saugatuck, there were fourteen people around the dining room table. And for fourteen days, wherever he went—the living room, the bathroom, the kitchen, the porch, the yard, downtown Saugatuck—D.J. was sure to run into at least one of his relatives. And as I watched D.J. ricochet from one uncle to another, I saw myself at his age.

Growing up, my aunts, uncles, and grandparents were a daily presence in my life, just as D.J.'s aunts, uncles, cousins, and grandparents were a daily presence for the two weeks in the summer of 2004. In 1918 my great-grandparents, James and Margaret Hollahan, purchased a two-flat at 6433 N. Glenwood Avenue in Rogers Park, an Irish-Catholic neighborhood on the north side of town. They paid $6,000 for it. Two-flats, for non-Chicagoans, are brick buildings with flat roofs and just two apartments, and they are to Chicago what brownstones are to New York City and Victorians are to San Francisco; comfortable, iconic, and, once upon a time, affordable. Both apartments had three bedrooms, one bathroom, enclosed porches at the back, and a sunroom at the front. There were formal front steps that linked the apartments, although I don't remember anyone ever actually using them. We came and went by the back steps. In the summers we lived on the back stoop. It was a time when six-year-old children not only walked to corner stores all by themselves, they were frequently sent by their parents to buy cigarettes.

My great-grandparents had six children when they moved into the upstairs apartment at 6433; they would have two more while they lived there. They rented the downstairs apartment to another Catholic family with eight children. For those of you doing the math at home, that means that in the 1920s and 1930s, sixteen children and four adults were sharing six bedrooms and two bathrooms. In the early 1950s, one of James and Margaret's daughters—my grandmother, Marijo—moved into the downstairs apartment with her husband, Ed. Marijo already had two children when she moved back into her childhood home—Judy, my mother, and her brother Walter—and would go on to have four more while she lived at 6433: Joie, Jimmy, Peggy, and Jerry. While my mother was a little girl at 6433, her grandmother and grandfather lived upstairs. Eventually James and Margaret bought an apartment in the Edgewater Beach Apartments nearby, and moved there with Katie, the only one of their eight children who didn't either marry or join a religious order. One of their sons moved into the empty upstairs apartment with his six children. Once again for those doing the math: That's twelve children and four adults packed into six bedrooms and two bathrooms. In prison that would be considered overcrowding.

When my mother moved out of 6433 as a young adult, she swore she would never move back, the same oath Marijo had sworn when she moved out twenty years earlier. But in the late 1960s, my parents were living in Skokie, Illinois, a suburb just over the Chicago city limits. My father had applied to join the Chicago Police Department, which has a residency requirement, and when his application was accepted, he had to quickly find an apartment in the city. The upstairs apartment at 6433 was empty, so my mother and father moved in with their four kids. My grandparents still lived downstairs with their younger children. A family with four children may be large by today's standards, but it was tiny by the standards set by two generations of Hollahans. Ours was the smallest family to live at 6433 N. Glenwood Avenue in the seven decades my family owned the building, and the amount of space my family had—there were "only" six of us in the apartment, my great-aunts used to marvel—seemed positively decadent to relatives who grew up sharing bedrooms with three or four siblings.

Like all small children, I assumed everyone lived like I did. Didn't every little boy live with his grandparents, aunts, and uncles, all under one roof? When I look at pictures taken at 6433 in the '40s, '50s, '60, and '70s, the number of people crowded into every photograph amazes me. Pictures taken in our house on Vashon Island seem so empty; there's only ever two of us in any given shot. Terry and D.J. skateboarding in front of the house, me and D.J. carving pumpkins on the kitchen floor, Stinker and D.J. on the porch swing. Comparing pictures taken at 6433 with pictures taken at Vashon makes me feel guilty for living so far from my family. I have to remind myself that for D.J., though, this is normal. He assumes that all kids live the way he does, the same assumption I made at his age. It's normal for him to spend more time with friends and neighbors than he does with grandparents, aunts, uncles, and cousins.

"You really thinking about getting a tattoo?"

Eddie dropped down beside me on the sand. We were at Saugatuck's Oval Beach, a long stretch of dunes and cottonwood trees. Terry had gone for a swim while Thor tossed D.J. into waves. Delsin, Eddie's infant son, was asleep under an umbrella. Mikki had gone back to the house to make sandwiches.

"Do you know what the guy who did my 'Jenny' tattoo said to me?" he asked. I shook my head. "He was a biker, a guy called Fat Joe, and he looked at me and said, 'Only a dumb fucking asshole gets a girl's name put on his arm.' But the fat bastard took my money anyway."

I laughed.

Eddie leaned back on his elbows.

"You're one of the people in my life who does the right thing,"

Eddie said, getting serious, "so it kind of flips me out that you would even be thinking about getting a tattoo."

In the narrative Eddie's constructed about our family, I'm the good son, the one who never made a mistake, the one who never gave our parents any trouble. A tattoo didn't jibe with the good-son role in which Eddie had cast me. I've attempted to explain to Eddie that I've made mistakes, too. Unlike Eddie, who spent his teens and twenties in Chicago, I was lucky enough to make my mistakes far from home. Most of mine took place in London, where I regularly passed out in Trafalgar Square, and Berlin, where, um, well, let's just say I did things a good son would never burden his dear mother with the knowledge of. Since my family isn't aware of most of my mistakes, they don't haunt me the way Eddie's mistakes haunt him. In his mind, Billy, the English professor, is the smart son; I'm the considerate son; and he, with his tattoos, his first marriage, his stint in the air force, is the prodigal son. The truth, of course, is more complicated. We have all been smart, considerate, and prodigal in turns, just as we've all made mistakes. Nevertheless, Eddie was having a hard time believing that I was on the verge of making the same mistake he once did. It doesn't fit his script.

"I don't get to play the wise big brother often, but on this issue, I will," he said. "Don't get a tattoo. I would hope that you and Terry would be together forever, but you never know, right?"

Pointing to his other tattoos, he said, "I think tattoos are cool," he continued. "I've got five. Or six. But I know you can't take them off."

I was away at college when Eddie made the mistake of getting his "Jenny" tattoo, so I told him I would tell him about one mistake I made if he told me about that day.

"You first," he said.

I walked him through a particularly harrowing day in Berlin, shortly after the Wall came down, involving a German, a French Canadian, a large, empty apartment, and some bungee cord. Like all stories involving unreasonable risk-taking and appalling stupidity, it's impossible to tell the story now without sounding like I'm bragging—how come stupid mistakes you survive become points of pride?—and I had to reassure Eddie that I wasn't proud of what I did, or of the bungee-cord burns that took almost six months to heal.

And then, after I swore Eddie to secrecy, it was his turn.

"When I got home and Mom saw the bandage, she said, 'That better say 'Mom' under there,' " he laughed. "Everyone told me I was a dumb fuck and they were right, you know. I am a dumb fuck. But it was something I did when I loved somebody, so I'm not ashamed of it. I don't regret it. It was a good time in my life, and I like to be reminded of it."

"It sounds like you're trying to talk me *into* getting a tattoo," I said. "He's not a German with a thing for bungee cord, but Terry's a pretty good time."

"If this is a person you're never going to leave, forever, I would say do it," Eddie said. "But you can't know that. My 'Jenny' tattoo reminds me of a time when I was young and stupid, and it's a fine thing to be young and stupid. If you get a 'Terry' and things come to shit, it's only going to remind you that you were stupid at a time in your life when you should've known better. You're almost forty? Know what I'm saying?"

Eddie pointed to one of his other tattoos—"Thor," his older son's name, written under a large hammer.

"I will get another tattoo sometime," he said. "I'll get 'Delsin' on me somewhere. Why don't you get a 'D.J.' tattoo?"

"So why don't you two get married?"

It was the first time on our summer vacation that the question wasn't being put to Terry and me. This time it was Billy, one of my two unmarried heterosexual siblings, who was on the spot. And I put him there.

"How come you're not married to Kelly?"

"I wouldn't marry her because I wouldn't be going out with her for this long if she wanted to get married," Billy replied.

"Oh, there's some circular logic," I said.

"Actually, no, it's not circular logic. It's a self-fulfilling prophecy. And it works for me," Billy said.

It had been raining heavily most of the day and Mom and Jerry offered to watch all the grandchildren, creating a free afternoon for the rest of us. Kelly and Terry drove to the nearest big town to get groceries; Eddie and Mikki, after a long night up with Delsin, took a nap; Laura and Joe went to a movie. Billy and I had originally opted to lie around and read, but when there was a break in the thunderstorm— bright sunlight, a nice cool breeze off the lake—we hopped on our bikes and rode to the bowling alley in Douglas, a little town less than a mile from Saugatuck. Our cunning plan worked beautifully: Moments after we locked our bikes, the thunder and lightning started up again, trapping us in the bowling alley. We had no choice but to wait out the storm in the bowling alley's small bar. Sometimes life sends you lemons and you make beer out of them.

"So how come you and Kelly not getting married works for you, and it works for Mom, but the same thing doesn't work for me and Terry? It doesn't seems fair that I'm the one Mom is pushing to get married when you and Kelly aren't married. And what about Laura and Joe?"

"As for Laura," Billy said, "Mom's not convinced that Laura and Joe should get married, so she doesn't push them. Mom's finally convinced I won't get married, so she's given up on me. But you and Terry are getting it with both barrels because she's convinced you should be married. And you've failed to convince her that you can't be convinced."

"What would it take?" I wondered aloud.

"Shit, for me all it took was elective surgery—my vasectomy. Having some stranger rummage around in my scrotum with a scalpel did the trick. Best money I ever spent."

Billy ordered us a couple of beers. I needed one after that mental image. "So tell me why you don't want to get married," I said after we had our first sips. "And spare me the circle-jerk self-fulfilling prophecy. Convince me."

"I don't want to get married because I don't believe that my life can be made complete by any one other person," Billy said. "There's a myth that goes back to Plato and beyond, that for every person there's a missing other half, and once you find your other half, you're going to want to spend the rest of your life with that person and that person alone, who will be everything for you, blah blah blah. I don't feel that way. I don't believe the myth that all my social, emotional, or physical needs can all be met through one person. And neither does Kelly."

I don't believe in that myth either, I said. I don't expect Terry to meet all my physical, emotional, and social needs, nor does he expect that I can meet all of his needs. "But even though it's not true, the myth of the other half," I said, "that is what true love feels like. I do feel like Terry's my 'other half,' even if I knew he's not, and that there's no such thing."

Billy took a swig.

"Well, sure. That emotional and physical response must have some basis or the myth would not have come into being. By 'myth' I don't mean 'lie,' I mean a story a culture uses to explain itself to itself. At the same time, this myth of true love, of this other half that completes you, it's only in the last couple of centuries that the marriage contract and the completion of the self with another have become one and the same thing. For the ancient Greeks, it was often a boy, or another male, that was your other half. But men didn't marry boys. The other half was about romantic love, and marriage wasn't a romance. Until modern times, marriage was an economic contract."

"We live in modern times. Provided you don't enter the marriage with unrealistic expectations about what you're going to mean to each other," I said, "why not get married? You and Kelly, two people who don't expect the other person to meet all their needs, would have a better chance at making a success of marriage than, say, a couple who believes in the myth of the other half and goes into marriage with unrealistic expectations."

"There are other myths to worry about," Billy replied, "like the myth of the marital bed: the presumption that every day, for the rest of your life, you will share the same bed with another person, and that it will never grow dull or oppressive. The proponents of this insane lifestyle will say that the more you get to know this person, the longer you're together, the deeper your erotic and emotional bond will grow. That might be true for some people, but it isn't true for everyone."

The marital bed, Billy believes, doesn't necessarily result in deeper knowledge and love—it can lead to boredom and ennui. As evidence, he cites divorce rates and the Western European literary tradition, with special emphasis on novels written in English or French since about 1920.

"Because Kelly and I are not together every night—our pattern is spending Friday, Saturday, and one weeknight with each other—when we are together, we're focused on each other. We don't do things together that we don't both enjoy—I don't drag her to Cubs games, she doesn't make me come out for live music. We don't even double-date much, since being together is special, and it's not routine, which makes our sex life special. It's not like, 'Oh, here it is, night again, and here we are in bed. Again.' It's like, 'Oh! It's Saturday night and here we are together in bed!' I call it Permanent Romance, like Trotsky's idea of Permanent Revolution. We don't take each other for granted, nothing is carved-in-stone, sworn-in-court routine, and that makes our time together fresh and fun, in bed and out."

I asked Billy if there were any circumstances under which he would get married.

"If I won the lottery. Kelly was bitching about work one time—not her job, but the need to have a job at all—and I promised to take care of her if I won the lottery. She said she wouldn't want to feel dependent on me for money, so I offered to marry her and then get a quickie divorce. That way she could take half the money and we could go back to our normal-slash-abnormal routine."

We got another beer and, with the thunderstorm booming along, decided to bowl a few games.

"What if you and Kelly are together thirty, forty years?" I asked between frames. "What about the right to make end-of-life decisions for each other?"

"I'm pretty confident that my siblings will respect the wishes of the woman I love," Billy said. "That's more of a worry for you guys. If you and Terry live to be a hundred, your only surviving 'legal' relative could be some distant cousin who's a born-again Christian asshole who disapproves of your relationship, and that could cause problems. But Kelly and I have a relationship that falls into the 'normal' range, even if we don't marry. If we live to be a hundred, our distant, born-again relatives will probably respect her wishes. And if I'm hit by a truck while riding my bike and put on life support now, I'm pretty confident that my immediate family will respect my living will and Kelly's wishes if she decides it's time to pull the plug."

"If it comes to that," I said, "one of your brothers will beat her to the wall socket before she can finish asking the question."

Billy laughed and missed his spare.

"You could have an eBay auction of the right to pull it," he said. "Just give Kelly the money. Donate my organs—except the liver, that'd be cruel to the recipient—cremate the remains, no open casket at the wake, and scatter the ashes on the warning track at Wrigley Field."

Eventually, the thunderstorm ended and, a wee bit tipsy, we headed out to our bikes.

"You know, I should have been the gay one," Billy said as he put on his helmet and pulled on his gloves. He leaned on his bike, and I leaned on mine, and we talked for a few more minutes under dripping trees in the parking lot overlooking the Kalamazoo River. "A lot of the assumptions that gay men bring to relationships would have made dating a lot easier for me."

Before he found a match in Kelly—not his other half, mind you, and not his match, singular, but "a" match, one of millions of potential matches he could have made—Billy had some rocky dating experiences. Like the Rocky Mountains have some rocks, and some mountains.

"Most women date with hopes that it will 'end in something real,' and by that they mean one thing and one thing only: marriage and kids. The implication is that the only 'real' or successful relationship is a marital one," Billy said. "If you don't get married and have kids and stay married till one of you croaks, the relationship has been a failure."

When Billy would explain to women that he wasn't interested in marriage, their first date was often their last. "They weren't primarily interested in me, they were interested in *it*." Because gay men do not—or did not—expect that their relationships would end in marriage; gay relationships were judged on their merits. "If you were happy, it was successful. If it wasn't, you ended it," Billy said. "Like gay you of old, Kelly and I don't have to talk about our love 'going anywhere.' It is what it is, and we like it this way. Permanent Romance. No kids, no marriage, no cohabitation. It doesn't have to become something else to be worthwhile."

We kicked off and rode back to the house. We were a little wobbly, but we had helmets on, and the streets were deserted after the storm. As we dismounted in the driveway, D.J. tore around the corner of the house.

"Daddy!" he screamed. I'm the rough-and-tumble parent, so I picked him up—all fifty pounds of him, who needs a gym?—and tossed him into the air. Thor ran up a second later, in hot pursuit of D.J. They were playing tag, like cousins from time immemorial. D.J. tried to declare me "base," but Thor wasn't buying it.

"People can't be base," he said. D.J. entered an appeal, but the Supreme Court of Uncles ruled unanimously that People Cannot Be Base, and so D.J. was now It. He chased Thor around the other side of the house.

"You realize we wouldn't even be having this conversation if it weren't for D.J.," Billy said as we locked the bikes up (some city habits cannot be dropped even in bucolic Saugatuck). "If D.J. weren't in the picture, Terry would be the kept boy, and Mom wouldn't be so interested in marrying you off."

"If D.J. weren't in the picture, Terry wouldn't be 'kept.' He'd be working," I said.

"Then you'd just be another cohabitating gay couple. But you wouldn't be parents, and in Mom's view, and the world's view—and your own, you hypocrite—parents are supposed to be married."

"My own view?"

"Does 'Why don't you marry my sister and *then* knock her up?' ring any bells?"

"Laura isn't married to Joe," I said, "and that doesn't seem to be an issue for anyone but me."

"Laura and Joe," Billy said, "well, that's a different thing."

And so it is.

My sister met her boyfriend via the Internet—but not, she's quick to point out, via an Internet personal ad. She was at a friend's house in July of 2001 and noticed an open e-mail on her friend's computer. It was a long list of jokes. "Funny ones," she says, "not the usual Web crap people forward to each other." The e-mail turned out to be from the friend's cousin, who lived in Texas. Laura sent him an e-mail, requesting that he include her on his mailing list.

He wrote back, she wrote back. In early August Joe flew up to Chicago so they could meet. Joe came back up for another visit over Thanksgiving, then Laura went to Texas for Christmas and wound up staying through New Year's. Then in January Joe moved up to Chicago to live with Laura, less than six months after they met.

Four weeks later Laura was pregnant. She was thirty-six, Joe was thirty-nine.

Laura had always wanted to have children, but she'd never met a man she could see herself married to. She had been engaged once, and backed out, and another guy asked her to marry him, but she turned him down. My parents' divorce hit Laura hard, and she has a hard time trusting men. At some point I think she made an unconscious decision to make herself downright unpleasant to the men who pursued her. There's no nice way to say this, so I'll just say it: By being a bitch, Laura hoped to drive off men who weren't really sure they wanted to be with her. But by the time a guy who stuck it out long enough to prove to her that, yes, he really wanted to be with her, she had lost all respect for him. How could she love a man with so little respect for himself that he would take so much crap from her? It was a cruel catch-22.

But Joe got Laura pregnant before any of these dynamics could play out, and while they were both sure they wanted the baby, they weren't sure they wanted each other. When Cody was born, Laura and Joe embarked on the courtship from hell: Confronting all the stresses of being new parents, Laura and Joe were also trying to determine if they were right for each other and if they should make some sort of formal commitment. My mother knew that Laura and Joe weren't ready to commit, and refrained from pressuring them to marry.

Almost three years later, Laura and Joe are still together, and they seemed at ease around each other in Saugatuck in a way that they hadn't the other times I'd visited with them. I slipped into the bathroom while Laura was giving Cody a bath and asked her if she and Joe were thinking about getting married.

"I haven't really thought about it," she said, and then a long string of clichés came tumbling out of her mouth. "I guess I like my last name. And it's not important, anyway. Marriage doesn't change the relationship. It's just a piece of paper. If you're committed, you're committed, and you don't need the state or the church to tell you how you feel."

We sat on the floor of the bathroom together, talking and keeping an eye on Cody while he took a bath.

"For a while I guess I didn't want to marry him because I felt like he was only around because of Cody," Laura continued, "and if it weren't for Cody, he'd be back in Texas."

Wouldn't that be a point in Joe's favor? Didn't that prove he was a stand-up guy? "If he could commit to his kid," I said, "wasn't that proof he could commit to you?"

"I wanted him to be there for me, too," she said, "not just for 'me and Cody.' Now I feel like he's there for me. It's not all about Cody anymore, but it's not all about me either. It's about us, the three of us, this thing we've created together."

This thing?

"You know, this family."

Laura asked me if she could tell me something without it getting back to Mom or our brothers. Sure, I lied.

"We're thinking about it now, about getting married," she said. "I'm kind of getting back into the church these days, the whole sacrament thing."

I told her it wasn't hard to picture her married, just hard to picture her *getting* married. My sister had always been a bit of a tomboy. She doesn't wear skirts or dresses, she's never worn makeup. I couldn't see her in big white wedding dress.

"Neither can I," she laughed. "I'd wear something simple, and Joe would be in a suit, not a tux. And I wouldn't want a fancy reception. I would just have the ceremony and then have everyone over to the house for some food. A big traditional wedding just wouldn't be my style."

Terry brought D.J. into the bathroom for his shower—he was a big boy now and refused to take baths anymore, but he still needed one of us in the bathroom to turn the tap on and off and wrap him in a towel when he was done.

"What are you guys talking about?" Terry asked.

"Marriage—what else?" Laura said.

"Are you getting married?" D.J. asked Laura.

"Not me," Laura said, "but maybe your dads will. Wouldn't that be nice?"

"No, it would *not*," D.J. replied. "It would be dumb and stupid and retarded and gross and dumb and stupid and retarded and gross and dumb."

"Your uncle Billy agrees with you," I said.

*   *   *

I won't bore you with more tales from my summer vacation. Suffice it to say, the beach was relaxing, the margaritas were not as expensive as first feared, and D.J. got to spend time with his relatives and meet other kids with gay parents—including some kids his own age with two dads, who were at gay family camp for the first time. And despite the impression created by this chapter, my family did occasionally discuss topics other than gay marriage. The whole family gathered around the television set to watch the Democratic National Convention; we discussed the latest Paris Hilton scandals; we debated the symbolic meaning of concrete chunks falling inside Wrigley Field. But those conversations aren't really relevant to the subject at hand, so I haven't included them.

Billy and Kelly left town first, followed by Eddie, Mikki, Thor, and Delsin. Then Laura, Joe, and Cody said good-bye, leaving D.J., his parents, and his grandparents alone in the big Victorian for a couple of days. On our last night, my mother insisted that Terry and I take advantage of the free child care and go out to dinner, just the two of us. We wound up at Phil's, a restaurant on Saugatuck's tiny main street. We ordered some margaritas—singles this time, not quads—and salads. Before our second drink arrived, we were talking about marriage again. After spending two weeks with my mother, my resistance was crumbling. Terry hadn't budged. He remained pro-tattoo, anti-marriage. Things were at an impasse when our third round of drinks arrived.

"What if we have that anniversary party we used to talk about?" Terry asked. "Just a party, not a ceremony."

Terry and I met at a Chinese New Year party in 1995, and we've always regarded Chinese New Year as our unofficial anniversary. Re-bar, the club where we met, isn't any more Asian than we are, but the popular rock/queer/hip-hop club in downtown Seattle opened on

Chinese New Year in 1990 and the club's owners throw a big anniversary party when that holiday rolls around. I was talking with a drag queen working the coat check booth at Re-bar's fifth anniversary party, when I noticed an impossibly sexy boy with long blond hair and a mouth like Carly Simon's. (I've always had a thing for guys with big teeth—sick, huh?) When the pretty boy came up to get something out of his coat, the drag queen—bless you, Ginger Vitas—said, "Talk to him!" in a loud voice.

"You have a pretty mouth," I said, which would have been permanently filed under "Worst Pick-Up Line Ever" if it hadn't worked.

"The better to eat you with," Terry replied. We wound up making out in Re-bar's tiny men's room before heading back to my place for what I assumed would be a one-night stand.

We used to joke that we would have a big Chinese New Year party if we made it to our tenth anniversary. At our gala Tenth Anniversary Party, we would serve Chinese food, hire Chinese performers, and pass out fortune cookies. And by having an anniversary party and not a wedding, we could avoid the big gay curse. We would pronounce the first 3,650 days a success without making any jinxy promises about the next ten years. In the rush of parenting, schooling, getting Terry's pottery career off the ground, and churning out columns and books, though, the tenth anniversary party plans had fallen by the wayside.

What seemed most appealing about throwing ourselves an anniversary party as opposed to, say, a wedding reception was that no one would arrive with any expectations. Nothing has to happen at an anniversary party: People don't give toasts, there are no bouquets to toss, no ceremonies to suffer through. Having a big anniversary party, we figured, would allow us to celebrate our relationship without feeling like we had to perform for anyone. At an anniversary party, the couple being celebrated mingles, drinks, eats, and visits, like any other guests. There's no head table, no spotlight.

Later that night, after we got home and put D.J. to bed, Terry and I sat down to play one last game of hearts with my mother. It was just the three of us. The cars were packed, the kitchen had been scrubbed, and Jerry had gone to bed. Then we popped the question.

"We're thinking of having a party, mom," I said.

"It would just be a party," Terry said, jumping in, "and not a wedding reception. Just a semi-big, semi-formal tenth anniversary party. Would you come?"

"Of course I would come," my mom said, shuffling the cards. She gave Terry the stink eye. "Would I come? Try and stop me. When's your tenth?"

"Chinese New Year," I said, "which is in January or February sometime. We met on Chinese New Year."

My mother rolled her eyes. She knew all about the day we met, "more than a mother should," she liked to say. My mother doesn't really approve of one-night stands, not even one-night stands that never end.

"We wouldn't be making any promises about the future, just safely celebrating the past," I said. "It wouldn't be a wedding, so D.J. wouldn't object. And since there would be no ceremony, Terry wouldn't have to make a spectacle of himself. No vows, no rings, no toasts, no preachers, no speeches, no gifts. Just a party. Maybe some new tattoos to show off. And an open bar, of course."

"All the Savages would have to do is show up and get hammered," Terry said.

"I think it's a wonderful idea," Mom said, dealing the cards.

"But if we have a party," Terry said, "I want *everyone* to come. I've lost count of the number of weddings, funerals, graduations, holidays, and christenings I've been to in Chicago in the winter. This is as close as we're ever going to get to a wedding. Besides, it's time that the entire family came out to Seattle. I want people to take this seriously."

Mom nodded, and shuffled the deck.

"If you want people to take it seriously, then you have to take it seriously," mom said without looking up. "That means sending out formal invitations well enough in advance that people can plan ahead and buy airline tickets and get hotel rooms. And you can't send out those kinds of invitations until after you've found a banquet room, a caterer, things like that. The kind of party you're talking about is an awful lot of work, my dears."

—5—

The Long Drive Home

I was convinced that there would be a knock on the door and we would both be arrested.

We were spending the night in small motel in Sioux Falls, South Dakota, that shared a parking lot with an enormous Home Depot. Seattle was still days away and Terry—He Who Has to Do All the Driving (HWHTDATD)—had collapsed into bed the moment we opened the door to our room. Despite the fact that Dan—He Who Reminds Terry Every Morning that We Could Have Flown to Michigan (HWRTEMTWCHFTM)—was just as exhausted as HWHTDATD, it was HWRTEMTWCHFTM who got stuck with walking the damn poodle and getting D.J. into pjs.

HWHTDATD refuses to believe that being a passenger is anywhere near as tiring as being a driver. HWRTEMTWCHFTM begs to differ. For while HWHTDATD sits in the driver's seat, concentrating on the road ahead and blocking out everything that's going on inside the car, HWRTEMTWCHFTM has to keep the six-year-old in the backseat entertained, which requires him to spend a lot of time twisted around in his seat, loading movies into a portable DVD player, offering snacks, and cleaning up spills. HWRTEMTWCHFTM also acts as valet and butler to HWHTDATD, getting him drinks and snacks, reading maps for him, and feeding CDs into the car stereo. And HWRTEMTWCHFTM is never allowed to put in a CD that he might like to listen to.

"The driver picks the music," says HWHTDATD. "If you want to pick the music, learn to drive."

After ten hours on the road, Terry—I'm retiring the acronyms—and I were barely speaking, so I was actually somewhat relieved when he went right to sleep. But then, in my hurry to get to bed, I made what turned out to be a near-fatal mistake. Instead of making D.J. take a shower before bed, after we had walked the dog around a couple of sad-looking shrubs in the Home Depot parking lot, I decided to let him take one in the morning before breakfast. Big mistake. D.J. had been sitting in a warm car all day long—air-conditioning can only do so much in July in the Midwest—and the combination of a six-year-old wipe job after a truck stop bathroom break and all that sweat and inactivity had tragic consequences.

Diaper rash.

Diaper rash on a kid who's been out of diapers for four years.

Now, I've felt like an incompetent parent on plenty of occasions. I didn't feel too bright, for instance, the time I left my overnight bag sitting open on the kitchen floor after returning home from a trip. After using the bathroom, I walked back into the kitchen to discover my two-year-old son gnawing on a full bottle of Xanax, looking for all the world like he was playing the lead in a preschool production of *Valley of the Dolls*. (Xanax is an anti-anxiety medication; I'm a nervous flyer). If the bottle had cracked open in his mouth, or if he had managed to chew the lid off, D.J. would have overdosed and, quite possibly, died before we could have gotten him to a hospital. (Perhaps Patty Duke could have played the E.R. doctor who saved his life and turned his parents in to Child Pro-

tective Services in the TV movie?) And there was the time I acci-
dentally put a five-dollar bill under D.J.'s pillow. His first baby
tooth had fallen out earlier in the day, and it was up to me, the resident insomniac, to replace the tooth under his pillow with a one-
dollar bill in the middle of the night. But in the dark I took a five
out of my pocket and put it under his pillow. This mistake not only
set an expensive precedent (there were lots of other baby teeth still
in D.J.'s mouth), it also earned me the lasting resentment of the
parents of D.J.'s friends. Most of his friends hadn't lost any of their
baby teeth yet and, after hearing about D.J.'s fiver, they expected
they would receive the same amount per tooth. When they didn't,
they were none too pleased with the Tooth Fairy, who unfairly
placed a higher value on D.J.'s teeth, and they took their displeasure out on the only handy targets—their parents, a.k.a. the Tooth
Fairies.

And then there was the time I almost taught D.J. how to set fires
in the house—that didn't win me any parenting prizes either. We
have a fireplace and D.J. likes to help bring in wood, bunch up newspapers, and stuff them under the logs when it's time to have a fire.
Clearly not thinking, one day when D.J. was five, I started to show
him how to perform the final task—here's how you light the match,
son. Luckily Terry was standing right there. He won't win any parenting prizes for shouting "What the *FUCK* are you doing!?" at the
top of his lungs, forever expanding D.J.'s vocabulary, but his outburst stopped me from showing D.J. how to play with matches. We
made a big production out of the serious talk we needed to have
about the word "fuck"—how it's only appropriate to use that word
when something terrible happens—in the hopes that using the word
"fuck" would seem like a larger, more tempting taboo than setting
newspapers on fire in the living room.

But my son waking up howling in the middle of the night with diaper rash at age six was a shameful new low. What kind of parents let their six-year-olds get diaper rash? Abusive, neglectful parents, that's what kind. But I hardly had time to beat myself up for allowing this to happen before the full horror of what was unfolding in our motel room began to dawn on me. Unlike most children who get diaper rash—preverbal infants—D.J. has a full and colorful command of the English language. So he wasn't just sobbing, which would have merely annoyed the people in nearby rooms, he was "using his words," something his parents had long encouraged him to do. Divorced of their context, overheard in a neighboring motel room, D.J.'s words had to be alarming.

"OOOOWWWWWW!" he screamed, waking us both up. "My butthole hurts! Daddy! It hurts! IT HURTS! DAAAADDDDYYYY! MY BUTTHOLE HURTS! MAKE IT STOP! OW! OW! OW!"

The walls were thin; I had a hard time falling asleep earlier that night because I could hear the TV in the next room, and as we rushed D.J. into the small bathroom, I worried that we weren't the only people D.J. woke up. And that it sounded to all the world like a small child was being murdered in our room.

Or worse.

And we're not even at the ugly part yet: After taking a quick look at his butt, we realized what the problem was. D.J. had the worst parents in the world *and* diaper rash. At age six. A few seconds later we were sitting on the bed, Terry holding D.J.'s arms so he couldn't cover his butt with his hands, as I attempted to pry D.J.'s clenched butt cheeks apart long enough to drag a wet, soapy, and, unfortunately, rough hotel washcloth across his burning butthole. This charming family tableau—D.J. howling and thrashing and continuing to use his words ("DON'T TOUCH MY BUTT, DADDY! IT HURTS! STOP, DADDY! OW! OW! OW!")—would make Gary

Bauer, Jerry Falwell, and other opponents of gay adoption howl at the top of their lungs, too.

After I washed D.J.'s butt, it was Terry's turn to pry D.J.'s butt cheeks apart, so that he could apply some antibacterial ointment he'd brought along in his bag. (I swore then and there to never again make fun of Terry for overpacking.) As the screaming and sobbing continued, I kept one eye on my suffering son and another on the door, waiting for the knock that would signal the arrival of the police.

"It's not what it looks or sounds like, officers," I would say to the South Dakota SWAT team as they burst into the room. "It's just diaper rash! We swear to God!"

But there was no knock on the door—not yet, anyway. Soon our poor, traumatized son and his poor, traumatized butthole began to settle down. His butt still burned, but it wasn't on fire. The conflagration passed. Sitting on Terry's lap, tears drying on his face, D.J. looked up at Terry.

"Was that terrible?" asked D.J., sniffling.

Yes it was, Terry assured him, it was terrible.

"Terrible enough to say the F-word?"

Terry looked at me. I shrugged. If not now, when? He nodded.

"Fuck," D.J. said, shaking his head. "Fuck! Fuck! Fuck!"

Terry laughed and kissed D.J. on the forehead.

"If I gotta drive," Terry said, turning to me, "I gotta sleep."

Terry stood up and passed D.J. to me, and then treated me to an awesome display of one of his parental superpowers: his ability to fall instantly asleep, no matter what the circumstances.

With Terry snoring softly on my right, D.J. cuddled up in the crook of my left arm, and my heart still pounding against my rib cage, I lay in bed waiting for the knock on the door that I still expected to come. Surely the police or whatever passes for Child Pro-tective Services in South Dakota were on their way—after all that screaming, sobbing, and yelling about buttholes and daddies, how could they not be?

Every minute that ticked away was a relief. Soon D.J. was asleep. Unable to sleep, I flipped on CNN, and caught up on the Scott Peterson trial.

"Gee," I thought to myself, "maybe we lucked out—maybe no one in the motel called the police."

About an hour and a half later—almost two hours after D.J. woke up screaming—my relief that no one had called the police was replaced by anger. A six-year-old boy screams bloody murder in a motel room for thirty minutes and no one calls the police? What the hell is wrong with people in South Dakota?

We left Saugatuck a couple of days before the Sioux Falls Ass Massacre, as it's come to be known. We were sad to say good-bye to Saugatuck, and to all the friends we'd made at gay family camp—and this year we actually did manage to meet some people. Thanks to the efforts of a pair of very outgoing lesbian moms, all the wallflowers at gay family camp got together for some big-ass parties. D.J. made some new friends he didn't want to say good-bye to, and we promised him we would come back again next year.

Mostly, though, it was hard to say good-bye to my mom. Her mortality is emphasized three times a week by the shots she needs to halt the progression of her lung disease, and when we left Saugatuck, I could no longer pretend that my mother was an eternal force of nature. It's hard to imagine the world without my mother in it, so for selfish reasons I want her to live forever. But I also want her to hang around for D.J.'s sake. My grandmother died when I was D.J.'s age, six years old, and my only vivid memory of her is this sweet-smelling old lady who pushed her dentures in and out of her mouth. I want D.J. to remember more of his grandmother.

My mother is a wonderful grandmother—she's warm and playful, and she showers D.J. with the kind of love that a kid can only get from a grandparent. Unlike his parents, D.J.'s grandmother isn't a constant presence; she doesn't have to correct him, which means he doesn't have to rebel against her authority, and he's actually better behaved around her as a result. When he's alone with Terry and me, D.J. makes sure we understand that he's a big kid now; a big kid with his own likes and dislikes. He's reached the age where, in order to forge a sense of his own autonomy, D.J. is instantly suspicious of everything his parents tell him. But when he's in my mother's lap, the kid he was at two or three surfaces, the kid who isn't worried about being cool. One of the deepest satisfactions of becoming a parent is the sight of my mother and D.J. together, enjoying each other's company, even if, on occasion, the two are clearly conspiring against Terry and me.

After D.J. was strapped into his car seat, my mother leaned in to give him a hug, and she presented him with a skateboarding magazine she had found at Saugatuck's five-and-dime. She hugged Terry, told him to drive safely, and then hugged me.

Then she handed me an envelope.

"The Mad Clipper strikes again," she said, pressing the envelope into my hand. "It's a few things I saw in the paper this morning that I thought you and Terry might find interesting." When I began to open the envelope, my mother said, "Don't read it now. Read it on the road. Let it be a conversation starter."

Two minutes after we waved good-bye to Mom and Jerry, before we even made it all the way out of Saugatuck, I tore the envelope open.

There was a handful of clippings—one about Ellen DeGeneres's new talk show, another about one of the guys on *Queer Eye for the Straight Guy*. In the margins she'd written "Why don't you have a talk show?" and "Did you know that the one who cooks is from Chicago?" This wasn't unusual; ever since I came out, my mother has been sending me clippings about gay issues and people. God help me if my mom ever discovers Lexis-Nexis. I wasn't sure what was so special about these clippings until I found the one she'd decorated with little exclamation points.

" 'Nick Carter Doesn't Regret 'Paris' Tattoo,' " I read out loud. Terry laughed. I continued to read: " 'Paris Hilton left a permanent impression on ex-boyfriend Nick Carter—literally. When the couple got tattoos together three weeks before their July 22 breakup, Backstreet Boy Nick Carter, 24, got 'Paris' tattooed on his wrist. The pop star says he's harboring no regrets about the untimely ink. 'No, I don't regret it because I love her. She'll always have a place in my heart, always.' "

"What message could your mother be trying to send?" Terry asked as he turned the car onto Michigan's Blue Star Highway. "A newspaper clipping, a tattoo, a failed relationship. Must your mother be so cryptic? Why can't she just come right out and tell us what she thinks?"

"You know, I'm starting to think my mother doesn't want us to get those tattoos after all," I offered. "She somehow managed to mask her true feelings for two long weeks, but apparently she's cracked under the strain."

Almost to spite my mother, we began to talk about our tattoos, sounding very much like two men who had made up their minds. But while Terry wanted his "Property of Dan Savage" tattoo to look like a blue USDA meat stamp, I was leaning toward having my "Property of Terry Miller" tattoo on my arm in Terry's handwriting, like something he might write on the inside cover of a book he owned.

"You know what tattoos you should get?" said D.J., looking up from the pictures in his skateboarding magazine. " 'Property of D.J.' because you're *my* dads."

"Your uncle Eddie told me the same thing," I said. "But grandma thinks we shouldn't get tattoos. Grandma thinks Terry and I should get married."

"Look at me, Daddy," D.J. said from the back seat. I twisted around in my seat and watched as D.J. attempted to roll his eyes.

Eye rolling is an important interpersonal skill that D.J. hasn't quite mastered yet. I roll my eyes constantly—I can't help it, it's a bad habit I can't break—and over the course of my life it's gotten me into no end of trouble with parents, teachers, managers, coaches, cops, boyfriends, and editors. When D.J. was four, he asked me to teach him how to roll his eyes; I think he knew how much it annoyed Terry, and he wanted to add that weapon to his arsenal. I tried to teach him how it's done, but he can't quite do it. Instead of rolling his eyes, he looks up and to the left, and slowly rolls his head around his fixed eyes.

"Are you trying to tell me something, D.J.?" I asked. He was attempting to express his disgust, of course, as D.J. objects to same-sex marriage. He wanted to make his objection clear nonverbally, in the hope that I would respond in kind, thereby sparing him from having to discuss all those lesbian wedding announcements we've shown him in the "Sunday Styles" section of the *New York Times*.

"You *know*," he answered.

"I know, but Terry doesn't. He can't see you, so I'll have to tell him. Terry, when I looked back, D.J. was nodding his head, which I guess means he wants us to get married."

"No!" D.J. said. "Rolling my eyes means I don't want you to get married."

"Why not?" I said.

"Hello?" he said. "Boys don't marry boys."

"So should we marry some girls?" Terry asked.

"No!" D.J. said.

"Why not?" Terry asked. "Aren't boys supposed to marry girls?"

D.J. thought about this for a second. Then he explained that we weren't the kind of boys who marry girls. Since we loved each other, and since we were his dads, we had to live together forever. Married people live together, and we wouldn't be able to do that, since we had to live with each other, and be his dads forever, and so we couldn't get married because then we would have to live with the girls we married, and not with each other, which we couldn't do because we were his dads, and had to live together forever, because we were his dads.

"The kid makes sense," Terry said.

Three days later we were in a small town just across the straight line that marks the border between South Dakota and Wyoming. We visited three of South Dakota's biggest tourist attractions on our way back through the state—the Corn Palace (not worth the trip), Wall Drugs (ditto), and Mount Rushmore (worth it)—but our first stop in Wyoming wasn't anyplace we'd read about in a guide book. We'd pulled into an impossibly beautiful little town to find some lunch and stumbled across an enormous outdoor community swimming pool. There was a water slide, and the pool was full of kids—and unlike pools in big cities, it was free of charge. (No doubt on account of that red-state welfare we would hear so much about after the election.) After three days of driving around South Dakota looking at stuff (and taking a bath every damn night), D.J. was anxious to actually *do* something. So while he and Terry splashed around, I walked to a little grocery store a few blocks away, pulled together a picnic, and headed back to the pool.

Sitting at a picnic table just outside the fence, I watched Terry climb the water slide's ladder. I haven't dwelled too much on the normal sniping that goes on during a long road trip. D.J. gets tired and grumpy and takes it out on us; Terry gets tired of driving and takes it out on me; I get tired waiting on both of them hand and foot and take it out on Terry. It gets tense in a car after a few days. So it was a blessing to get a good, long look at Terry in his Speedo climbing the water slide's ladder again and again. I needed to be reminded that I'm one of those insanely fortunate people who somehow managed to fall in love with, be loved in return by, and build something lasting with, my physical ideal. If I may be crude: Terry is the guy I had been masturbating about since I hit puberty. He has my fantasy man's build, hair color, eye color, cheekbones, and, er, other physical attributes. He's also got the temperament, sense of humor, and character that I had been looking for all my life. So staring at my soaking wet boyfriend in deepest, darkest Wyoming, the tension of the drive melted away as I counted my blessings. (I'd like to read this into the record: Terry and I are not Speedo fetishists—not that there's anything wrong with being a Speedo fetishist, of course. Terry wears Speedos because he swims, I admire him in a Speedo because, well, because I have a pulse.)

Then it occurred to me that staring at a soaking wet guy in a Speedo at a crowded public pool in deepest, darkest Wyoming wasn't a very good idea. When I looked around, a few of the locals were staring at me. So I tore my eyes off of Terry's backside. Searching around for something to distract myself, I noticed a newspaper box by the concession stand.

Could it be?

Way out here?

In the middle of nowhere?

In a red state?

A *New York Times* newspaper box!

I ran to the car and got four quarters, and bought myself the last—maybe the only—copy of the *New York Times* in this part of Wyoming. As I strolled back to the pool, I wondered if maybe David Letterman or Oprah Winfrey or Demi & Ashton had a ranch nearby and the *New York Times* flew in a couple of copies a day just for them.

About the only thing that could distract me from the sight of Terry in a swimsuit is an unread copy of a daily newspaper; if you're going to be addicted to something, it might as well be newsprint. So while Terry and D.J. splashed around, I read about Lance Armstrong's lead in the Tour de France, Iraqi insurgents running circles around George W. Bush's cheery rhetoric, and those wacky, binge-drinking Brits. Then a story at the bottom of page A4 caught my eye. Apparently a couple of Canadian lesbians were preparing to make history. They weren't making history by trying to get married. Oh, no. By late July of 2004, same-sex marriage in Canada was so six weeks ago. Lesbian and gay couples had been getting hitched up north since June 11.

"Gay Pair Seeks Canada's First Same-Sex Divorce," read the headline. "The women married on June 18, 2003, a week after a landmark court decision legalized same-sex marriage in Ontario, Canada's most populous province." Marrying, as it turned out, was the easy part. What the couple couldn't do under Canadian law was divorce. "While more than 3,000 same-sex couples married in the last year in Canada, the Canadian Divorce Act had not been amended to reflect the new reality of gay marriage. . . . To divorce, the couple must have a judge with the Ontario Superior Court of Justice rule that the current divorce act is unconstitutional. . . . Their hasty split, after such a long premarital relationship, raised questions as to whether the women were divorcing simply to test

Canada's divorce laws. Martha McCarthy, a lawyer for [one of] the women said they were parting over differences, just as any couple might."

It seems that when the courts in Ontario ruled on gay marriage, they didn't rule on gay divorce—they couldn't. Divorce is covered under a different statute. While marriage laws had been rendered gender-neutral by the courts, ". . . the divorce act still refers to a spouse as 'a man or a woman who are married to each other.' "

I knew it was coming, of course. No one expects gay and lesbian couples to be any better at marriage than straight couples. I, in fact, fully expect us to be worse at it. With so many homos forced to sit at dinner tables and in pews listening to parents and preachers dismiss same-sex love as diseased or nonexistent, it's highly likely that thousands of immature and/or insecure homos will marry to prove to themselves, to their families, and to their preachers that gay love is *so* real. "Our love is *so* real," these couples will tell themselves, "that we got married even though we've only been together for six weeks! That's how real our love is!"

These marriages, needless to say, *so* won't last.

But the Canadian lesbians who wanted to make history by being the first same-sex married couple in North America to obtain a legal divorce hadn't been together a mere six weeks. They didn't impulsively tie the knot. "They had been together for nearly 10 years, but separated after five days of marriage." Ten years. The number jumped off the page and danced around the picnic table where I was sitting: a same-sex couple, together ten years, they wed to celebrate their anniversary . . . and five days later—five days!— they break up!

I was lost in thought when I felt some water splash my face. When I looked up, Terry was standing at the fence. In his Speedo.

"Your son is calling you," he said, pointing at D.J., who was standing at the top of the water slide.

"Watch me, Daddy!" D.J. yelled, waving from the top of the water slide. Then he jumped sideways off the slide and did a cannonball into the pool.

I clapped for D.J. then excused myself. While Terry and D.J. sat at the picnic table, wrapped in towels and eating their sandwiches, I went back to the car. After carefully clipping the story of the two unhappy Canadian lesbians out of the paper, I drew some exclamation points above the headline. Then I put the clipping in the envelope my mother had handed me three days before. I wrote her address on it and affixed three postcard stamps from the roll that Terry brought along for the trip. I walked to a mailbox across the street from the pool. I didn't write our return address on the envelope, figuring my mother would know that the clipping was from me. But just in case, I wrote JINX! in large letters on the back of the envelope. That would make us even.

But a week after we arrived back in Seattle, a letter came for me in the mail. There was no return address, just "The Mad Clipper" written in black ink in the upper left-hand corner. The clipping read . . .

CARTER COVERS HILTON TATTOO

Pop heartthrob Nick Carter has covered up a tattoo honoring ex-girlfriend Paris Hilton, which was inked onto his wrist just three weeks before they broke up. Backstreet Boys hunk Carter and hotel heiress Hilton went their separate ways in the summer after a brief romance. At the time, the singer insisted he didn't regret the body marking—which reads "Paris"—because he still loved her. But Carter recently had a change of heart and went to a Marathon, Florida, parlor to cover up the tattoo with another one—of a skull and crossbones.

The phone rang.

We'd been home for a month before my mother called to ask what progress we were making on our plans for our tenth anniversary party. Waiting four whole weeks to make this call must have been a real strain for her. She wanted to make sure we understood the importance of making plans sooner rather than later. If we wanted people to come—if Terry wanted people to treat our big gay anniversary party with the same seriousness that we've treated their big straight weddings—we had to get serious about this party. We needed to settle on a date; our guests, particularly my relatives in Chicago, would need their invitations months in advance.

"You're not just asking people to come to a party, Daniel, you're asking them to *travel* to a party," she said.

"We're working on it, Mom," I lied. "We're going out to look at some banquet rooms next week."

In actual fact, we hadn't even discussed the party since we got home. Or the tattoos, for that matter. D.J. had just started first grade and the presidential election was heating up. Frankly, the gay marriage issue—to say nothing of the gay tenth anniversary party issue— was shrinking in importance. Yes, there were anti–gay marriage initiatives on the ballots in eleven states, and yes, they were probably going to pass. But all anyone I knew, gay or straight, could think about was getting George W. Bush out of the White House. Terry and I knew we couldn't wait until after November 2 to start making concrete plans, but we were having trouble concentrating on anything else.

"Maybe you should hire someone," Mom suggested. "A party planner, someone who can take care of the details."

"It's going to be expensive enough without paying someone to screw it up for us," I said. "We can screw it up all by ourselves."

"Oh, Danny," Mom sighed. "You and Terry want people to take this party seriously, to treat it like the wedding reception you're determined not to have—"

"The take-it-seriously thing is more Terry's issue than mine—"

"—and if people don't take it seriously, if they don't make the effort to come, Terry's going to be upset, and if Terry's upset, he'll make sure you're upset. But you can't expect people to be there if you don't, at the very least, give them enough notice."

My mother was correct, maddeningly enough.

"We'll get on it," I said, unsure if I was lying or not.

"Of course, there's one way you could make sure your family and friends treat this party no differently than they would any wedding reception."

There was a short silence.

"You could get married," mom said. "Then no one would be confused. The party you're talking about sounds more like a wedding reception than an anniversary party anyway. Why not do the deed?"

"Stop pressuring us, Mom."

My mom was silent for a moment, but I'm pretty sure I heard the Diet Coke in her hand freeze solid.

"Daniel," Mom said. "Do. What. You. Want. I'm not pressuring you one way or another."

"Mom, I didn't mean you were pressuring us," I said, "only that you would clearly like us to marry, and we're feeling a bit of pressure to 'do the deed.' And not just from you, Mom, it's coming from all sides. And you can't deny that, all things being equal, you would rather your children married than not. That comes across, Mom. It's a subtle kind of pressure, but it's pressure."

"I have four children, my dear," Mom interrupted. "Of the four, three of you aren't married. Only Eddie has been married—twice, just like his dear ol' ma. So if I'm subtly pressuring my children to marry, then I'm doing a pretty lousy job of it."

She actually does a pretty effective job of it—it's just that some of her children do a better job of resisting pressure than others. When my brother Billy, for example, resolved in his late teens never to marry or have children, my mother spent a decade wondering aloud about his reasons. He had to be unhappy about his childhood, she would say, if by age twenty he had ruled out children. It's one of my mother's Catholic judo moves: She can turn any decision one of her children makes into a referendum on her parenting skills. With Billy, she kept it up for years, asking my eldest brother again and again what she had done wrong. He had to reassure her again and again that his choice not to have children had nothing to do with her. She wasn't angry, she would tell him, just worried—worried that he was angry with her. When he would tell her that he enjoyed his childhood and thought she was a great parent, she would be mollified—for the moment. Then, like some endless game of maternal Whack-a-Mole, the subject would pop up again. Perhaps Billy was angry with her and was simply afraid to tell her the truth? Maybe he was too thoughtful and too considerate to tell her that he was, in actual fact, absolutely furious with her about his childhood. How else could he be contemplating getting a vasectomy at his age?

Ultimately, Billy had two options: 1) he could have a child to reassure her that he remembered his childhood fondly and was in awe of her skills as a parent, or 2) he could go get the fucking vasectomy already. Billy went with option 2, and my mother dropped the subject. She knows when she's been beat.

Which is probably why she was keeping after Terry and me about marriage. Of all her children, she knows that I am easily—and ironically—the most traditional. Sometimes I get down on my knees and thank the God-I'm-no-longer-convinced-exists that I'm gay. If I weren't so attracted to tall blond guys who look good in Speedos, I would probably have grown up to be an insufferable, judgmental prude, instead of the insufferable, judgmental libertine that I became—and, yes, it is possible to be an insufferable, judgmental libertine. Respecting the rights of others to make their own choices doesn't mean you can't make judgments, or form and share opinions. This sometimes makes me insufferable—just ask my nephew Cody's father, Joe. My sister was eight months pregnant by her live-in boyfriend when I met him for the first time. "Nice to meet you, Joe," I said after my sister introduced us. "But did you ever think of maybe marrying my sister first and *then* getting her pregnant?" I didn't know at the time that Joe had asked Laura to marry him and she had turned him down. My mother and brothers gasped—they had been thinking the same thing, but only the insufferable, judgmental libertine had said it out loud.

For while I'm untraditional in my sexual desires—desires that, for the record, I didn't choose—I'm extremely traditional when it comes to family. I feel that straight people who have children should *get* married and *stay* married. So my mother doubtless assumes that, on some level, the idea of marrying Terry is deeply appealing to me. Shouldn't the same moral compass that prompted me to direct the father of my nephew to marry my sister also direct me to marry the (other) father of my own child? My mother was going to keep at us, because there was no option 2, no equivalent to Billy's vasectomy, no way of effectively shutting down the conversation about Terry and me marrying. We might not get married in time for our anniversary party, we might maintain that we would only get married if and when it's legal, but marriage—legal or not—would always be floating out there; it would always be an option. On the marriage issue, my mother could never be beat.

I told my mother that I needed to get off the phone—I had to get right on planning the big party.

"All right, my dear, I'll let you go," she said. "But let's make a deal: I promise not to bring up marriage if you'll do one thing for me."

"What's that?"

"Just think about marriage."

PART II

Engagement

—6—
Old

The groom looks smashing in his morning coat. He's long-waisted, broad-shouldered, and has a full head of thick brown hair. He's virile, young, and handsome. His face, though, is a little too delicate for a man who towers over his bride. His eyes, staring out into the middle distance, are soft and brown, and his eyebrows have a feminine arch. He leans in toward his bride, hips cocked. He's disturbingly sensuous.

His bride stands beside him, a tiny hand resting in the crook of his arm. She's impossibly slim, with small breasts and a long, graceful neck. She's looking at the same spot off in the distance. Her eyebrows are almost identical to those of her groom, with the same graceful arch, as if the same artist painted them on her face.

Which is probably the case.

The bride and groom figurines sitting on my desk once sat on top of my grandparent's wedding cake. It's remarkable that these figurines still exist—do you know where your grandparent's wedding cake figurines are?—but more remarkable to me is what they're made of: They're porcelain. I'd never seen a pair of porcelain wedding cake figurines until the day my mother showed me these. I haven't seen another pair since.

My mom and stepdad are moving into a smaller house, and I've been on the receiving end of a long stream of boxes for the last few months. Rotting prayer books, deeds to gravesites no one visits anymore, fur hats that once belonged to my great-grandmother—these worthless family "treasures" take up a lot of space, but my mother doesn't have the heart to throw them away, and neither, she knows, do I. Not only am I the least likely of all of her children to toss out a pair of kid gloves that haven't been worn for half a century, I'm the only one of her children with enough space to let the pack-rat gene all four of us inherited from Mom fully express itself. Not only can I tuck the boxes onto shelves in our closets and put them in the attic, I'm happy to do so. I like the idea of having things that belonged to my grandparents and great-grandparents in the house. As far as I'm concerned, they can safely sit in their boxes for another five decades. Then one day my children, or my children's children, will have to decide what to do with them.

I don't have the heart to put my grandparents' wedding figurines in the attic or the basement. They look so happy to be out in the light, staring at the back of my laptop from under matching arched eyebrows. But they're not safe on my desk, not with a six-year-old running around the house, nor are they safe sitting out in a house sitting atop the Puget Sound Fault. Even a tiny earthquake, the smallest tremor, could destroy them. So I tell myself again and again that I should wrap them back up in the tissue they came in, the same tissue my grandmother herself wrapped them in after her wedding reception, and return them to the safety of their box.

And the box? Even that's something of a treasure. The figurines were purchased at C. D. Peacock's, which for 150 years was Chicago's answer to Tiffany. The store was located in the once-grand Palmer House Hotel on State Street, right around the corner from the offices of my great-grandfather's millinery company, but both are gone now. I don't know when C. D. Peacock's closed, but the last time I was at the Palmer House I noticed that a tacky chain jewelry store had taken over Peacock's ornate salesroom. It looks like a Taco Bell plopped into the Hall of Mirrors.

When my mother told me to think about marriage, the first one that came to mind was my grandparents'.

My grandfather, Ed Schneider, grew up on the south side of Chicago, the only son of Walter Schneider and Nellie O'Brien. (Nellie O'Brien—do names get much more Irish than that?) Walter Schneider owned a number of apartment buildings on the south side before the Great Depression. After the crash of 1929, Walter refused to collect rent from his unemployed tenants, and he wouldn't evict people, and as a result he gradually lost his buildings. Soon my great-grandfather Walter was running booze—this was Chicago during the Al Capone era—and gangsters threatened the life of Walter's only son. Walter and Nellie moved to the north side of Chicago and packed their son, Edward, off to the safety of a boarding school in Indiana.

Ed Schneider went to high school with one of my grandmother's brothers, which is how he met a nice Irish girl named Marijo. They dated throughout college. When they got out of college, Marijo worked as a lab technician at a hospital. When Ed found a job as the sports information director at Loyola University, his alma mater, Ed and Marijo were finally able to get married. They were both twenty-five. Marijo quit her job at the hospital—she was married now, and married Irish Catholic girls didn't work. They stayed home and made more Catholics.

My grandparents were married at St. Ignatius, one of the largest parish churches in Chicago, a block and a half from 6433. I have a picture of Ed and Marijo that was taken in the church on their wedding day. They're walking back down the aisle, moments after being pronounced man and wife by the priest. My grandfather, a tall, athletic man, is wearing a morning jacket and a silk vest. He's smiling into the camera. My grandmother is in a cream-colored satin wedding dress and pearls, is holding a bouquet of lilies of the valley, and is looking up toward heaven, beaming. They look remarkably similar to the bride and groom that sat on top of their wedding cake, and they couldn't look happier.

The cake was served at a breakfast held at the Edgewater Beach Hotel immediately after the ceremony; formal wedding portraits were taken later in the afternoon at the Drake Hotel in downtown Chicago. My grandparents honeymooned in Detroit, Michigan. I found their train tickets in a box my mother sent me, along with a note from one of my great-grandfather's employees—the employee, per my great-grandfather's orders, had made all the arrangements for the honeymoon: hotel reservations, train tickets, a sleeping car.

My grandmother's wedding dress is in another box in my basement, along with a scrapbook filled with telegrams and letters that arrived on their wedding day. It was, judging from the evidence stored in my house, the kind of big, glamorous wedding that Americans aspire to, very *Father of the Bride*, very royal wedding, the kind of ceremony and reception the marital-industry complex strives to sell to all brides and grooms, regardless of their means.

Unfortunately for my grandmother, her wedding day marked the end of the royal treatment. Although she grew up in an upper-middle-class home (she went to private schools, took riding lessons, wore expensive clothes), she married a man who didn't want much more than marriage and family. The priest my grandparents went to for premarital counseling warned Marijo that Ed wasn't the sort of man who would make a lot of money. Ed would make a good husband and father, the priest told Marijo, but he would not provide her with the same sort of life that her father had given her. All Ed wanted, he told Marijo, was food on the table, more than one child, and a home to which his children felt comfortable bringing their friends.

When I was a child, my grandfather left 6433 every day and rode the "L" downtown, where he worked as a sportswriter and editor at the *Chicago Tribune* and later the *Chicago American*. But my grandmother was a constant presence at the apartment. She kept a jar of hard candy in her kitchen and would pass it out to us and other neighborhood children when we came to the back door. As a child, I hadn't learned to regard marriage as a perishable, like milk left out on the counter. I hadn't learned to scrutinize a marriage and wonder if it was happy or unhappy, if it was one that would last or one that would fail. Until I was ten years old, I didn't even know what divorce was. In my mind, my grandparents could no more stop being husband and wife than I could stop being my sister's brother or my mother's son.

Looking at their wedding photos, I wonder if they were content, if they had a good relationship, if they had a happy marriage.

"They used to sing and dance in the house, and Dad used to come up behind Mom and give her a kiss and a hug. I can still hear her say, 'Oh, Edward, stop it, stop it!' " my mom tells me on the phone when I called to ask. "They were very loving to each other—when mother was sober."

My grandmother was born in 1914; I was born fifty years later in 1964. The summer I was six, she was fifty-six. People in their fifties aren't old anymore; judging from the television commercials selling the latest prescription drugs, people in their fifties are too busy practicing yoga, riding bikes, and taking up Thai kick-boxing to get old. But in 1970, fifty-six was *old*. My grandmother had dentures, she wore housedresses. It's easier to picture her with a third eye in the middle of her forehead than it is to picture her in "downward dog" or some other yoga position. Even so, she seemed like a contented old lady to me. In the mornings, she would sit in her kitchen and drink coffee. At night she would sit in her living room smoking Herbert Tareyton cigarettes, reading the papers, occasionally popping her dentures in and out her mouth to entertain her grandchildren. At Christmas she decorated her apartment as if it were a department store, with an elaborately trimmed tree on the sun porch, red bows on every framed photograph in the house, and velvet stockings that she made herself hanging from her mantel, one for every member of her family, including her ever-expanding number of grandchildren.

It would be years before I learned that she wasn't a well woman, that she lived in mortal fear of her own mother, and that she had a combative relationship with my mother. When I was old enough to be let in on various family secrets, the fact that my grandmother drank was the first one I was told. Later I would learn that she had a habit of making dramatic suicide threats and half-hearted suicide attempts. I didn't know when I was six that one of my mother's responsibilities as a teenager was turning off the gas after her mother, who had been drinking, put her head in the oven and passed out. And I didn't know that when my grandmother graduated from college in 1936 and announced that she wanted to study to go to medical school to become a doctor, her parents—her feared mother, her beloved father—didn't support her aspirations. She was engaged to my grandfather Ed, and married Catholic women didn't work. They stayed home and had babies—however many God sent them, however miserable it made them, however far it stretched the family's resources.

"She wasn't a happy woman," my mother says. The drinking started after she had her third child. "People didn't know about things like postpartum depression back then."

Even after it was clear that my grandmother shouldn't have more children, she continued to have babies. Ed was getting the large family he wanted, while Marijo was growing increasingly miserable. In my grandfather's defense, he and my grandmother were devout Catholics. My grandmother would walk down alleys on her way to church because she knew that, due to morning sickness, she was going to be sick—throwing up in a neighbor's trash can was an option, skipping Mass wasn't. Both believed they were supposed to have just as many children as God saw fit to give them, however problematic the pregnancies, however much it unhinged my grandmother. And while the idea of having six children seems crushing by the standards of today's smaller families, Marijo had two fewer children than her own mother, my great-grandmother, did. I wonder if my great-grandmother ever asked her, How hard could six be?

If my grandmother were a young woman today, she probably wouldn't have made the same choices. She would have stayed in school and pursued a career in medicine—as a doctor, not a technician. And if and when she decided to marry, she wouldn't necessarily have been compelled to have children. If she did decide to have children, she, not God or chance, would determine how many. Like most modern American Catholics, Marijo would have rolled her eyes when celibate priests insisted that birth control was immoral, and then gone right on taking the Pill, and she probably would have stopped at two children. So it's too bad for Marijo that she was a young adult in the first half of the twentieth century, and not the first half of the twenty-first, although it's good for her six children and thirteen grandchildren and eleven great-grandchildren that she lived when she did. If Marijo had been free to make her own choices, if marriage and kids hadn't been compulsory, if her family's values hadn't been so traditional, it's likely that none of us—not me, my mother, aunts, uncles, siblings, or cousins—would even exist.

*   *   *

"Look at the bottoms of the bride and groom's feet," read the note my mother had tucked inside the box. "That's icing from their wedding cake!"

Seventy years ago the icing was cream-colored, like my grandmother's wedding dress, but now the icing on the bottoms of the bride and groom's feet is dark brown. Through the thin layer of icing on the bottoms of the groom's shoes you can just make out the word GERMANY stamped in red ink. Since my grandparents were married in 1939, it's entirely possible that the person who painted the bride and groom's identical eyebrows was a member of the Nazi party. Holding them in my hand, I wondered how little bride and groom figurines came to sit on top of so many wedding cakes—were they one of those ancient wedding traditions that homos wanted to piss all over? Or were they a more recent phenomenon? And what the hell happened to them?

Like many American wedding traditions, the use of wedding cake figurines—known as "toppers" in the trade—got its start in Victorian England. In 1840, Prince Albert and Queen Victoria's wedding cake featured statues of the royal couple in Roman togas, with cupids and bouquets of white flowers arranged at their feet. Like the Victorian Christmas we're still celebrating more than 150 years after Charles Dickens invented it in *A Christmas Carol*, Americans stage and re-stage Queen Victoria's wedding more than a century after her death. Only we, as is our custom, have taken the Victorian White Wedding to ridiculous extremes. The huge—and hugely expensive—wedding dress, the big public ceremony, the horse and carriage, the cost-is-no-object reception, the massive, architectural cake: Our weddings are traditional British weddings crossed with traditional American hyper-consumption. Royal Wedding, Ltd.

While toppers were popular in England, they never came to dominate British wedding cakes they way they did wedding cakes in the

United States. By the 1890s, toppers were being mass-produced in England, Japan, and Germany for sale here. In the fifty years between 1920 and 1970, it was unthinkable for Americans to marry without bride and groom figurines on top of their wedding cakes. And with the wedding cake's starring role in the bride's big day—"The bride's cake should be the gala attraction of the entire occasion," wrote author Mary Woods in *Your Wedding* (1949)—fathers of the brides, men like my great-grandfather, were willing to splurge on expensive toppers from high-end jewelry stores.

Flipping through a wedding magazine that I found in the seat back of an airplane, I noticed that none of the wedding cakes shown in the ads for caterers have brides and grooms on top. Somehow I missed the memo on brides and grooms—apparently they're out. Thinking back over the weddings I've attended in my life, I can't recall ever seeing a pair of toppers on a cake. About the only time I have seen bride and groom figurines on cakes is when the editors of *Time* or *Newsweek* or the *New Republic* or the *Nation* stick a pair of grooms or a pair of brides on top of a cake to illustrate a story about gay marriage.

It's hard not to see my grandparents' German toppers as a metaphor not only for their marriage—fragile, but something of value, something lasting, but with a little touch of fascism about it—but for the whole idea of marriage circa 1939. Back then you got married, and you stayed married. If your wife drank, you made excuses and stayed married. If your marriage made you miserable, if you were bearing more children than you could physically care for, you stayed married. Marriage wasn't cheap and disposable like, say, the toppers sold today. It took two days of looking before I found a pair of toppers in a dollar store in downtown Seattle; they were covered in dust, the base was cracked, and they cost $2.99. (Whatever happened to things costing a dollar at a dollar store?) They're a sad sight, with jagged mold lines and lumpy faces. The bride doesn't even have eyebrows, and the groom's brows were slapped on at a 45-degree angle. One eyebrow cuts across his left eye, the other moves up and over his forehead. They're slapdash, a grand tradition laid low.

"For my mother, everything was sin and church and sin and church."

My mother and I are sitting in a pew at St. Ignatius, our old family church, on a warm Sunday morning in the fall. My grandparents married in the huge main church at St. Ignatius; my parents married in the small side chapel. My grandmother had her First Communion here, as did my mother, as did I. My grandmother went to St. Ignatius grade school, my mother went to St. Ignatius grade school, and I went to St. Ignatius grade school. I hadn't been back to St. Ignatius since my grandfather's funeral in 1991. Besides some announcements posted in Spanish, the main church hadn't changed much since I was a boy.

"Those were her major themes," Mom continued. "Premarital sex was wrong. That was a biggie. I always thought that if I killed somebody, she would stand by me, but if I had sex with someone, it would be unforgivable."

We got up and walked up to the old white marble Communion rail, a pre–Vatican II relic.

"She had a big wedding," my mother said. "My wedding was small because it had to be put together quickly."

My mother wore a borrowed dress, and at the last minute her mother canceled a planned reception.

"Mother insisted that only champagne would be served and Bill's family wouldn't come in that case because they were all drinkers. So my mother called it off. Then Grandma Hollahan stepped in. She was not going to let her first grandchild get married without having a wedding breakfast, so she and my grandfather hosted a reception breakfast for us."

The reason for the last-minute rearrangements?

My mother and father were already engaged to be married when they discovered that my mother was pregnant. The late February date, the borrowed dress, the quickie reception—it was all thrown together in a desperate effort to prevent my grandmother from discovering that, despite her constant warnings about the dangers of premarital sex, her eldest daughter was pregnant on her wedding day.

"We told my father, and your father's parents, but not my mother, because we knew she'd go crazy," my mother says, shaking her head. Two weeks after the wedding my mother had a miscarriage. "Seven years later Grandma Savage got mad at your father and me so she wrote my mother a letter telling her that I was pregnant the day I got married. My mother didn't speak to me for two years."

Luckily for my siblings and me, my mother didn't expect us to be virgins when we married. Like any sensible 1960s mom—excuse me, *parent*—my mother wanted us to view sex as healthy and natural. She fully expected that all four of her children would have premarital sex, like she did, and while she didn't do anything to facilitate our premarital sexual experiences—one of the house rules when we were teenagers was no sleepovers with friends of the opposite sex (a rule that suited my purposes just fine)—she didn't want us to be afraid to tell her when we became sexually active. She didn't want to hear any gory details, just enough to know that we were being safe and responsible.

"She didn't seem to like sex," my mother said, as we walked out of the old family church. "I remember the night my mother told me the facts of life. I was eleven. We were walking down Arthur Avenue delivering Girl Scout cookies. She said it was time I knew this stuff and explained to me that being someone's wife meant enduring sex. Your grandmother used the term 'wifely duty' to describe it."

Even as a young woman my mother didn't see sex the same way—and her mother knew it, and didn't approve.

"We called the day after the wedding," my mother said. "Your grandmother asked me, 'So how's married life?' I said, 'Fantastic! Wonderful!' She said, 'Here, talk to your father. You're obviously his daughter, not mine,' and handed the phone to your grandfather."

As we walked to the car, I asked my mother if she regretted marrying my father. Setting aside the fact that her four adult children wouldn't exist if she hadn't married my father at St. Ignatius, knowing what she knows now, would she still have married him way back in 1961?

"Yes, yes I would," she says. "We were very much in love. We had the same outlook on life. He wanted a lot of kids, I wanted a lot of kids. And we were happy for a long time. That marriage was not miserable. You kids were all wanted children, you were all loved, and your father was superb with children. There were many, many good years before things turned sour and our marriage ended."

My grandparents' marriage ended in the summer of 1970. It was Labor Day weekend. The war in Vietnam had spread into Cambodia that summer, and four students had been killed at Kent State. Billy, Laura, and I spent most of the weekend at one of the neighborhood beaches with our parents, while my brother Eddie, who was ill, was at 6433 with my grandmother. My mother remembers walking home in the middle of the day to check on Eddie; she sensed that her mother was upset about something. When we all returned home from the beach for dinner later that night, my grandmother was already in bed.

A few hours later my grandfather came upstairs and woke my mother and father.

"I think your mother is dead," Ed told my mom.

There's still some controversy in the family about whether my grandmother passed away in her sleep or finally succeeded in killing herself with booze and pills. My uncle Jerry, who was still living at 6433 when his mother died, recalls three rare "Silver Certificates," each redeemable for two dollars' worth of silver, that his mother owned. "She used tell me that I could have them when she died," he says. "She had been drinking that night and she gave me the certificates. I tried to give them back, told her not to be silly. She insisted, and I put them in my pocket." Jerry went out that night to see his older brother Jimmy, a longhaired musician, do a show with his band, C. W. Moss. "That night we came back to 6433 and went to bed. Dad woke us up and told us Mom was dead."

When I woke up the next morning, my mother wasn't in the kitchen, where I could usually find her in the morning, drinking coffee. She was in the living room, lying on the couch, head in her hands, sobbing. Spooked by the sight of my mother crying, something I don't think I'd ever seen before, I stood there, paralyzed, before I worked up the courage to ask her what was wrong. She sat up on the couch and took me onto her lap.

"Your grandma died last night," she said.

I couldn't understand why that would make her cry.

"Aren't we supposed to be happy when people go to heaven?" my mother tells me I said. "Isn't that what Grandma wanted?"

Blame my insensitivity on my early exposure to Catholicism. I was still in the "Jesus loves me, this I know . . ." stage of my religious education, and nuns, neighbors, and my own grandmother had drummed into my head that good Catholics—*and only Catholics*—went to heaven when they died. They described heaven to us as the biggest toy store we'd ever seen combined with the biggest candy shop we'd ever been in. Every day in heaven was Christmas and your birthday rolled into one. If I were a good Catholic, my grandmother used to tell me, then one day I would get to live in that toy store/sweet shop/Christmas party in the sky with Jesus Christ. Consequently, at six, I couldn't see a downside to Grandma—or anyone else—going to heaven. Hell, I wanted to go with her.

"You can be happy when someone dies because they're in heaven," my mother replied, "and sad at the same time because they're no longer with you."

Downstairs that morning, my aunt Joie was arguing with her father. Joie wanted an autopsy performed; her father refused. Ed had been making excuses for Marijo for two decades, minimizing her drinking, covering up for her, and pretending that nothing was wrong. Today that's known called "enabling behavior," and it's a no-no. Now husbands whose wives drink too much are told to stage interventions, join support groups, and march the whole family to a therapist's office. But my grandmother drank at a time when the people you loved showed their love by covering for you. They lied, they threw out the cans of Schlitz you hid in the piano, they dumped your vodka down the sink and filled the bottle back up with water, they pulled your head out of the oven, put you to bed, and the next day pretended that nothing had happened.

Refusing to allow an autopsy to be performed was my grandfather's final loving act, his final bit of enabling behavior. It was his way of protecting his wife from the stigma of suicide, a mortal sin. It was an act of love.

My mother didn't go downstairs with my grandfather that night. Once a doctor arrived to pronounce my grandmother dead, my grandfather called Maloney's, the funeral home at the end of the block, and they came and took her body away. Joie went to the funeral home and fixed Marijo's hair, and cut some locks for Marijo's children.

The two-flat at 6433 N. Glenwood was in my family from 1918 until 1978, exactly sixty years, but my grandmother was the only member of the family who passed away there. She was the only casualty. It was an old-fashioned end to an old-fashioned marriage. Gramps and Grandma had honored their vows and stayed together until death parted them.

There was something else we could be happy about that morning besides Grandma getting to go to heaven. I wouldn't realize it until long after my friends' parents started getting divorces in the early 1970s, which was soon followed by my aunts' and uncles' divorces, and finally my own parents' divorce in 1984.

The instant my grandmother died, her marriage became a success.

Death parted my grandparents, not divorce, and death is the sole measure of a successful marriage. When a marriage ends in divorce, we say that it's failed. The marriage was a failure. Why? Because both parties got out alive. It doesn't matter if the parting is amicable, it doesn't matter if the exes are happier apart, it doesn't matter if two happy marriages take the place of one unhappy marriage. A marriage that ends in divorce *failed*. Only a marriage that ends with someone in the cooler down at Maloney's is a success.

It's a rather perverse measure of success.

My grandparents had been married for thirty-one years when my grandmother either passed away in her sleep or finally succeeded in killing herself. They loved each other, and there was a lot that was right about their marriage, but it's safe to say that my grandmother was far from content. My parents had been married for twenty-two years when they divorced. My parents survived their first marriage—they survived the divorce, and both went on to remarry. They were happy together for two decades, they raised four children together, and then, when their children were all practically adults, they parted.

That doesn't look like a marriage that failed to me. It looks more like a marriage that reached its expiration date, something more marriages do as our life expectancies increase. My parents' parting, finding new partners, and embarking on succesful second marriages was a long, painful process, but it was preferable to one of them drinking themselves to death.

On the same visit to Chicago that had I dragged my mother to St. Ignatius, I also dragged my brother Billy off his barstool at Bruno's, a neighborhood tavern where we used to buy cans of sodas and bags of Jays potato chips on our way to the beach when we were children. The church was locked when we showed up—a nice metaphor, Billy thought—so we sat on a bench built into the wall of the enormous brick assembly hall. Our great-grandfather helped raise the money to build the assembly hall. On our left was St. Ignatius' school building, where we'd both gone to grade school. To our right was the church, its Italianate bell tower looming over us.

It rang on the hour, and I was reminded of how on the morning of my grandmother's funeral, my first grade teacher, Mrs. Kampman, told me the bell was ringing just for my grandmother, whose funeral was taking place. This is all lost now, I said to Billy, this connection to one particular place. Our grandmother died in her bed, in the building she grew up in. Her body was taken to one end of the block for her wake; two days later, her body was driven to the church at the other end of the block for her funeral. A life could be lived, a person could grow up, have and raise her own children, entertain her grandchildren with her dentures, and then die, be waked, and be mourned, all on the same block. That kind of life is lost now, that sense of place, that kind of connectedness.

Naturally, he disagreed. "I have some of that connectedness. I still buy meat from Bornhofen's, where Uncle Jimmy used to work. Last summer I took Thor in there—that makes five generations of the family getting steaks and hamburger from the same butcher shop. Every day I see people I went to grade school with, and I walk streets I've walked my entire life."

"You're the exception," I said. "You're the only one of us left in a neighborhood that used to be lousy with our family. That's lost, that family connection."

"But think of what we've gained," he said. "Space, freedom, and privacy. I'm in Rogers Park still, but I'm not in a two-flat crowded with relatives. Thank God."

"We've lost intimacy and familiarity," I said, "not to mention a sense of our own family history."

Billy delivered a reality check. It's easy to be nostalgic, he pointed out, now that staying in the old neighborhood is an option. You can live like your parents and grandparents, you can live where they lived, but you don't have to anymore, and that makes all the difference. Choice. Unlike me, my brother has chosen to live where his grandparents lived, even though he's not living as they lived. He went to Loyola University, a short walk from 6433, and went on to get a Ph.D. at Northwestern University, a short bike ride from 6433. He's never lived more than a few blocks from 6433; and despite his administrative and professorial work at Northwestern, he tends bar one night a week at a tavern around the corner from 6433 for extra income and the laughs. He's familiar with every inch of the neighborhood, and while he travels—to Ireland, to Italy, to Spain—he wouldn't live anywhere else on earth.

"I get along here fine, Danny, but it would have killed you if you had stayed," he said. "And that would be bad, because I'd miss your idiotic sentimentality. On the other hand, I would get to sit on this bench and feel all sentimental about your funeral. So I guess it would be a wash."

*   *   *

The letter was in one of the boxes of my grandmother's things that my mother sent me. It was in a stack of telegrams and birthday and Christmas cards, and it stuck out because it was the only letter that wasn't just a line or two long. Immediately after reading it, I called my mother.

"Mom, who is Lenthal?"

"Lenthal?" she said. "He's someone your grandmother worked with at Michael Reese Hospital. He was this great cancer researcher from England. He thought highly of your grandmother. He gave her his Knight's Cross."

"I found a letter he sent Grandma in one of the boxes," I said. "It doesn't sound like a letter from a colleague, Mom. It sounds like a love letter."

My mother laughed. It was impossible. Lenthal—Sir Lenthal of Westgate-on-Sea, according to the return address—was a married man. He was much older than my grandmother when they worked together in the late 1930s.

I told Mom to sit down, and I read her the letter:

> August 1938 (Sunday)
> My dearest,
>
> I do want you to feel in your innermost self that you are absolutely sacred to me from the top of your dear head to the soles of your feet. So sacred that sometimes I dare not to think of it all. My memories will always and for ever be sweet ones. You will always be [sublime?] and the novelty of you can never grow less or dim. Much too sacred to talk about.
>
> I am happy, too happy to believe that you are unhappy. I presumptuously hope that you are not unhappy.
>
> You asked me if I were too "jittery" to work. My happiness makes me want to work the harder. Every thought of

you is beautiful and constantly stimulating me to strive to be a better man. I can drive you home tomorrow when the day's course is over.

You didn't give me one of your farewell waves yesterday. I will remember the handkerchief and the tablecloth for your hope chest. Mine will be full of memories if I can get one big enough to hold them, and a lock to which I only have the key. Chicago, America, and the world contain only Marijo.

Lenthal

" 'Chicago, America, and the world contain only Marijo?' " I repeated. " 'Every thought of you is beautiful and constantly stimulating? You're sacred to me, from the top of your head to the soles of your feet?' I know I have a filthy mind, Mom, but people just don't write letters like that to colleagues. They were fucking."

There was a long silence.

"I think that letter explains a lot," I said, "don't you?"

There was another long silence. I listened closely, but I didn't hear any Diet Coke freezing.

"Maybe your mother was paranoid about the dangers of premarital sex because she'd had a little premarital sex herself," I said. "Maybe she knew firsthand how risky it could be."

There was another long pause—the longest yet. My mother is rarely silent, and I was afraid that I'd offended her.

"That would explain a lot," she finally said. "Your grandmother was forever warning people about the dangers of drink."

It doesn't take much to make me obsess about death, so when I heard that my cousin Debbie crossed that grim matrimonial finish line a month shy of her twentieth wedding anniversary, I began to obsess. Debbie's husband, Michael, had died in his sleep after a long illness, leaving Debbie a widow at thirty-nine, with one kid in grammar school and two kids in college. This was the second big marital success story in my extended family in under a month: ten days before Debbie's husband died, my uncle Walter's wife, my aunt Cheryl, had died. The loss of two members of my extended family in less than two weeks—or, for those who prefer to accentuate the positive, the sudden addition of a widow and a widower to my extended family—sent me over the edge. Deaths come in threes . . . Walter lost Cheryl shortly before their fortieth anniversary . . . Debbie lost Michael shortly before their twentieth anniversary . . . our tenth anniversary was fast approaching. That couldn't be a good sign. Cheryl married in to the family . . . so did Michael. That had to be a worse sign. Terry seemed the obvious third death . . . but only if I married him.

While Terry and I have avoided muttering "until death do us part," we have made each other a long series of extremely jinxy promises. Did I say promises? It would be more accurate to say we've told each other a series of comforting lies—whoppers like, "I'll always be there for you," and, "We'll be together forever." Not only are these the same lies that all ex-husbands once told their ex-wives and vice-versa, they're also biological impossibilities. Even if we never break up, even if he never leaves me for someone saner, death will eventually part us, vows or no vows. One of us is going to outlive the other. One of us will be left behind.

Being the morbid type, I've pictured Terry's death down to the last detail: There's a knock at the door and a police officer is standing there. He asks me if Terry Miller lives at this address. Yes, I whisper, he does. The officer asks me if I'm related to Terry Miller. While I usually describe Terry as my boyfriend—I can't stand the term "partner"—I want the police officer to know that I'm the person he's looking for. Even if I'm not legally entitled to hear the bad news first, I want him to know that I'm emotionally entitled. So I tell him

Terry's my partner—and I say it with a manic look in my eye. I want to make it clear that I'm not about to get Terry's mother on the phone and eavesdrop while he delivers the bad news to her. Then the officer—assuming he's not an asshole, assuming he doesn't insist on going by the book, assuming he's willing to treat me like Terry's next of kin—gives me the bad news. There's been an accident. Terry was driving while talking on his cell phone, putting a CD into the stereo, and drinking a double-tall vanilla latte, and this time—not the first time he performed this dangerous driving trifecta—he lost control of his car. He's sorry, the policeman says. Terry is dead.

And that's just one of my fantasies about Terry's death—there are dozens more. Terry's gayer than I am, and I worry about him getting bashed when he goes out clubbing with his friends; Terry snowboards, and I worry about him smashing into a tree; Terry ogles men at lumberjackoffs and I worry about a homophobe attacking him with a chain saw.

When I can't sleep—something that happens at least three nights a week—I sometimes just sit and watch Terry sleeping. He takes a breath, there's a pause, he exhales, there's another pause. What, I wonder, would I do if this man stopped breathing? Can the day-to-day misery of being alone be worth the risk of being absolutely shattered if Terry should die before me? If Terry were to die today, if a knock came at the door tonight, if some stranger arrived to tell me that I would never be able to speak to Terry again, or hold him, or look into his eyes, or smell him, or listen to him breathe—just writing these words makes my stomach hurt.

Being single visits a kind of constant, low-intensity misery on a person—at least on a person who doesn't want to be single. Coming home to an empty house, not having anyone to confide in, facing illnesses on your own—being alone hurts, but people can get used to it. But being in a long-term relationship doesn't spare you from all that day-to-day pain. It just banks it. Every day I'm with Terry, every day I'm not alone, a little misery gets put into a savings account, where interest is compounded hourly. The day Terry dies, all the pain I avoided when I was with him will be paid out all at once; I will suffer a windfall of misery. I imagine the pain would feel literally like being torn in two. Maybe that's what people mean when they talk about "one flesh"?

Opponents of gay marriage will object to my use of that image to describe my feelings for Terry. They insist that only a male and a female can become one flesh. Only God, through the sacred institution of marriage, can make one flesh out of two individuals, just as only one man and one woman can come together to make one child, one flesh created by their two bodies. But the notion that two people in love are one flesh predates Christianity by five centuries, just as the notion that marriage has anything to do with love postdates Christianity by nineteen.

In his *Symposium*, which my brother Billy brought up earlier—and let me just say that Billy is the only regular at Bruno's who casually brings up the *Symposium*—Plato attempts to explain romantic love. Human beings were once two people combined, Plato wrote, with two heads, two sets of legs, and two sets of arms. There were three sexes: humans with two male halves; humans with two female halves; and humans with one male and one female half. Zeus punished humanity for some imagined slight by cutting all the two-headed, four-legged people in half, condemning us to wander the earth in search of our missing other halves. Homosexuals were originally part of a male/male whole, lesbians are were part of a female/female whole; and heterosexuals were part of a male/female whole.

"And so," Plato wrote, "when a person meets the half that is his very own, whatever his orientation . . . something wonderful happens: The two are struck from their senses by love, by a sense of belonging to one another, and by desire, and they don't want to be separated from one another, not even for a moment. These are the people who finish out their lives together." (A generation of hipsters and musical-theater fans were made familiar with this story in John Cameron Mitchell's *Hedwig and the Angry Inch*, which includes a song called "The Origins of Love," based on Plato's theory of romantic love.)

Even if we're lucky enough to find our other halves, though, being in two separate bodies means that one half is fated to die before the other, leaving behind countless Debbies and Walters.

Plato addressed this, too. "What is it you human beings want from each other?" a god asks a young couple. "Is this your heart's desire then—for the two of you to become parts of the same whole, as near as can be, never to separate day or night? Because if that's your desire, I'll weld you together and join you into something naturally whole, so that the two of you are made into one." No couple that received such an offer would turn it down, Plato wrote, because "No one would find anything else that he wanted."

It's a nice thought, but the ever-so-sweet-to-think-about "one flesh" idea falls apart when you threaten to actually make one flesh out of two people. I don't think it's possible for me to be more in love with Terry than I am now—whistle, whistle, whistle past the graveyard—but I can't imagine a worse fate than being welded to my boyfriend. Like all sane couples, we have to spend time apart. I may live in fear of being permanently separated from Terry, but that doesn't mean I want to permanently joined to him, either.

A much better way to go, I think, is laid out in Book Eight of Ovid's *Metamorphoses* (also brought to my attention by my brother Billy, the damn scholar). In "The Story of Baucis and Philemon," the gods Jupiter and Mercury are traveling in disguise, and no one gives them any hospitality except a poor couple. After the gods reveal themselves, Jupiter says:

"You are good people, worthy of each other
Good man, good wife—ask us for any favor,
And you shall have it." And they hesitated,
Asked, "Could we talk it over just a little?"
And talked together apart, and then Philemon
Spoke for them both: "What we would like to be
Is to be priests of yours, and guard the temple,
And since we have spent our happy years together,
May one hour take us both away; let neither
Outlive the other, that I may never see
The burial of my wife, nor she perform
That office for me."

The old couple are made priests of the temple, and years later, at the moment of their deaths, both are turned into trees, their roots and limbs forever intertwined.

That's how I want to go—with Terry, not before him, neither of us outliving the other. Death is a perverse measure of success, as I said, and I don't believe that someone has to die in order for a relationship to be considered a success. But I live in hope that when our time comes, after many more happy years together, we're both taken to Maloney's on the same day, at the same hour.

—7—
New

What the hell is wrong with straight people?

We were having dinner at the house of some friends, a nice married straight couple, terrific parents to three girls. The kids were tearing around in the yard and the adults were well into our third bottle of wine when the conversation turned to sex. We knew the wife was relatively young and sexually inexperienced when she married—she confided as much in us the first time we'd been over to dinner, almost a year before. She felt as if she'd missed out, she told us. She never really had any sexual adventures; she had never done anything she regretted or looked back on and thought, "Wow! Was that me?!?"

We were the only gay couple she knew, and she had been initiating awkward conversations about sex with us ever since we met. She seemed hung up on our gayness, but not in a bad way. What she seemed was jealous. She assumed that, because we were gay, we had both had wild sexual experiences, the kind of adventures she had missed out on, and after two or three glasses of wine she would start demanding the details. Tonight she wanted to talk about infidelity.

"Have you ever cheated on Terry?" she asked me.

I looked at Terry and made my "am I allowed to answer this question truthfully?" face. He nodded and made his "if you must" face.

"Sure, I've cheated on Terry," I said, after checking to make sure the kids were all out of earshot. "But only in front of him."

She laughed and looked at Terry, then me, then Terry again. Were we joking? I shrugged my shoulders. It wasn't a joke, the shrug said. I had "cheated" on Terry—but only in front of him, only with his permission, only with someone we both liked and trusted, only when we were in one place and our son was in another. We've had a three-way—actually we've had a couple. While three-ways hardly register on the kink-o-meter anymore, they're considered the absolute height of kink for people like us—for parents, I mean, not for gay people. As parents we're not supposed to be having sex with each other anymore, much less be having sex with other people.

She demanded the details, but I would only give her a basic outline. One was a nice French guy we met on a just-the-two-of-us vacation. He looked a lot like Tom Cruise, which was nice, and was practically a gay virgin, which for safety reasons was even nicer. The other was with an ex-boyfriend of mine, a tech millionaire who spent hundreds of thousands of dollars building a playroom in his basement, a sex toy wonderland. After hearing a friend rave about David's playroom, Terry wanted to see it for himself, so we went over for dinner . . . and one thing led to another . . . and that's as much as I'm willing to reveal.

We told our friends that we regarded three-ways the same way Bill Clinton regarded abortion—it's best when they're safe, legal, and rare. Really rare—two in ten years? We get to vote for a president more often. And with less pleasant outcomes.

When we were done, our neighbor's eyes widened and she leaned in and grabbed my arm.

"That's wonderful," she said, a little too loudly. "I would love to have a three-way. But I wouldn't want my husband to know the details."

She said all of this in front of her husband, who laughed. He thought it was a joke.

A couple of bizarre double standards have been getting a lot of press since those "activist judges" in Vermont, Massachusetts, Hawaii, New York, California, and Washington discovered a "new" right to same-sex marriage in their state constitutions.

The double standard relentlessly promoted by opponents of gay marriage—and attacked just as relentlessly by supporters—is that marriage is about raising children. Since gays and lesbians can't have children, opponents argue, we shouldn't be allowed to marry. It has been almost comically easy to punch holes in this argument. Not all married straight couples can have children. My eldest brother and his girlfriend, Kelly, could marry tomorrow, despite Billy's vasectomy. After Marijo's death, my grandfather Ed married an elderly widow. Both of my parents are currently in childless marriages.

And it's not exactly a secret that thousands of gay and lesbian couples have had children or plan to have children through adoption or artificial insemination. If marriage is about children, how is it that childless straight couples can marry, but same-sex couples with children cannot? By promoting this double standard, social conservatives have unwittingly exposed the shocking truth about straight marriage in America, never mind what us homos will or won't or can't do.

The institution of marriage, as straight people currently understand and practice it, is terrifically elastic and hard to define. Marriage is whatever two straight people say that it is. Kids? Optional. Honor? Let's hope so. Till death do us part? There's a 50/50 chance of that. Obey? Only if you're a Southern Baptist with two X chromosomes.

A modern marriage ceremony can be sacred (church, family, preacher), or profane (Vegas, strangers, Elvis). What makes a straight couple married—in their own eyes, in the eyes of the state—is a license issued by a state and the couple's willingness to commit to each other. They don't have to be in love, they don't have to have children, they don't even have to have sex. Just exactly what a straight couple is committing to when they marry is entirely up to them. It's not up to the state, their reproductive systems, or the church that solemnizes their vows.

This is the reason so many defenders of "traditional marriage" sputtered their way through their appearances on *Nightline* and the Sunday morning news programs in 2004. Traditional marriage is just one option available to straight couples. A religious straight couple can have a big church wedding and kids and the wife can submit to the husband and they can stay married until death parts them—provided that's what they both want when they marry, and that's what both of them continue to want throughout the marriage. Or a couple of straight secular humanists can get married in a tank full of dolphins and never have kids and treat each other as equals and split up if they decide their marriage isn't working out—again, if that's what they both want. (It should be pointed out, however, that a religious couple is likelier to divorce than a couple who marries in a tank full of dolphins. Divorce rates in the United States are highest in conservative red states, and lowest in—it's almost too good to be true—true blue Massachusetts, the only state in the union that currently offers full marriage rights to gays and lesbians.) The problem for opponents of gay marriage isn't that gay people are trying to redefine marriage in some new, scary way, but that straight people have redefined marriage to a point that it no longer makes any logical sense to exclude same-sex couples. Gay people can love, gay people can commit. Some of us even have children. So why can't we get married?

But supporters of gay marriage have been peddling a double standard of their own, one that's just as easy to punch holes in.

Gene Robinson, the openly gay Episcopal bishop of New Hampshire, told the Associated Press that "it serves the common good also to support same-gender couples who wish to pledge fidelity, monogamy, and lifelong commitment." On *Larry King Live*, Gavin Newsom, the mayor of San Francisco, claimed that he was only "advancing the bond of love and monogamy." On CNN *Newsnight* with Aaron Brown, conservative commentator and leading gay marriage advocate Andrew Sullivan described the gay marriage movement as "a very conservative thing. . . . We're arguing for the same conservative values of family and responsibility and monogamy that everybody else is." In the *Washington Times*, Democratic consultant Michael Goldman encouraged Democrats to defend civil unions for gays by saying, "[They're] about two things, which I favor—monogamy and accountability."

Excuse me?

Straight couples don't have to be monogamous to be married or married to be monogamous. Monogamy no more defines marriage than the presence of children does. Monogamy isn't compulsory and its absence doesn't invalidate a marriage. There are hundreds of thousands of heterosexual married couples involved in the organized swinging movement—which I explored in my last book, *Skipping Towards Gomorrah*—and God alone knows how many disorganized swingers there are out there. Married straight couples are presumed to be monogamous until proven otherwise, of course, and that assumption serves as a powerful inducement to be (or appear to be) monogamous. Even most swinging couples prefer that their family, friends, and associates see them as monogamous. But as with children, monogamy is optional. As much as it may piss William "The Gambler" Bennett off, each individual married couple gets to decide for themselves if monogamy is a part of their commitment. Or slots, for that matter.

By promoting the erroneous notion that monogamy defines marriage, and that all gay couples who want to marry want to be monogamous, supporters of gay marriage are creating and, in some cases, attempting to enforce a double standard of their own—one that opponents of gay marriage can poke holes in pretty easily. Just as supporters of gay marriage can produce gay and lesbian couples with children, opponents of gay marriage won't have to search for long before they find nonmonogamous gay couples among the thousands of same-sex couples who have wed in Canada and Massachusetts.

Indeed, my own relationship presents a tough case for opponents and supporters of gay marriage alike. My boyfriend and I have a child; we're thinking of adopting another. If children are the gold standard, we should be married. But if monogamy is the gold standard, then the couple of three-ways we admit to having disqualifies us.

All sorts of nightmare scenarios play out in people's minds when a male couple—particularly one with a child—admits to being nonmonogamous. (Maybe that's why so few will admit to it.) While married couples are presumed to be sober monogamists until proven otherwise, nonmonogamous gay male couples are presumed to be reckless drunken sluts until proven otherwise. "Children will suffer the most [if gay marriage is legalized]," says James Dobson, the conservative Christian leader who unmasked deep-cover homosexual operative SpongeBob SquarePants. "Homosexuals are rarely monogamous," Dobson has warned, and children, "who by their nature are naturally conservative creatures, will be traumatized by the ever-changing sexual partners of their parents and the instability of home life. Foster care and homelessness among children will rise."

Dobson paints a scary portrait of gay parents, one that's shaped by stereotypes about gay men, monogamy, and promiscuity. In Dobson's world, a gay man is either a one-guy-kinda-guy (and a one-in-a-zillion rarity), or one-thousand-guy-kinda-guy, and there's no in between.

Before I argue with Dobson, I would like to agree with him on one point: Dobson is absolutely correct when he says that children are naturally conservative creatures—but not in the modern sense of the term "conservative." I've never met a child who took a strong position on tax cuts, and most of the children I know are budding welfare queens. (Allowances, like welfare, can create a troubling culture of dependency.) Children are also instinctively horrified by the death penalty. Children are conservative inasmuch as they require stability in order to feel secure and therefore generally prefer things to stay the same. They need ritual and familiarity. One of the most underrated virtues—one I'd like to see virtuecrats promote to parents everywhere, and a virtue many homos have a problem with—is constancy. Once you're a parent, you simply have to stop reinventing yourself while your children are young. Parents who burn through a series of religions or change partners every six months or switch genders are, in my opinion, terrorizing their small children. Children not only need their parents to stay together, they need their parents to stay relatively the same. I've got your back on that one, Jimmy.

Now, back to those reckless drunken sluts:

Dobson believes that there are two kinds of gay male couples out there: so-rare-they're-hardly-worth-discussing monogamous gay male couples, and gay male couples whose home lives are characterized by an ever-changing roster of sexual partners. Dobson isn't alone in assuming that nonmonogamous gay men are always and everywhere appallingly promiscuous; other gay people make the same assumption when a gay couple admits to being nonmonogamous. So I feel obligated to paint a more detailed picture of our non-monogamous behavior: My boyfriend and I don't hang out in sleazy bars at all hours, we don't have intercourse with men we've met on the Internet, and neither of us is willing to take irrational risks for the sake of the next orgasm. Like a huge number of straight couples, however, we have an *understanding*. We're allowed to "cheat" under a set of highly unlikely circumstances, and all outside sexual contact has to be very safe—indeed, it has to be hyper-safe, almost comically safe. We've never done anything, nor would we ever do anything, that would put our child at risk. (There will be no *Kramer vs. Kramer* moments, i.e., no strange adults wandering nude through our house in the middle of the night.) For all intents and purposes, the limits we've placed on outside sexual contact have resulted in a sort of de facto monogamy. In the ten years we've been together, the planets have aligned on only a handful of occasions. We're more non-monogamous in theory than in practice. If I had to pick one word to describe our approach to nonmonogamy it would be "conservative." Unfortunately, the word "conservative" has been hijacked—and ruined—by sex-obsessed, puritanical asswipes like Dobson.

Far from undermining the stable home we've built for our child, the controlled way in which we manage our desire for outside sexual contact has made our home more stable, not less. Unlike most couples, we're not going to break up over an infidelity. We've already been there, done that, had a very nice, very safe time, thanks, and might want to do it again sometime.

Depending on who you're listening to at any given time, you're either going to hear that marriage will change gay men, making us more monogamous, or that gay men are going to change marriage, making it less monogamous. On NPR's *Talk of the Nation*, Jonathan Katz, executive coordinator of Larry Kramer Initiative for Lesbian and Gay Studies at Yale, made the case for the latter. "[Monogamy is] one of the pillars of heterosexual marriage and perhaps its key source of trauma," Katz said. "Could it be that the inclusion of lesbian and gay same-sex marriage may, in fact, sort of de-center the no-tion of monogamy and allow the prospect that marriage need not be an exclusive sexual relationship among people?" In his book *Gay Marriage: Why It Is Good for Gays, Good for Straights, and Good for America*, Jonathan Rauch writes for the former: ". . . once gay cou-ples are equipped with the entitlements and entanglements of legal marriage, same-sex relationships will continue to move toward both durability and exclusivity."

I think it's possible that Katz and Rauch are both right. If gay mar-riage is legalized, not all gay married couples will choose to be monoga-mous, just as not all straight married couples choose to be monogamous now. I expect that married gay male couples will be nonmonogamous at higher rates than married straight couples. Gay men are men, first and foremost, and men place a lower value on sexual exclusivity than women do. (Lesbian couples, on other hand, are monogamous at higher rates than straight or gay male couples.) But with marriage comes the as-sumption of monogamy and, if a couple has kids, a host of logistical and ethical road blocks to being nonmonogamous. Marriage may not trans-form gay men into models of monogamous behavior, but marriage and family life will nudge us in that direction, moving us toward durability and exclusivity in some cases, decorum and hypocrisy in others. In other words, married gay men will most likely act more like married straight men, i.e., likelier to cheat than married women, but motivated to cover it up. And like most swinging straight couples, nonmonogamous gay couples will probably keep their mouths shut.

So why not keep my mouth shut and let people assume Terry and I are strictly monogamous? That's what Terry would have preferred. And it is what most nonmonogamous couples do—gay or straight, it's how most couples with understandings handle it. Like most long-term couples, my boyfriend and I don't rub our friends' and neigh-bors' noses in the details of our private life. But no one gets to be openly gay unless they're willing to be honest about who they are sexually, and that kind of honesty is a hard habit to break. (Plus, I've got a book to write.) Once you've told people that you're gay, telling them that you're nonmonogamous seems like pretty small beans. And with so many supporters of gay marriage pointing to gay men with kids to attack the right's double standard, while at the same time promoting a double standard of their own about monogamy, I felt obligated to go on the record. We want equal marriage rights, after all, not the right to be held to a higher standard than straight people hold themselves to, whether it's in regard to being parents or being strictly monogamous.

I also feel obligated to point out that nonmonogamy in marriage, at least for males, is more "traditional" than the expectation of life-long sexual exclusivity. The idea that married men were bound by monogamous marriage vows is itself a relatively new concept—and its rise seems to correlate with rising divorce rates. Social conservatives describe marriage as an ancient institution, and openly call for a return to traditional gender roles. But in the old days—the really old days—men weren't expected to be monogamous. The Greeks and Romans passed laws punishing female adultery, not male adultery. Jews had the right to several wives and concubines and Greek men to one wife and several concubines. While Roman law allowed a man only one wife or concubine, adultery and prostitution were widespread and not a legal or moral issue. Matters didn't change much until the twentieth century.

Perhaps the Greeks and Romans were wise to value the survival of marriages over sexual exclusivity, although they should lose points for owning slaves, treating women as property, praticing infanticide, and punishing female adultery. But they were on to something, I think. When the demands and pressures of monogamy threaten the survival of a relationship, it's better to toss the baggage of monogamy overboard than to sacrifice the ship of the relationship itself. But I'm a conservative; what do I know?

As it turns out, I'm not the only one of my mother's children in a nonmonogamous relationship.

Back at the bowling alley at Saugatuck, Billy and I, in the course of our conversation about why he isn't marrying Kelly, also discussed the rather queer "understanding" that they have.

It's not the only queer thing about my oldest brother. Billy and Kelly met in a library, for one, which is about the gayest way two people can meet outside of the Marines. Unlike most gay men who meet in libraries, however, Billy and Kelly didn't consummate their relationship in the men's room on the third floor. They dated for a while and then took it home, to Billy's apartment, which is filled with original art and his collection of books. Being childless, Billy has disposable income, most of which he spends on books, art, and theater, which is also pretty damn gay. (If he didn't have Cubs season tickets, I'd really be worried he was just very deeply closeted.) But the single gayest thing about Billy is that he's in an openly nonmonogamous relationship.

"We both acknowledge that we're going to find other people attractive," Billy told me over beers back in the Douglas bowling alley, as the thunderstorm roared outside. I'd known this for a while, but we hadn't discussed it at length, so I offered to tell him about my understanding with Terry if he told me about his with Kelly. "It's like this," he said, before shifting into what sounded like well-rehearsed remarks. "Should an opportunity arise or present itself in such a way that it can be taken advantage of discreetly, without doing emotional harm to the other person, or endangering the other person, then either of us can take advantage of the opportunity."

Billy and Kelly are more nonmonogamous in theory than they are in practice, just like Terry and I.

"It's a logical extension of not buying the myth of completion. That myth requires couples to pretend that they find no other person on the planet attractive in any way. That's one-hundred-proof, copper-plated, rock-ribbed bullshit." To prove this point, he cited the multi-billion-dollar pornography industry, the existence of prostitution, and the *Sports Illustrated* swimsuit issue. "What our understanding mostly comes down to is this: If Kelly and I are at a restaurant and the waitress is really hot, I don't have to act like I don't notice. We spare each other the trauma of pretending. Saul Bellow has a line in *The Adventures of Augie March*: 'Everybody knows there is no fineness or accuracy of suppression; if you hold down one thing you hold down the adjoining.' Now, I despise Bellow—he's proof that despite free love and socialized medicine, the Swedes can be very wrong." (Bellow wasn't Swedish; Billy is referring to the fact that the Swedes gave Bellow a Nobel Prize.) But he's right here: When people have to pretend that they find no one else attractive, they have to suppress a large part of their sex drive, and that means suppressing (unconsciously, sure, but definitely) their sexual feelings about their partner. Hence, I would argue, sexless marriages and lesbian bed death.

How does Kelly react when he notices another attractive woman?

"A few weeks ago, this tall redhead was standing at a bus stop outside the restaurant we were eating at. She was in my peripheral vision, and I kept having a Pavlovian response of turning my head to look over my shoulder at her. For lots of couples I know, that's a recipe for a snarling fight at dinner and no sex for a good long time. Kelly laughed at me, said 'You are so busted,' and offered to switch seats so I'd have a better view. Best girlfriend ever, or what?"

"Best doormat ever, some women might say."

"Yeah, but I'm a doormat too—albeit it a bigger, lumpier, one—since this rule applies to her as well. She can have extracurricular fun.

And while I would have brought up nonmonogamy eventually, she beat me to the punch. The freedom we allow each other was a much her idea and her attitude as mine."

How would this more freedom work on a practical level?

"See those women over there? Try to turn off your gay male pixilation." I tend not to notice women, attractive or not; it's as though they're pixilated, like the bad guys on *Cops*. Two lanes down were four women, maybe in their late twenties, one of them redheaded, Billy's biggest weakness. "If this bowling alley were in Chicago, and I was out with some friends while Kelly was out of town or having her own girls' night out, and Red over there and I hit it off, and things proceeded as things sometimes proceed, I could take advantage of the situation without guilt."

Why so little actual action?

"Nonmonogamy is not a ready narrative for straight couples, or for single straight women," Billy says, shifting from his bartender mode—noticing every woman in the place—to English professor. "Particularly the kind of nonmonogamy we practice. I'm crazy in love with Kelly. Yet if a woman comes along who wants to sleep with me, and I want to sleep with her, I can do that." Red bowled a strike, and Billy joined her friends in applause. "But I'm not looking to leave Kelly, and most straight women don't go for that. If they're going to sleep with you, it's got to be the first step in the direction of a relationship. Even Laura Kipnis's book, *Against Love*, which comes out in favor of adultery, is really more about forming another intense, all-consuming couple bond than it is about finding a different way to structure relationships, to allow for both being happily part of a couple and nonetheless seeing someone else occasionally. For most straight women, sleeping with a man in a non-monogamous relationship who isn't potentially going to fall in love with her and leave the girlfriend or wife and marry her and have kids? That's not part of their script."

Billy rolled a 7–10 split, and shook his head wearily. Red didn't seem to notice his bowling failure.

"If Kelly and I were two gay men, and we were together three nights a week, and spent the rest of the time socializing in a world filled with gay men, we would have more opportunities. In the hetero world, very few women are in line to sign up to be a bit of recreational sex on the side. Unless you're willing to have sex with some of the ever-available women who live in saloons, which I'm not because it would be endangering and I can't stand smokers, opportunities don't arise very often. Gay men go into casual sex expecting there will be no strings."

"Which has its good points and its bad points—"

"Sure, but if you want to have sex with someone else, you benefit from that assumption. It makes it easier for you."

"The trouble for me and Terry is that the only narrative out there for nonmonogamous gay male couples involves a degree of promiscuity that we don't want to be associated with. I wish there was a narrative out there for a 'mostly' monogamous gay male couple."

"But there isn't," Billy said, which makes it less risky for him to be open about his understanding with Kelly than it is for me to be open about mine with Terry. If Billy and Kelly ever decide to marry, James Dobson won't jump up and object; William Bennett won't condemn them for introducing nonmonogamy into decent, God-fearing heterosexual society.

"For straight couples," I tell Billy, "it's anything goes as far as marriage is concerned. It's only when gay people want to get married that marriage is all about children or all about monogamy. It doesn't matter how many three-ways you and Kelly—"

"Just a minute there, gay boy," Billy interrupts. "Who said anything about three-ways? Kelly says, rightly, that having sex with a man is the one time she's sure she has his undivided attention. She's not about to give that up. Three-ways are out. And, frankly, I'm getting too old for that kind of exertion anyway." Hmm. My brother assumes that all heterosexual three-ways involve two women and one man. I would have pointed out that Kelly could be the center of attention in a boy-girl-boy three-way, but Red was walking past us on her way out of the bowling alley and my brother's brain had shut down.

I have to agree with Jonathan Katz when he says that monogamy is "one of the pillars of heterosexual marriage and perhaps its key source of trauma." It's impossible for two people to be all things to each other sexually, and the expectation that two people *must* be all things to each other sexually—that they should never find another person attractive or act on that attraction—does a great deal of harm. Human beings didn't evolve to be monogamous, and everything from divorce rates to the impeachment of William Jefferson Clinton proves, I think, that the expectation of lifelong monogamy places an incredible strain on a marriage. Monogamy is hard work; it's not natural (even disgraced virtuecrat William Bennett concedes this point!) and it doesn't come easily to human beings or many other mammals. But our modern concept of love has at its foundation not only the expectation of monogamy, but the idea that where there's love, monogamy should be easy and joyful.

This is, in a word, batshitcrazy.

If we want to promote stable, lasting relationships—particularly for all those naturally conservative kids out there—we shouldn't encourage people to have unrealistic expectations about sex, love, and desire. Since I don't demand or expect complete fidelity from my boyfriend, I'm not traumatized when he finds another guy attractive; nor have I been traumatized when he's acted on an attraction to someone else—provided that all of our rules have been followed to the letter, as they always have been. Unlike many straight couples, we've found a way to make our desire for others a non-issue. Indeed, as most heterosexual swingers report, the times we've had sex with other guys have actually enhanced our desire for each other. Far from tearing us apart, the times we've have sex with another person—the times we've gone and had a sexual adventure together—have renewed and refreshed our intimate life. It's made our home life more stable, not less, and that's good for us and good for D.J., naturally conservative creature that he is.

All of this came rushing into my head when our friends—the wife who wanted to have a three-way and her husband—announced a few months later that they were divorcing. The wife wants to have her sexual adventures, the ones she missed out on by marrying so young. Since there's no room in their marriage for a little constructive, conservative, stabilizing nonmonogamy—and since they can't have their sexual adventures together—their marriage has to end. It's a shame, isn't it? A little nonmonogamy could have saved their marriage, I'm convinced, but they can't conceive of being married without being sexually exclusive.

It's too bad for their three traumatized little girls that their parents aren't gay men, isn't it?

—8—

Borrowed

We're not even inside the convention hall when I start to feel my chest hair falling out, like I've just undergone some radical, fast-acting form of chemotherapy. I look over at Terry, and there's a look of panic on his face. "What's he so afraid of?" I wonder to myself. "He doesn't have any chest hair to lose."

No wait, he's not panicked. . . . I know that look. . . . He's *pissed*.

We were home on a Saturday morning, just the three of us, a rare enough occurrence, when the phone rang. It was Alex's mom; was D.J. available for a playdate? Suddenly Terry and I had a Saturday afternoon off—an even rarer occurrence. After some horizontal time, I suggested we head downtown to catch a movie. But what did we see when we walked past the Washington State Convention Center on our way to the movie theater?

SEATTLE WEDDING EXPO.

I pointed out the banner.

"No. No, no, no." Terry said. "No."

We could see the movie any time, I said.

"No!" he said.

"I want to write about it."

There isn't much that I can't get Terry to agree to when I toss out an "I want to write about it." Those six magic words have secured me Terry's permission to visit prostitutes, vacation at a recreational prison run for incarceration fetishists, and conduct experiments on him with sex toys that can't be sent through the mail. The three of us live pretty well, I'm not above reminding him, because people pay me to "write about it."

"Besides," I said, "it'll be fun."

But it wasn't fun—is anything ever fun after someone says "it'll be fun" out loud?

Upon entering the Washington State Convention Center, we were immediately swept along in a fast-flowing current of women. I didn't spot another male until after we entered the expo hall—and he wasn't a groom, just a young guy with a chain saw carving up a block of ice at an ice sculpture company's booth. There were grooms at the Seattle Wedding Show; they were just a little harder to spot than a boy using a chain saw. Every once in a while I would see a heterosexual male being dragged along in the wake of his bride-to-be, his future mother-in-law, and two or three of his future wife's friends. Getting a marriage license in Washington State still requires one man and one woman but there's no similar restriction on tickets to wedding shows. The crowd was so far from gender parity that estrogen levels in the room were reaching dangerous highs. With my chest hair falling out in clumps, I avoided breathing too deeply for fear of sprouting breasts.

I've attended a few weddings in my life, but this was the first time I got to witness the making of the wedding sausage. Under the din, in the maze of booths, a not-so-subliminal message could be heard over the chain saws and sales pitches. "It's not enough to make a commitment," the room murmured. "People won't take your commitment seriously if you just run down to city hall or fly off to

Vegas. If you want people to take your relationship seriously, if you want them to believe you're really in love, then you need to marry in the presence of God, friends, family, ministers, caterers, waiters, banquet hall managers, bakers, bartenders, disc jockeys, jewelers, florists, wedding consultants, limo drivers, photographers, videographers, and Web designers. Oh, and ice sculptors—don't forget the ice sculptors."

But what really struck me about the wedding show was the look of resignation and defeat evident on the faces of all the grooms-to-be. Most were happy about getting married, without a doubt, but not one looked happy to be spending his Saturday afternoon at a wedding expo.

"If we do have this anniversary party," Terry suddenly said, "can we get an ice sculpture?"

We had circled back to the ice sculpture booth.

"Why would we do that?" I asked.

"Because they're hilarious!" he said. "How many other opportunities will we have in our lives to get an ice sculpture?"

"We're not buying an ice sculpture," I said, "unless it comes with the boy with the chain saw."

"I thought you were afraid of boys with chain saws."

"This is where it starts," I said, attempting to change the subject. Yes, I'm afraid of boys with chain saws—who in their right mind isn't?—but I didn't want to discuss it. "This is where the long, slow castration of the heterosexual male begins."

Terry rolled his eyes and grabbed a brochure from the boy with the chain saw. What a jerk—the boyfriend, not the boy with the chain saw. After the grief he gave me outside, he had the nerve to enjoy himself! And all he wanted to do was shop! He didn't want to listen to my trenchant observations about the chaos we were witnessing! To hell with him, I thought, and I started jotting my thoughts down instead of sharing them with Terry, who apparently couldn't care less when and where straight boys get castrated. I, however, have a soft spot in my heart for straight boys. So I not only found myself pitying the poor straight boys at the wedding expo, I also started to feel a bond with them. Modern marriage, I realized, as we strolled around trying wedding cake samples, isn't about men—gay men *or* straight men. It's about women. It's by women, for women, all about women.

Now maybe everyone knows this already, but it's not something that had ever occurred to me. I've been to plenty of weddings, but since I was never planning on actually getting married myself I didn't think too deeply about what I was witnessing. I spent most of my time at weddings looking forward to the cake. (Mmm . . . cake.) The wedding expo changed that. Each and every vendor, from the lowliest florist to the highest-end caterer, was selling the fairy-tale princess wedding, the wedding that almost all straight girls grow up fantasizing about. For the women in the room, this was their one and only chance to be the princess in the Disney movie and they were determined not to fuck it up—and "it" refers to the ceremony and the reception, and not the choice of a mate, as divorce rates would seem to indicate. (The wedding industry rakes in billions annually at a time when one out of every two marriages ends in divorce. Isn't it about time some trial lawyers slapped *Brides* magazine, Vera Wang, and the rest of "big marriage" with a class action lawsuit modeled on the ones filed against big tobacco?)

Back to the boys: As we worked our way up and down the rows of vendors, I caught sight of the same guys again and again. Every time their fiancées or future mothers-in-law looked away, the boys would send out subtle distress signals, like a kidnap victim in a ransom video, blinking messages in Morse code. "Oh my God, what have I done?" the looks on their faces said. "What did that marriage proposal get me in to?" As they were dragged from florist to caterer to limo, they looked like pawns. No, it was worse than that: They looked like hostages. No, worse still: The men at the expo looked like *afterthoughts*. You don't need men to have weddings! You need women and their mothers and their sisters and their best friends and container ships full of machine-made lace from China and towering ice sculptures and enormous white canvas tents and karaoke machines and stretch Hummer limos and bouquets and chocolate fountains and cover bands and garter belts and veils and trains and engraved champagne glasses and sterling silver cake knives and on and on and on. Same-sex marriage, at least where male couples are concerned, had never seemed so ridiculous to me as it did that day at the wedding expo. You need a boy at a wedding like you need a stalk of celery in a Bloody Mary: It looks nice, and it makes things official, but it's not crucial and probably wouldn't be missed if you left it out.

But a wedding—as currently understood, practiced, and marketed in America—without a bride? Unthinkable.

Because I believe gay men should be held to the same basic standards (not double standards) of morality as everyone else—do unto others, more or less—I think that gay men who maliciously infect other men with HIV should be locked up, just as straight men who infect women are. For this and other positions I've taken in my advice column, "Savage Love," over the years, I'm frequently accused of suffering from internalized homophobia. For those of you who don't know what internalized homophobia is, it's the state of being insufficiently enamored of homosexuality and, as a consequence, hating yourself for being gay. I don't see how finding fault with the behavior of *other* gay men—gay men who aren't, you know, *me*—can be classified as internalized self-hatred. But who am I to question the gay thought police and homophobia diagnosticians?

So I fully expect this next couple of paragraphs will get my ass roasted by my friends in the gay media, but what the hey: I think it looks silly when two men ballroom dance. There. I said it. Men's ballroom dancing is a sport at the Gay Games (which were once called the Gay Olympics, but the International Olympic Committee didn't want an athletic competition founded by the ancient Greeks associated with homosexuality, so they sued and the name was changed), and I've caught this dubious gay "sport" on cable. And I'm sorry, gay ballroom dancers, but you look ridiculous. And do you know why? Because ballroom dancing is a parody of heterosexual courtship and mating, an elaborate send-up of male and female sex roles, and it just looks strange when two men in tuxedos float around the dance floor together doing the fox trot.

I don't have the same reaction when I watch, say, two hot men fucking one another's brains out. I will happily watch two hot dudes make out, roll around, suck each other off, and screw each other's brains out for hours at a time—provided, of course, that they're two dudes I find attractive. (Brad Pitt on top of Gael García Martinez? No problem. Tom DeLay on top of Bill Frist? I would have to avert my eyes.) When two men have sex, neither is wearing a tuxedo and neither is playing the part of the woman. Gay sex, unlike ballroom dancing, is not a parody of straight sex. Two men having sex look like two men having sex; contrary to popular misconception, neither one is playing the woman's role. There is no role for women in gay male sex. It's two guys. Fucking.

But you can't ballroom dance without a woman and, walking

around the wedding expo, it seemed like you couldn't have a wedding without one either.

Thousands of male couples have been married in North America in the last two years, of course, so I know for a fact that you can have a wedding without a woman. But the question I put to Terry as we left the wedding expo wasn't whether gay men should marry—they're already getting hitched in Toronto and Vancouver, Provincetown and Boston, Amsterdam and Madrid—but what kind of wedding a gay male couple should have. Unlike same-sex ballroom dancing, which can't really evolve into something more egalitarian and, therefore, less gendered (someone has to lead, someone has to follow; the traditional sex roles are hard-wired into its DNA), marriage can evolve and change. Indeed, it has been evolving and changing since the beginning of time. Nevertheless, the wedding expo convinced me that same-sex couples couldn't just borrow heterosexual wedding ceremonies, receptions, traditions, and ice sculptures. We would have to create our own rituals, not just appropriate rituals pregnant with heterosexual symbolism. (Pregnant? Get it?) Wouldn't two gay men walking down the aisle together look just as silly as two gay men doing the fox-trot?

"If two people want to get married, they should get married," said Terry. "Making up new 'traditions' never works."

He was right, something he occasionally is. Nontraditional weddings can never really free themselves from the specter of a traditional wedding. When straight couples promise to "love and honor" each other, everyone in the pews immediately thinks, "Hey, they dropped 'obey.' " If the bride walks down the aisle in a hula skirt, it only draws attention to the fact that she opted not to wear a traditional wedding gown. The sole measure of a nontraditional wedding cake is its distance from a traditional wedding cake, and to calculate that distance, you have to call up a mental image of a traditional wedding cake. So powerful are wedding rituals and symbols that even their absence evokes them! And if straight people can't come up with original, nontraditional wedding rituals that don't make their guests cringe, what hope is there for gay couples?

"We're not getting married," Terry said. "That's what will save us. But if we were to get married, there's a simple solution."

"What's that?"

"We get to pick," he said, "and we get to make fun."

We were sitting in a crowd of women listening to a glamorous "personal shopper" from Nordstrom give advice to the brides-to-be about putting together their gift registries. "Don't ask for common things like backpacks or mountain bikes," she said. "Ask for china, serving dishes, fine silver, crystal vases—think heirlooms. And don't be shy. It's your day! Think of it as a thousand Christmases and your guests as a thousand Santas."

Ugh.

People arrive at straight weddings with expectations, Terry sighed. Since it's a traditional relationship, they expect a traditional wedding, a traditional reception, traditional gifts. "But people don't come to gay weddings with the same expectations," he said. "They don't come with any expectations at all. Which means gay people can pretty much do whatever the hell we want. We can borrow what we want, and ignore what we don't want. We can take what works and leave the rest of it alone. And no one is going to wonder why we didn't have flower girls or chocolate fountains or any of that shit."

"But how do you avoid looking like two men doing a fox-trot when you do the shit you do want?" I asked.

"By making fun of it," Terry said. "By being ironic, by mocking it while you do it. Two men in tuxedos doing the fox-trot look silly and wrong. But one man in a tuxedo and another in drag doing the fox-trot? They look silly and *right*. They're in on the joke."

"So we can have our weddings and our dignity, too, but only if we mock the traditions we want to borrow?"

"Precisely."

Embrace and inhabit sex roles while mocking them at the same time? We've had some experience with that. Ever since we became parents and Terry quit his job, we've joked about being "husband" and "wife." While the roles we play in our family have traditional outlines, we don't feel oppressed by them, and we don't feel like fox-trotters. It helps that these are roles we play willingly, not roles we're obligated or expected to play because of our gender. Since he isn't actually a woman, Terry doesn't spend a lot of time wondering if being the stay-at-home "mom" is something he freely chose, or if he finally succumbed to cultural pressures beyond his control. And while my "daddy" role is more traditionally male, I'm not a traditional male, and I was never expected to play this role. We borrowed these roles from straight people first because they work—I don't know how single parents or couples who both work outside the home do it—but mostly because they work for us. We never neglect to put quotation marks around them, however, and we never stop mocking them, or ourselves for playing them, no matter how closely we hew to them.

We're not the only borrowers.

Think about the way many straight people live today. After college, straight men and women move to the big city. Their first orders of business are landing good jobs and finding cool apartments. Then the hunt for sex begins. Most young straights aren't interested in anything serious, so they avoid dating and look for "friends with benefits," or they just "hook up," a.k.a. engage in no-strings-attached sex with anonymous or nearly anonymous partners. Some want to have relationships, but find it hard to make a commitment, so they engage in what's known as "serial monogamy," i.e., they have a series of sexually exclusive, short-term relationships. When they're not having sex, they're going to gyms, drinking, and dancing. And since they don't have kids, these young, hip, urban straight people have lots of disposable income to spend on art, travel, clothes, restaurants, booze and other recreational drugs.

And do you know what all of that hooking up, drinking, and partying used to be called? "The Gay Lifestyle." Substitute "trick" for "hook-up," and "fuck buddies" for "friends with benefits," and "unstable relationships" for "serial monogamy," and straight people all over the United States are living the Gay Lifestyle, circa 1978. The only difference is that social conservatives don't condemn straights for being hedonists or attempt to legislate against the straight version of the Gay Lifestyle.

What prompted so many young straights to run off and live like homos? I have a theory: A lot of the early opposition to the gay lifestyle was motivated by envy. Straight people resented gay people for giving themselves permission to do what a lot of straight people wanted to do but couldn't—have fun while you're young, sleep around while you're hot, and live someplace more interesting than the suburbs. When the first post-Stonewall generation of young straights came to adulthood, they decided they wanted to get in on the action. They could put off having kids and live a little before they settled down. They could be gay, too.

At the same time that young straights were coveting the gay lifestyle, a growing number of gays were coveting the straight lifestyle. While tricks and fuck buddies are fun, even hedonism can lose its appeal after a while—particularly after the AIDS crisis drove home the fact that hedonism can have consequences here on earth, not just in some imagined afterlife. As individual gays and lesbians matured along with the gay and lesbian civil rights movement, many of us began to realize that we wanted more out of life than tea dances and club nights for fist-fuckers. Some of us wanted a commitment, a home, maybe some kids. We wanted the Straight Lifestyle.

You would think that after spending three decades arguing that the Gay Lifestyle was a threat to the traditional family because it was so appealingly hedonistic—yes, appealingly: the fear was that straights would be tempted to live like gays, a fear that was not entirely irrational, as it turned out—social conservatives would be delighted when huge numbers of gays and lesbians decided to embrace the Straight Lifestyle and marry. What a victory for traditional family values! So attractive was commitment, so appealing was the prospect of family life, that even gay men and lesbians were embracing them! But unlike all the good-looking straight guys out there who've come to see being lusted after by gay men as a compliment (hello there, Ashton Kutcher), social conservatives refuse to take the compliment. Gay people who want to settle down and live like straights are not an affirmation of the Straight Lifestyle, they insist, just another attack on it.

You would think conservatives would declare victory and take the freakin' compliment. (Defenders of Traditional Family Values! We who are about to suck cock salute thee!) But no. Instead, social conservatives moved the goalposts. From Anita Bryant through early Jerry Falwell, gay people were a threat because we didn't live like straight people. Now we've got Rick Santorum and late Jerry Falwell running around arguing that gay people are a threat because some of us do live like straight people. It's not on the hedonism charge that the religious right has attempted to move the goalposts. Anti-gay leaders used to argue that homosexuality was so disgusting a perversion that not even animals engaged in it. When researchers admitted that many other animals—from white-tailed deer to pygmy chimpanzees to hooded warblers—engage in homosexual sex acts and, in some instances, form lasting homosexual bonds, anti-gay leaders declared that gay sex was a disgusting perversion *because* animals engaged in it. I suspect that Kathleen Parker, the conservative commentator who accuses gay parents of being "selfish," would condemn me for being a selfish, self-indulgent gay man if I were childless and spending $1,000 a month on, say, male prostitutes in leather hot pants and not on D.J.'s school tuition.

The religious right moves the goalposts so often that they sometimes forget where they were left last.

The religious right still levels the hedonism charge when it suits them. Robert H. Knight, director of the Culture and Family Institute, a conservative Christian group, attempted to pin the blame for skyrocketing housing costs on gays and lesbians in an interview with a Christian news service. "The homosexual lifestyle is about pleasing oneself," Knight said, "not planning for the future, not setting aside money for the kids, not creating a situation where the generations come together. It's about having fun. It's about indulging in whatever desire you want at any given time." With no kids or generations to worry about, we have more money to spend on housing, and drive up home prices.

Or maybe there are multiple sets of anti-gay goalposts on the field. Homosexuals who do set aside money for the kids and bring the generations together are a threat to the American family; homosexuals who don't do those thing are a threat to the American family's home.

And all those straight people living the Gay Lifestyle in cities like New York, Chicago, Boston, San Francisco, Los Angeles, Atlanta, Miami, Seattle, Portland—basically any city with a population over 250,000? Social conservatives don't have much to say about their hedonism. They want to prevent gay people from acting like straight people (by banning same-sex marriage, gay adoptions, civil unions, and domestic partnerships), but there's no concurrent effort to ban straight people from acting like gay people. This hardly seems fair. If we can't get married, at the very least, all the straight people who've moved into gay neighborhoods should have to go back to the 'burbs, where they should be forced to marry young and make babies. If we can't have marriage, can we at least have our neighborhoods, gyms, bars, and lifestyle back? Oh, and let's not forget about sex. When a straight girl fucks her boyfriend in the ass with strap-on dildo, a gay angel gets his wings—but I don't think straight people should get to enjoy sex acts pioneered and popularized by gays if we can't get married. Fair's fair, breeders. Back to missionary position sex for you.

If gays living like straights and straights living like gays proves anything, it's that there really is no such thing as "The Gay Lifestyle"—or "The Straight Lifestyle," for that matter. My life proves there's nothing inherently "straight" about making a commitment or starting a family; my brother Billy's life proves there's nothing inherently gay about being urban and childless and having an "understanding." (Although it is fun to accuse Billy of being a bigger fag than I am.) The Straight Lifestyle was only "straight" because gay people weren't allowed to form lasting relationships, or to have families, things we weren't allowed to do because for centuries straight people insisted we were incapable of it. And how did straight people know we couldn't form lasting relationships? Because we didn't form them. And why didn't we? Because discrimination, hatred, and bigotry warped our lives. Until very recently it was illegal for us to have relationships at all. You could be jailed for being openly gay, your family could have you committed, you could be lobotomized. And our relationships—all conducted under the threat of imprisonment, some conducted post-lobotomy—because *these* relationships weren't perfect in every possible way, that imperfection used to justify the very persecution that warped our lives in the first place.

"We're not in complete agreement about the chairs-on-the-beach thing."

After we left the wedding expo—even after the estrogen drained from our systems—I could tell Terry was tempted. There's nothing he loves more than spending money, and he had never realized how much could be spent on a single wedding. While I had grown less comfortable with the idea of marriage at the expo, he had grown more comfortable with it. So we decided to take a look at some same-sex marriage ceremonies. Since we didn't know any gay couples about to marry, we rented *Gay Weddings*, a Bravo documentary about four same-sex couples, and invited a younger lesbian couple— Amy and Sonia—over for a gay marriage marathon.

The couple in conflict over chairs on the beach was one of four couples that the filmmakers followed. There were two male couples and two female couples, and we got to see each pair go from the wedding planning stage through their wedding receptions. There were two working-class, mixed-race lesbians; two white gay men who fought constantly; two professional lesbians with a purple house and purple living room walls and a purple living room sofa; and two wealthy gay men who hired Merv Griffin Productions to stage their wedding, an event that cost $250,000 if it cost a cent.

The combative couple couldn't agree about the chairs when they met with the event planner at the Mexican resort where they were to be married. After fighting over chairs on the beach, the couple went on to fight over whether they should wear matching or different Hawaiian shirts during the ceremony, the number of times God would be invoked during the service (one of the men was a practicing Catholic), and finally they fought with their florist over the height of the flower arrangements. "You're a pushy little bitch, aren't you?" one of the men said to the florist, at which point I was ready to vote for an anti–gay marriage amendment myself.

"Maybe we're just not the type of people who would ever get married, gay or not," Terry said about halfway through the DVD.

"Yeah, us either," said Amy.

Then we watched all four couples celebrate Valentine's Day by showering each other with presents—romantic dinners, flowers, candles, chocolates, *helicopter rides.*

We've never been big on the Grand Romantic Gesture. Flowers, chocolates, canoodling in the backseat of a limo—that's just not who either of us is, and while that makes us perfect for each other, we wondered if it didn't make us wrong for marriage. Valentine's Day at our house usually comes and goes without either of us saying a word about it. For nine of the ten years that we've been together, I've hosted an annual party in Seattle for the single and the broken-hearted called the Valentine's Day Bash. Recently dumped and divorced people bring a memento—a wedding invitation, a mix tape, photos, complete sets of china—of their failed relationship to a night-club. I bring them up on stage, ask them a few questions about their failed relationship, and then destroy the memento in some spectacular fashion. After spending the last nine V-Days talking with broken-hearted folks who smile though the tears as I melt down engagement rings, smash their mix tapes and CDs, and shred their wedding invitations before feeding them to dogs, maybe Valentine's Day is permanently ruined for me.

Don't get me wrong: Terry and I show each other affection all the time. We kiss good-bye in airports, we kiss when I get home from work, and we lean into each other on the couch. We don't hold hands when we walk down the street—we're not teenagers, after all—but we're intimate in small, subtle ways all the time. But a wedding . . . a wedding . . . what is a wedding but one long, drawn-out, well-attended, hugely expensive Grand Romantic Gesture? If we couldn't picture ourselves celebrating Valentine's Day as formally as the couples in *Gay Weddings*, how could we possibly celebrate a wedding?

If we thought we weren't cut out for marriage halfway through *Gay Weddings*, by the end we were utterly convinced of it. Apparently getting married is a stressful business, as you have to make tons of choices about momentarily consequential matters like, oh, pastry chefs and the height of flowers and whether your parents are going to freak out at the post–rehearsal dinner drag show you've got planned. The entire process seems designed to create as much conflict as possible—who knew?

I should have. I've been a professional advice columnist for more than a decade now, and while I don't get a lot of mail about the issues raised by weddings—my mail runs toward questions about welts raised by floggings—my colleagues who write for more mainstream papers are constantly fielding questions about weddings. "My dad who abandoned me as a child wants to give me away at my wedding, but I want my stepfather who was always there for me to do it, and now everyone is mad at me. . . ." "I'm supposed to be the maid of honor but I know the groom is cheating on his bride (he's cheating on her with me), and I don't know what to do. . . ." "I want a simple ceremony with just close family and friends, but my parents want a big wedding so they can invite everyone they know. . . ." I don't get to answer questions like these, but I grew up reading them in Ann and Abby and today I read them in "Dear Prudence," "Tell Me About It," and "Ask Amy."

By the end of *Gay Weddings*, the rich grooms were unhappy about seating arrangements and the fact that some of their relatives weren't going to come to the wedding, and the other gay male couple was unhappy about absolutely everything. One set of lesbians was in tears after encountering homophobic hotel managers who didn't want their business, and the other pair of lesbians was unhappy when their New Age minister revealed herself to be just as controlling and judgmental as any Catholic priest. (The only thing worse than organized religion? Disorganized religion.) And for what? For a wedding, a ceremony, a big production that—now let's be frank—never measures up, always disappoints, whether it's a straight couple getting married or a gay couple getting married. If you're over twenty-five you've been to at least three or four weddings, and it's always the same: a little formal, a little awkward, a little clunky. And how could it not be? A wedding is a really big show with a lot of production numbers staged by and starring a cast of rank amateurs. The bride, the groom, the parents, the flower girls, the ring bearers, the maids of honor, the groomsmen, the minister—they all assemble the night before the event for one perfunctory rehearsal and then it's show time! How could it not be a disaster?

And what's the show about? Love. People marry for love, and a wedding is supposed to put that love on display for all to see. You have to kiss in front of everyone during the service and at the reception, you have to choke up during your vows, you have to endure having your very special love toasted at the reception by your very drunk relatives.

By the time we turned off the TV we all agreed that watching other people get married is an effective form of marital aversion therapy.

"We are not putting ourselves through that bullshit," Terry said, clearly no longer tempted, as we cleared up the wineglasses. "We're not putting our families through that."

If we did decide to marry, if we decided to delight my mother and torment our son by making a huge public spectacle of our love, there were so many questions we would have to answer:

If we married, where would we marry?

If we married, how much money would we have to spend?

If we married, who would officiate?

If we married, how much would we fight?

If we married, what on earth would we wear?

If we married, would our relationship survive the Grand Romantic Gesture?

And if we married, what would we do about D.J.? Our last conversation about marriage didn't go well. Despite the fact that neither of us was sure we wanted to get married, we nevertheless initiated conversations with D.J. about the possibility that we might get married because, well, because it just felt so weird to be a gay couple with a six-year-old kid who opposed same-sex marriage. We sort of wanted him to want us to get married even if we didn't want to get married.

So sitting at the kitchen counter, reading the "Sunday Styles" section of the *New York Times*, Terry pointed out yet another same-sex couple's photo, two lesbians, who had married in Boston that weekend.

"We might get married someday," Terry said.

"I'm not going to go if there's a guy who goes 'Do you take blah blah blah? And do you take blah blah blah?' " D.J. said.

"Well, if we get married, there will be someone who says that," I said, "although it might not be a guy."

"Then I'm definitely not going," D.J. said.

We also weren't sure we were prepared to sacrifice the one thing gay relationships have always had over straight relationships: their quiet dignity.

Before gay marriage became an option, no one expected a same-sex couple to put on a floor show for our families and friends about how much we really, truly loved each other. Straight couples that want their relationships to be taken seriously have always had to jump through the marital hoop, but not gay couples. We couldn't cut to the front of the take-my-relationship-seriously line by getting married two days or two months or two years after we met. Unlike heterosexuals, we had to do the hard work of building a life together in order to be taken seriously, something we did without any legal entanglements or incentives. Without the option of making a spectacle out of our commitment—no vows, no cakes, no rings, no toasts, no limos, no helicopters—we were forced to simply live our commitments. We might not be able to inherit each other's property or make medical decisions in an emergency or collect each other's pensions, but when our relationships were taken seriously it was by virtue of their *duration,* by virtue of the lives we were living, not by virtue of promises we made before the Solid Gold Dancers jumped out of the wedding cake at the reception.

My relationship with Terry has always been our own creation, the product of a love some people believe isn't even supposed to exist. With state and church against us, there's a kind of dignity in loving each other anyway. Sometimes when we're introduced as a couple, straight couples will ask how long we've been together. Often they're shocked and delighted to learn that we've been together such a long time. At first I assumed many were shocked because they believed that gay men weren't good at forming stable relationships. But when I've pried—and I tend to pry—I've found myself listening to straight people explain that it means something different to them when a gay couple hangs in there long enough to get into the double digits. We could walk away from each other at any time, but we don't. That can mean only one thing: We really, truly love each other. Married straight couples don't benefit from the same assumption. They might stay together for love or they might stay together because they take their vows seriously, because they do see themselves as "bound together in holy matrimony." They've tied the knot and the bitch in the house is stuck with the bastard on the couch. Divorce is an option, of course, but the awareness of how awful an experience divorce is works to keep some couples together.

Yes, yes: The quiet dignity of a long-term gay relationship isn't worth the stigma of being treated as second-class citizens. The inability of stable, long-term gay couples to tie the knot is discriminatory and unfair. A straight couple could meet and marry in one drunken evening in Las Vegas (how about a constitutional amendment to put a stop to that?), and their relationship has more legal standing than, say, the fifty-one-year relationship of Phyllis Lyon and Del Martin, the first same-sex couple to marry in San Francisco. Then there's Julie and Hillary Goodridge, one of the same-sex couples who successfully sued the state of Massachusetts for the right to marry. They'd been together seventeen years on their wedding day. If a groom in Las Vegas were to be hit by a car leaving the chapel with his bride, his new wife—not his parents, not his siblings—would have the legal right to direct his medical care and, if necessary, pull the plug. But after fifty-one years, Phyllis and Del may not be able to make those end-of-life decisions for each other. Distant cousins who might be hostile to the surviving partner could blow into town and make all the medical decisions. While the arrival of gay marriage will correct this injustice, something else will be lost, something intangible, something that used to be uniquely our own.

In bed later that night, Terry was reading a mystery novel by a Swedish writer and I was reading about—what else?—marriage.

When a Christian is in trouble, he'll often pick up a Bible and start flipping around. If he finds a passage or a psalm or a parable that speaks to his predicament, he'll take it as a sign from God. Of course, if the Christian picked up some other book—*The Origin of Species*, for instance, or *Dr. Phil's Weight Loss Solution*—he might chance upon a passage that might seem equally relevant, but he would never take that as a sign that Darwin was right about evolution or that he should take weight loss advice from a man who appears to be over-weight.

Anyway, I was reading E. J. Graff's excellent book *What is Marriage For? The Strange Social History of Our Most Intimate Institution* when Terry amended his previous objection to marriage. He no longer objected to marriage on the grounds that he didn't want to act like straight people. "I don't want to get married because I don't want to act like *gay* people," he said. "I don't want to act like those guys in *Gay Weddings*. I love you, honey, I really do, but I can't do it. I don't want to wear matching tuxes and I don't want to listen to your father offer us a toast and I don't want to shove cake in each other's faces. If getting married means making an ass out of myself in front of everyone I know, then tell your mother I'm sorry. I can't do it."

He went back to his book, I went back to mine. I was reading Graff's chapter about the moment the Catholic Church stepped in to regulate marriage in the thirteenth century. Early Christians rejected marriage, sex, and children, Graff writes, as a way of turning their backs on Roman and Jewish society and, they hoped, destroying the social order and bringing about the second coming of Christ. Then Christ didn't show, the Roman Empire collapsed, and the Church inherited Europe, and with it the responsibility to run the very society it had hoped to destroy.

"It wasn't until 1215 that the Church finally decreed marriage a sacrament," Graff writes, ". . . and according to the Church, what turned two individuals into a married couple? It was—drumroll, please—the couple's private vows. Why a drumroll? Because the Church insisted that a private promise was an unbreakable sacrament. . . . After a great many theological volleys and debates, theologians decided that a marriage was made and permanently sealed at the moment that the pair knowingly and willingly said 'I marry you.' *Even if they said their vows in absolute secrecy, with no witnesses.*"

The emphasis is mine.

I grabbed the Henning Mankell novel out of Terry's hands and handed him Graff's book.

"You have to read this," I said.

Here was a marriage ceremony we could get behind. It had the added benefit of being a more traditional, ancient, and sacred marriage ceremony, a marriage ceremony that predated cake toppers and florists and obviated the need for seating charts. If marriage was a promise two people made to each other, and if you didn't have to make it in front of anyone else, then here was a marriage ceremony infused with quiet dignity. All we had to do to turn our anniversary party into our wedding reception was mutter "I marry you" to each other before we walked in the door. We wouldn't even have to tell anyone we did it.

—9—

Blue

There's this little restaurant in Vancouver, British Columbia, called Dish. They serve organic food and fresh-squeezed juices and everything I've ever had there has been absolutely delicious. Well, not the teriyaki chicken. It was dry. But I can't hold the chicken against Dish because their tofu scramble is too good to pass up. I'm not a big fan of tofu—is anyone, really?—but the cooks at Dish have managed to crack the tofu-scramble code. Unlike tofu scrambles in other restaurants, the one they serve at Dish doesn't taste like a two-year-old airline omelet. I think the trick is that the cooks at Dish aren't trying to pass their tofu off as eggs. It's tofu, damn it, and Dish lets it taste like tofu. I'm such a fan that, whenever I'm in Vancouver, I stay in a hotel near Dish so I can go and have the tofu scramble and some fresh-squeezed orange juice for breakfast.

Dry chicken, tofu scrambles—this is not the stuff of bestselling memoirs. This is a literary genre dominated by people who've endured spectacularly abusive childhoods (God help the aspiring memoirist who endured run-of-the-mill abuse as a child), mind- and soul-deadening oppression in Iran, and rock climbers forced to cut off their own arms. But I'm actually going somewhere depressing with this tofu stuff, so please bear with me. There were a lot of things I could've obsessed about after George W. Bush was re-elected—the eleven states that passed state constitutional amendments banning same-sex marriage, for instance, or the likelihood of the draft coming back, or the coming war with North Korea or Iran or Syria or all of the above, or what I would say if I ran into the Bush twins in a bar in New York City.

But it was the tofu scramble at Dish that kept intruding on my thoughts. The last time Terry and I were in Vancouver, we had breakfast at Dish and then walked around Stanley Park and talked about how nice it would be to actually live in Vancouver. It's everything we like in a big city: It's dense, it's cosmopolitan, it's got great public transit, it's laid back. It doesn't hurt that every other guy in Vancouver is a snowboarder either, and guys with great butts are literally everywhere you look. And it certainly doesn't hurt that most Canadian men with great butts don't seem to mind being checked out by other guys. You see, up in Canada, no one really cares who you sleep with so long as you're not sleeping with someone who doesn't want to sleep with you. National political parties in Canada don't win elections by bashing gays and lesbians; they lose them. In Vancouver gays and lesbians can enjoy a tofu scramble in the morning, get married at lunchtime, and check out male and female snowboarders' butts until dinner. It's that kind of place. Why shouldn't we move there?

I know, I know, I KNOW: Everyone in the United States is sick of listening to disappointed Democrats, liberals, and progressives threatening to move to Canada. With so many liberals threatening to go and so few actually going, it's hard to take anyone who makes the threat seriously. When I hear a straight person swear they're thinking about moving to Canada I think, "Yeah, right: You're moving to Canada. Say hello to Tim Robbins for me."

But I don't have that reaction when I hear a gay person threaten to move to Canada. When a gay or lesbian person threatens to move to Canada I think, "I'm right there with you, pal." For us, the move to Canada—home of legal gay marriage, edible tofu scrambles, snowboard-sculpted butts, and decriminalized marijuana—isn't an overreaction to George W. Bush's re-election. American liberals may be blue, but American gays and lesbians are a deeper, darker shade of blue. Living in a country with a two-party system in which one of the political parties—the one that just so happens to control all three branches of the federal government and dominates the supposedly "liberal" mainstream media—"activates" its base by beating up on us year after year has left American gays and lesbians feeling battered and imperiled. Straight liberals are blue; gays and lesbians are black and blue.

It's not just exhaustion that has many American gays and lesbians eyeing the exits, but a real fear of where the Republican right's never-ending campaign against gays and lesbians will ultimately lead. Republicans tell their religious supporters that the existence of gays and lesbians is a threat to the American family, western civilization, and, as influential conservative Christian leader James Dobson claimed, "the survival of the earth." We're godless commies, marauding Visigoths, and global warming all rolled up into one great big mirrored disco ball.

You typically hear one of two things when you press a Dobson supporter about the threat that homosexuality supposedly presents to the planet. "The practice of homosexuality is potentially lethal to the human race," Rev. Rolfe F. Westendorf wrote in *The Northwest Lutheran*, a religious paper. "It is activity which precludes the possibility of procreation. Hence, if everyone were gay, the human race would be finished in fifty years."

The assumption at the base of the "if everyone were gay . . ." argument is a compliment, if a back-handed one. People like Dobson and Westendorf apparently believe that homosexuality is so tempting that pretty soon no one is going to want to be heterosexual. A sane person might think that the long, sordid history of heterosexuality, and the current human population of six billion, is all the evidence we need that human beings will never tire of heterosexual sex, but not Dobson or Westendorf.

And what of all those straight people out there who live near, work beside, and hang out with gays and lesbians for years without ever succumbing to our charms? I've shared an office with a straight guy for eight years, and he's still sleeping with women; according to *New York* magazine, straight women are still finding husbands in Manhattan; and the last time I was in San Francisco, I actually saw a man and a woman making out in a cab. If heterosexuality can thrive in seemingly inhospitable places like my office, Manhattan, and San Francisco, it's a hardier weed than hysterics like Dobson and Westendorf give it credit for being.

The other argument for the threat homosexuality presents to the planet is harder to refute. God hates gays—it's right there in the Bible, along with "God hates shrimp" (Leviticus 11:9–12), "God hates poly-cotton blends" (Leviticus 19:19), "God approves of slavery" (Exodus 21:20–21; Ephesians 6:5–6), "God wants you to pay your taxes without griping about it" (Matthew 22:17–21), and "God approves of killing women and children" (Deuteronomy 2:33–34). God destroyed Sodom and Gomorrah because of the homos, Christian conservatives insist, and if we're not careful we're going to reach some sort of mincing critical mass and God will lose his shit and destroy the planet. God is already mighty annoyed with current levels of gay and lesbian activity on our planet and, according to prominent Christian conservatives, He's trying to let us know. Sitting in a hotel room in Portland, Oregon, I listened to a "Christian leader" on a cable news shoutfest describe the December 26, 2004, earthquake and tsunami that killed a quarter of a million people in Asia as evidence of God's displeasure. With Asians? No, with same-sex marriage. "We can't allow things that offend God to flourish without expecting to incur the wrath of God," she said. She cited gay and lesbian marriages in Canada, San Francisco, and Massachusetts. "Gay marriage offends God deeply," hence the killer wave.

God may be all-knowing and all-powerful, but He is, it seems, a lousy shot, the Mr. Magoo of higher powers. Same-sex couples get married in Boston, Toronto, and San Francisco, and a vengeful, nearsighted God triggers an earthquake that slams a killer wave into Indonesia, Thailand, India, and Sri Lanka, killing a quarter of a million people who weren't even invited to the wedding.

But perhaps I'm being unfair to God: Sometimes He does manage to score a direct hit. The 1993 Northridge Earthquake, measuring 6.7 on the Richter scale, scored a direct hit to the San Fernando Valley in Los Angeles, California. Christian conservative leader Pat Robertson was quick to blame the multi-billion-dollar porn industry, which is based in the San Fernando Valley, for an earthquake that took fifty-seven lives and caused billions of dollars in damage. God doesn't like pornography, you see, and while not one of the people who died that day was a porn star, a porn director, or a porn producer, God's message was clear: Stop making dirty movies in the San Fernando Valley or I'll drop some more houses on innocent bystanders.

The funny thing about God and natural disasters, though, is that He sometimes strikes the faithful, too. So we can only wonder about what, exactly, God's message was on March 27, 1994.

Less than three months after God slapped the San Fernando Valley with an earthquake, God slammed a tornado into a church in Piedmont, Alabama. The Goshen Methodist Church was completely destroyed during Palm Sunday services. Twenty people were killed and ninety were injured. Among the dead was the four-year-old daughter of the pastor. The same Christian conservatives who pointed to the earthquake that hit Los Angeles as a condemnation of the porn industry, and a decade later claimed that the Asian tsunami was God's vote against same-sex marriage, get awfully quiet when the subject of the Piedmont Palm Sunday Tornado is raised. The best they can do is this: God was testing the faith of His flock.

How do you even reason with people who believe that, when something bad happens to you, it's God's wrath, but when something bad happens to me, it's God's pop quiz?

And if you believe their rhetoric, not only are gays and lesbians a threat to the long-term survival of the planet, as Dobson claims, but an immediate threat to our own children. When Republicans in Texas began to push for a ban on gay and lesbian foster parents (there are 16,000 children in foster care in Texas), supporters of the ban pointed to a study that allegedly showed that children being raised by gay and lesbian parents are eleven times more likely to be sexually abused. This bogus statistic was repeated on CNN, where it went unchallenged. And the source of this Big Lie? Paul Cameron, an anti-gay shrink who was expelled by the American Psychological Association. Cameron was also censured by the American Sociological Association in 1985 because he "consistently misinterpreted and misrepresented sociological research on sexuality, homosexuality, and lesbianism." Cameron's study credits every incident of sexual abuse committed by an adult on a child of the same sex to out gays and lesbians despite the fact that the overwhelming majority of child rapes are committed by heterosexual parents or other family members. Out gays and lesbians—the kind of parents who would be banned from serving as foster parents under Texas's proposed law—are statistically less likely to abuse children in their care. Cameron's widely disseminated lie is an outrage and it will, without a doubt, provoke violence against gay and lesbian parents.

Living in a country that would re-elect a proven incompetent whose political base includes irrational whackjobs like Dobson, Robertson, and Cameron frightens gay and lesbian Americans in ways that straight liberals can't begin to fathom. Gay and lesbian Americans are eyeing the exits more intently because we worry that the day is rapidly coming when the Republican party will have to make good on its rhetoric and actually do something about the threat we supposedly represent. If homos are imperiling the survival of the planet, and if one party wins national elections stoking fear and hatred of homos, sooner or later that party is going to take action, right? You can't run around screaming that gay and lesbian Americans are a threat to the American family and then just stand there and let us adopt children, move to the suburbs, and mow our lawns.

Republicans are already making good on their anti-gay rhetoric. Voters have approved Republican-backed anti–gay marriage amendments to state constitutions in Utah, Oregon, Oklahoma, Ohio, North Dakota, Montana, Mississippi, Michigan, Kentucky, Georgia, Missouri, Louisiana, Kansas, and Arkansas. The National Conference of State Legislatures says that seventeen more states have constitutional amendments pending that would ban gay marriage. And there are a lot more anti-gay laws in the works. In Texas, school officials are censoring textbooks that dare to acknowledge the existence of gays and lesbians. One targeted passage explained that adolescence brings the onset of "attraction to others," but it was revised to read "attraction to the opposite sex," in order to further isolate and terrify teenage gays and lesbians in Texas. (As if being a gay teenager in Texas wasn't already bad enough!) In Alabama, the Republican-controlled state legislature is moving to ban any and all books from that state's libraries—both of them—that portray being gay as acceptable. Oh, and they're moving to ban gay people from adopting children, too, in a state with more than 5,000 kids in the foster care system, each and every one abandoned, abused, or neglected by heterosexual parents.

Over in sunny Utah, where a state law bans teachers from "advocating homosexuality" (read: mentioning homosexuality), high schools are searching for an honors-level psychology textbook that doesn't discuss homosexuality, which is apparently hard to find. "Most publishers have now included small amounts—a paragraph or a couple of pages—in texts about homosexuality," one teacher on the search committee complained to the *Salt Lake Tribune*. "I don't teach homosexuality. But if it appears in a textbook, there's nothing I can do to keep students from reading it." Maybe God will express His displeasure with textbook publishers, most of which are based in California, by starving hundreds of thousands of Africans to death in a famine. Hell, maybe He already has.

Meanwhile in Michigan, Democratic governor Jennifer Granholm, who opposed the state's gay marriage ban, now appears to be its biggest fan. Granholm ordered state and local governments to stop providing partner benefits to public employees after that state's anti–gay marriage amendment passed. The courts in Michigan are currently determining if the anti–gay marriage amendment requires the state to deny domestic-partner benefits to same-sex couples, and the governor didn't have to act until the courts issued a ruling. But Granholm, a true profile in courage, decided to err on the side of doing maximum harm to gay and lesbian couples in Michigan and yanked the benefits.

The worst of the worst, however, is Virginia. In July 2004, the Marriage Affirmation Act took effect, which not only banned civil unions *but any contract between people of the same sex that might bestow a marriage-like privilege.* The law says: "A civil union, partnership contract or other arrangement between persons of the same sex purporting to bestow the privileges and obligations of marriage is prohibited." Gay couples living in Virginia can't sign durable powers of attorney, and they can't leave each other their property in their wills. Writing in the *Washington Post*, Jonathan Rauch noted that the law in Virginia, where he lives with his partner, heralded a new era of Jim Crow. "Slaves could not enter into contracts because they were the property of others rather than themselves; nor could children, who were wards of their parents," Rauch writes. "To abridge the right of contract for same-sex partners, then, is to deny not just gay coupledom, in the law's eyes, but gay personhood. It disenfranchises gay people as individuals. It makes us nonpersons, subcitizens. By stripping us of our bonds to each other, it strips us even of ownership of ourselves."

Stripping gay people of their personhood wasn't enough for legislators in Virginia. Conservatives in that state are pushing two more anti-gay bills. One would ban gay support groups in high schools; the other would ban adoptions by same-sex couples. (There are currently 7,000 children in foster care in Virginia.) The proposed anti–gay adoption law would require judges to ask prospective adoptive parents if they are "known to engage in current voluntary homosexual activity" (involuntary homosexual activity isn't a problem, I guess), or if they are "unmarried and cohabiting with another adult to whom he is not related by blood or marriage."

Of course, every once in a while the Universal Law of Unintended

Consequences comes into play, and that's some small consolation. In March 2005, a judge in Ohio said the state's new constitutional amendment banning gay marriage invalidates part of the state's domestic violence law. Until March, Ohio's domestic violence law was seen as treating married and unmarried couples equally. But the judge, ruling that the equal treatment of married and unmarried couples was forbidden by the state's anti–gay marriage law, set a precedent sure to be welcomed by abusive partners everywhere. He decided that a man who was accused of slapping around his live-in girlfriend over a pack of cigarettes could not be found guilty of domestic violence, but only of misdemeanor assault. "Dozens of Ohio men charged with domestic abuse," says *Time* magazine, "are prepared to argue in court that domestic-violence laws, which carry stiffer penalties than standard assault charges, no longer apply to them, since they are not married to the women they're accused of beating." Nice job, Ohio.

Not content to leave gay bashing to the states, Christian conservatives and their allies in the Republican party are pushing an amendment to the U.S. Constitution—an amendment so broad that, as currently written, it would not only ban gay marriage, civil unions, and domestic partnerships, but make it illegal for private companies to offer domestic partner benefits, which would deprive Terry of his health insurance. Prominent conservative commentator Andrew Sullivan describes these efforts as a "war on gay relationships."

What's the point of all of this anti-gay legislating, besides the sheer delight that comes with tormenting a relatively powerless, if fabulously accessorized, minority group? The claim is that persecuting gay people, particularly gay couples, somehow demonstrates our society's support for traditional families. How's that work exactly?

On ABC News's *This Week* a few years ago, William "The Gambler" Bennett explained it all for us: "I think the best state-of-the-art science right now is the belief that some people are hard-wired this way," he admitted, thereby separating himself from Dobson and the rest of the "It's a choice!" crowd. (Isn't it ironic that, on the subject of homosexuality, so many religious leaders believe so passionately in choice?) Nevertheless, society should actively persecute homosexuals, Bennett believes, in order to convince "wavering" bisexuals not to identify as gay. "There are a lot of people in the middle," Bennett said, ". . . a lot of waverers. We should be sending signals of what society needs to prefer. And it needs to prefer heterosexuality."

So society should "send signals" to bisexual guys by beating up on out gays and lesbians, all in an effort to keep dicks out of their mouths. It's seems reasonable enough—if you hate gay people, that is, or if you fear that your son or daughter is bisexual and you would rather have him or her terrified and closeted than out and gay. But where does the signal-sending stop? While the rest of the world moves toward full civil rights for gays and lesbians (even overwhelmingly Catholic Spain has legalized gay marriage!), here in the United States we're banning books with gay characters, relegating gays and lesbians to second-class citizenship, and doing all we can to further isolate and terrorize gay and lesbian teenagers.

And you know what? It's not going to work.

"What social conservatives have to grapple with," Andrew Sullivan writes on his blog, www.andrewsullivan.com, "is that openly gay people are not going away," and homosexuals "going away" is what those who make the "choice" argument are lobbying for. Their message to homosexuals is, "If we can just make things unpleasant enough for you, perhaps you will choose to be straight." To heterosexuals their message is, "You shouldn't have to think about gay people, much less gay marriage, because no one is essentially gay and no one has to remain gay."

Christian conservatives and their allies in the Republican party are trying to avoid certain questions about homosexuals, Sullivan writes. "Where do these people fit in? How can they be integrated into family life? How do we acknowledge their citizenship? And their humanity? The pro–gay marriage forces have an argument: We want full integration into civil institutions, the same rules, the same principles of responsibility. The anti–gay marriage forces have—what exactly? They are against civil unions, against domestic partnerships, against military service, against any form of recognition. They want to create a shadow class of people operating somehow in a cultural and social limbo. That strategy may have worked as long as gay people cooperated—by staying in the closet, keeping their heads down, playing the euphemism game. But the cooperation is over."

The cooperation ended decades ago. Laws like those being passed in Virginia and Ohio may cause more gays and lesbians to flee those states for more welcoming places, but they're not going to stop gays and lesbians from living our lives. We are going to continue having sex and falling in love and starting families. And what, I wonder, will the social conservatives do after they realize that their "Nuremburg-lite" laws have failed? Round us up and put us in camps? Pack us onto boxcars heading north to Canada? Line us up against walls and shoot us?

Okay, so I'm being hysterical again. There will be no camps—I have my father's word on that.

My dad voted for George W. Bush in 2000 and 2004, votes he doesn't want me to hold against him. Whenever we go to San Diego to visit, my dad goes out of his way to assure us that reasonable, rank-and-file Republicans like him don't hate homosexuals. It's just a symbolic "values" issue that the Republicans exploit for electoral advantage. They're never going to toss us into camps, my dad tells me, and he should know: He watches Fox News twenty-four hours a day and if the Republicans were planning to round us all up, the news would probably break on Fox. Oh, and they're not going to take our kids away either, my dad tells me. They beat up gay parents, but they know that there are more kids out there needing homes than there are homes for kids, and if Republicans are anything, they're fiscal conservatives—Bush's record debts notwithstanding—and they don't want to create more kids who are dependent on the state for services. They're just going to go on bashing gays and lesbians for as long as it wins them elections. It's not personal, he insists, just politics.

"It's like abortion," Dad says. "Republicans run against it, but it's not like they're ever going to do anything about it. Most people are pro-choice, but the anti-abortion rhetoric motivates the pro-lifers to vote Republican. It's the same with homosexuality. The Republicans aren't going to do anything about it, they're just going to work up the anti-gay voters in their base."

There's one big problem with my dad's analysis. Republicans *are* doing something about homosexuality in Virginia, Kansas, Ohio, Michigan, and other states. Some of the gay couples we've gotten to know at gay family camp in Saugatuck lost their health benefits after the Republican-backed anti–gay marriage amendment passed in Michigan. But, hey, look on the bright side: Our gay friends in Michigan may now be free to beat each other up without running afoul of Michigan's domestic violence laws.

The last time my father and I argued about the election in person, we were driving to LegoLand in San Diego. We were on day three of a conversation about the presidential race: I was imploring him not to vote Republican for my sake, for his grandson's sake, and he was once again telling me not to take the Republican party's anti-gay rhetoric, legislation, and party platform planks too seriously. Terry and D.J. were in the backseat looking at a LegoLand map Terry had downloaded from the Internet, deciding which rides to run to first. I didn't think D.J. was listening to my father and me discuss the election until he chimed in from the backseat.

"George Bush is a weasel!" D.J. shouted.

My father was silent for a moment and I was transported back to 6433. One of my earliest childhood memories is my father and mother fighting about another Republican president, Richard M. Nixon. My mother hated Nixon and would mock Tricky Dick in front of her children during the day; at night we would repeat her insults in front of my father, who at the time was a Chicago cop and a Democrat. One evening at dinner, one of the four of us kids, I don't remember who, said something rude about the president—I don't remember what—and my father exploded.

"Damn it, Judy!" he said. "You may not like him, but he's the president of the United States, and we should teach our children to have some respect!"

So I half-expected my father to slap the steering wheel and shout at me for teaching D.J. to insult the president. I was preparing to defend myself during the long silence; I was going to tell him that we didn't teach D.J. to call George W. Bush a weasel. That was something he picked up at school, from an older kid, a kid with straight parents who hated George W. Bush as much or more than we did. But my dad didn't explode. He chuckled.

"He's not a bad man, D.J.," my father said, "and he's certainly not a weasel. He's trying to do his best for your family and for all Americans—"

"No. He's a bad man, a very bad man."

D.J. didn't cut off my father. It was Terry. He usually held his tongue or walked out of the room when my father defended George W. Bush, but he wasn't going to let my dad tell D.J. that George W. Bush was working hard to protect his family.

"I'm sorry, Bill, but you can't tell D.J. that George Bush is working hard for his family," Terry said, addressing my father. Then he turned back to D.J. "George Bush is a bad man who is doing everything he can to hurt your family. You can call him a weasel whenever you want."

My dad cocked his head, sucked a little air between his teeth, and kept driving. We managed to avoid the subject of the election for the rest of the trip.

It wasn't just the re-election of the weasel that had us wondering if it might be nice to have Dish's tofu scramble for breakfast every day. Eleven anti-gay amendments to state constitutions passed on November 2, 2004, as "values voters" poured into polling places to take a stand against—well, I'm not sure exactly what they were taking a stand against. Election day polls showed that one-third of Americans are opposed to gay marriage, but fully one-third are for it, and another third are for marriage-in-all-but-name civil unions. That means that more than sixty percent favor legal recognition of same-sex relationships. Yet at every opportunity, Americans vote against legal recognition for same-sex relationships.

But as the talking heads on Fox News like to point out, a majority of Americans are opposed to gay people getting to use the "m" word, *marriage*, and it's gay marriage that was put to a vote in eleven states. That a majority of Americans are opposed to same-sex marriage is often trotted out as conclusive proof that same-sex marriage is beyond the pale. Since public opinion polls show that Americans aren't ready, those judges in Massachusetts and that mayor in San Francisco and that county clerk in Portland, Oregon, all jumped the gun when they recognized the rights of gay and lesbian Americans to marry. But what if a majority of Americans are wrong? Is it even possible? Yes, in a word. A majority of Americans have been wrong on issues ranging from slavery (which a majority of Americans once supported) to votes for women (which a majority of Americans once opposed) to the internment of Japanese Americans during World War II (which a majority of Americas once supported) to interracial marriage (which a majority of Americans once opposed). The American public's track record on civil rights issues is so uniformly terrible that anything a majority of Americans oppose automatically deserves the benefit of the doubt.

But why should we give a shit? Terry and I don't want to get married. We just want to live our lives, maybe get a couple of tattoos, keep being D.J.'s parents, maybe adopt again, and what difference does it make to us if that weasel George W. Bush goes on running/ruining the country? We can keep living the lives we've been living without having to go to Canada.

Well, maybe not. In an interview with the *New York Times* after the election, George W. Bush went on the record—again—opposing adoptions by gay and lesbian couples. "Studies have shown," Mr. Bush told the reporter, "that the ideal is where a child is raised in a married family with a man and a woman."

"Studies" have shown no such thing. "Experts say there is no scientific evidence that children raised by gay couples do any worse—socially, academically, or emotionally—than their peers raised in more traditional households," the *New York Times*, to its credit, reported. But George W. Bush never lets little things like facts get in his way. Even after the *New York Times* reported that he had his facts wrong, even after no studies were found that supported the president's position, Bush repeated his attack on gay families—on D.J.'s family.

At the same time that our president was attacking gay parents and renewing his call for an anti–gay marriage amendment to the U.S. Constitution, Canadian Prime Minister Paul Martin was speaking out in favor of gay marriage in Canadian House of Commons.

"For a prime minister to use the powers of his office to explicitly deny rather than affirm a right . . . would serve as a signal to all minorities that no longer can they look to the nation's leader and to the nation's Constitution for protection, for security, for the guarantee of their freedoms. We would risk becoming a country in which the defense of rights is weighed, calculated, and debated based on electoral or other considerations. That would set us back decades as a nation. It would be wrong for the minorities of this country. It would be wrong for Canada."

Delicious tofu scrambles, national leaders who won't attack a tiny minority group for electoral advantage, snowboarders' firm butts—Canada, what's not to like?

PART III

The Slippery Slope

—10—
The Non-Wedding Planner

A few weeks after the election, my mother called and demanded that we finally set a firm date for our tenth anniversary party. We had told the whole family back in July that we expected them to come to Seattle for our whatever-it-was-going-to-be, and everyone had agreed to come. But people needed to buy airline tickets and make hotel reservations and get time off work. We had to pick a date, my mother insisted, and give people at least three months' notice.

I apologized and tried to explain that we were having a hard time making concrete plans because we couldn't decide what kind of party we were planning to have. An anniversary party? A wedding reception? A farewell-we're-moving-to-Canada party?

"Does it matter?" my mother said. "You're having a party—a Chinese New Year party, as I was led to believe. So select a date, make plans, and then decide whether it's a celebration of your marriage, which I would prefer, or an anniversary party, which I've resigned myself to. But pick a date, Daniel."

"Okay, I will," I said.

"I mean now," Mom said. "I'm not hanging up until I get a date from you. You're going to have to bite the bullet and pick a date or spend eternity with me on the phone."

I shouted down to Terry to bring me the calendar from the fridge. Chinese New Year fell on February 9. The nearest Saturday was February 12.

"The party is on February 12, Mom," I said. "Feel free to tell everyone on earth."

"Thank you, my dear. See you in February."

"Holy shit," I said. I thought my mother had hung up, but she hadn't, and she heard me.

"What? What's wrong?" she asked.

"Nothing, Mom, it's all good. I just noticed something on the, um, calendar that we forgot about. Bye."

I ran down the stairs with the calendar and showed Terry what really made me swear. The Chinese calendar assigns an animal mascot to each year, with twelve animals doing the honors in rotation.

"I think it's a good omen that 2005 is the Year of the Cock," I said to Terry. "Don't you?"

If I may paraphrase Samuel Johnson, nothing concentrates the mind like knowing your entire family will be arriving in twelve weeks' time expecting an open bar.

We sat down and made a list of everything we needed to accomplish in the next twelve weeks and realized it was more than we could possibly do on our own. I'm not an organized person. I've never balanced a checkbook; I can't keep an appointment calendar; I've signed contracts I didn't read (book deals, speaking gigs, adoption decrees); and I've never met a deadline I could actually meet (hello there, Brian). I always wanted a boyfriend who was hyper-organized, someone who kept neat files, the kind of guy who would balance my checkbook and make sure I didn't lose my passport every six months. Sadly, I didn't wind up with a hyper-organized guy.

If we were going to pull together an anniversary party/potential wedding reception in twelve weeks, we were going to need help.

Enter Caroline.

Caroline had planned some parties and special events for *The Stranger*, the paper I edit in Seattle, and I called to ask if she might be interested in helping us plan our might-be-an-anniversary-party/might-be-a-wedding-reception. She would be delighted, she said, even after we explained to her what it was we wanted: A banquet room in a Chinese restaurant, some Chinese food, maybe a Chinese performer or two.

"How soon?" she asked.

"On the Saturday after Chinese New Year," I said. "Which is, um, February 12. Twelve weeks away."

"Are you out of your fucking minds?" she asked.

I assumed Caroline's outburst had something to do how quickly she would have to pull this party together, or maybe the fact that neither of us was Chinese. But the problem, like Caroline, was more practical.

"Has it occurred to you guys that you live in a city with a huge Chinese community?"

No, we hadn't really thought about that. Would they be offended?

"No," she said. "It's just that Chinese people actually have non-ironic Chinese New Year's parties and Chinese restaurants with banquet rooms are all going to be booked up that weekend, to say nothing of traditional Chinese performers."

None of that occurred to us, I had to admit, but I told Caroline it was too late to change the date. We'd already told my mother that it was February 12, and she had already booked her airline tickets.

"We can't move the party," I said, a note of desperation creeping into my voice. "My mother will kill me."

"Let me make some calls," Caroline said.

"The Mad Clipper strikes again," Terry said when I walked in the door. He handed me an envelope that had arrived in the mail that afternoon. There was a single clipping inside.

"Married People are Healthier, Study Finds," read the headline on the Associated Press story. "Married people are healthier than other adults and less likely to engage in risky behavior, the National Center for Health Statistics reported. The report, based on a survey of 127,545 people conducted from 1999 to 2002, found that married people said they had less low-back pain, fewer headaches, and less psychological stress. They also were less likely to drink and smoke. . . ."

I didn't have to work hard to find a retaliatory anti-marriage news clipping to send off my mother. It was right there in the clipping she sent me. ". . . husbands have a tendency to put on *extra pounds*," the report went on (emphasis added). As I read on, I learned that "extra pounds" was a great, big, lardy, fat-assed understatement: "The report said 70.6 percent of husbands were overweight or obese. . . ." I was shocked she would send me this clipping at all. It was as if she didn't know me as well as I thought she did.

She knows I live in terror of getting fat. Had the Mad Clipper at last gone truly mad?

I underlined that line in the story about obesity, put the clipping in a new envelope, and mailed it back to my mother.

"The Slim Bachelor," I wrote in the return address.

"You're either going to have to move the party or change your theme," Caroline said. "Every Chinese restaurant in town with a banquet room is booked solid the weekend before and the weekend after Chinese New Year. You're pretty much fucked."

I looked at Terry, my blond-haired, blue-eyed boyfriend.

"Maybe we're not destined to have a Chinese New Year's party to celebrate our anniversary," I said. "Maybe we should think about something a little more Caucasian."

"We're moving the party," he said.

"Terry, my mother—"

"I want a Chinese party, and if we have to move the party to have one, we're going to move the party," he said, "and that's that."

"I already made some inquiries about the following two week-ends," Caroline said, without waiting for me to respond to Terry's unilateral move. We were only two minutes in to our first formal sit-down with Caroline, and she already knew who was in charge. Terry was calling the shots. "You can get in just about anywhere the fol-lowing Saturday, February 19," she said, "but I know of an awesome place that's free on February 26, which would give us two more weeks to pull this puppy together. It's not a Chinese restaurant, but it's—"

"It has to be a Chinese restaurant," Terry said, cutting Caroline off. "A big, tacky, red-and-black décor kind of place. I want the cliché Chinese restaurant."

Caroline handed us a list of Chinese restaurants in Seattle that had banquet rooms available on the 19th and the 26th.

"You guys are going to be eating a lot of Chinese food over the next couple of weeks," she said. "I want you to check these places out, see if you like the rooms and the food."

"Here's the funny thing," I said to no one in particular. Caroline and Terry weren't listening. "Neither of us really likes Chinese food that much. We've been together ten years, and I don't think we've ever gone out for Chinese food even once."

"Well, we're going to be eating a lot over the next two weeks," Terry said.

"No, *you're* going to be eating lot of Chinese food, Terry, because I'm too busy to go to all these places," I said. "I have a paper to edit, a column to write, money to make to pay for all this."

Caroline saw that things were getting tense and jumped in with an alternative. "Let me take you to this place I know. It's awesome. It's not a Chinese restaurant, and it's not red-and-black tacky Chinese, but it might be Chinese enough for you. And it's pretty stunning."

Before I go on to describe how we managed to pull together our Big Chinese Anniversary Party/Possible Wedding Reception in a few short weeks, I would like to take a moment to apologize to my brother Eddie for the three years I spent making fun of his wedding.

My mother takes full credit for bringing Eddie and Mikki together. Eddie wanted to go back to college to finish up his bachelor's degree when he was in his late thirties, but told my mother he was too old to go back to school. "That's bullshit," my mother told him, reminding Eddie that she didn't get her bachelor's degree until she was in her forties. Mikki was one of Eddie's instructors, and he likes to say he was hot for teacher from day one. But Eddie waited until class was over before he asked Mikki out to a ballgame. A month later, he hired a small plane and took Mikki for a sunrise flight over Lake Michigan. As they watched the sun come up, Eddie proposed. Another impulsive marriage? Not this time. He and Mikki got engaged in the summer of 2000, but didn't marry until the summer of 2001.

In Iowa.

In July.

In a cornfield.

At noon.

Just the location of Eddie and Mikki's wedding provided his siblings with decade's worth of material. What kind of idiot gets married in a cornfield in Iowa? In July? At noon? Okay, so it's the cornfield behind the house where the bride grew up and her parents still live—but it's freaking hot in July in Iowa! As we drove through Iowa on the morning of Eddie's wedding, the sun was beating down mercilessly on the state's cornfields, meth labs, and pig manure lagoons. By the time we arrived in Waterloo, Iowa, at ten in the morning, it was already 80 degrees. By noon, it was nearly 100 degrees. By the end of the ceremony, three bridesmaids had collapsed (including my then-pregnant sister), and the guests who hadn't collapsed were light-headed from having their blood drained away by the mosquitoes flying over from the muddy river that ran along the edge of the cornfield.

But it wasn't just the cornfield or the hot summer day or the mosquitoes or our pregnant sister taking a header during the vows that made Eddie's second wedding so . . . so . . . *memorable*. It was the ceremony.

Eddie is only a year older than I am, and we shared so much growing up—bedrooms, toys, friends, teachers, scout troops, and on and on—that despite our different temperaments (I was sensitive, he was a jock), we were very similar people until age eighteen. We went to the same schools, watched the same TV shows, and endured the same religious education. But then we moved out of our childhood home and began to lead separate lives. Like all siblings, we grew apart in ways that were at once predictable and unexpected. It happens to everyone who isn't an only child—we watched it happen to my parents and their siblings—but it's not something you think will ever happen to you and your siblings. So I arrived in Iowa unprepared for the change my brother had undergone.

It was hard to stifle a laugh when I saw my Irish Catholic, blue-eyed brother in a traditional Native American wedding smock. Picture a big poncho with a lot of ribbons and feathers and beads hanging from it, my brother's sunburned, mosquito-bitten face poking through the neck hole. One of his groomsmen, a Chicago cop and the son of one of my dad's former police partners, took one look at Eddie in his wedding smock and said, "That's nice, Ed, does it come in a men's?"

My brother had developed an interest in Native-American spirituality in the year or two since we'd seen each other last. He had even gotten a dream catcher tattoo on his arm. And his bride, Mikki, had a tiny bit of Native-American blood in her; Mikki's father's great-grandfather married a Sioux.

Before the ceremony began, one of Eddie's friends, who was not Native American, conducted a "ritual smudging." It involved him waving a bundle of burning sage branches under the noses of the entire wedding party—a wedding party that included Eddie's asthmatic younger brother, Dan. The smudging ceremony induced an asthma attack that sent me running for my inhaler.

Standing in a field of corn, an Indian crop, in the middle of the Great Plains, which had once been Indian land, watching a white guy marry an almost entirely white girl in a Native-American ceremony . . . well, it felt like a poltergeist moment, the kind of cultural appropriation that might cause the spirits of Native Americans to emerge from the rows of corn and scalp us all. Eddie's sincere appreciation for Native-American culture couldn't erase the sinister subtext of what we were doing. European Americans stole the continent from Native Americans, drove them from their land, herded the handful of tribes we didn't exterminate onto reservations, and finally hybridized and patented their staple crop, corn. White Americans getting married in a traditional Native-American ceremony in a cornfield in Iowa was like a couple of Germans get married under a huppah in the ruins of a Berlin synagogue in 1946. It seemed a tad insensitive.

Hot and sweaty or tense and guilt-wracked, Eddie's friends and family reacted to his wedding the only way we knew how: We spent the day gently mocking where, when, and how he and Mikki chose to marry. Eddie has never forgiven us for making fun of his wedding, just as we've never forgiven him for getting married in a cornfield in Iowa in the middle of the summer. Eddie was sincere about his new-found Native-American spirituality, and the rituals, smocks, and burning sage were all deeply meaningful for him. Unfortunately, they were all foreign and strange to his Irish Catholic family and friends. So it was with some trepidation that I contemplated inviting my brother Eddie—and the rest of my family—to a Chinese New Year Party to celebrate our ten-year anniversary. I'm no more Chinese than Eddie is Chippewa, and I felt that we were setting ourselves up for some ribbing of our own.

"Gorgeous, huh? Didn't I tell ya?"

We were standing with Caroline on the balcony that wrapped all the way around the observation deck at the top of Seattle's Smith Tower, a forty-two-story office building that for fifty years was the tallest structure west of the Mississippi. The Smith Tower opened in 1914 and is named for L. C. Smith, a gun manufacturer. After seeing skyscrapers going up in New York and Chicago, Smith put up 1.5 million dollars to build a tall, terra-cotta tower topped by a seven-story pyramid. The observation deck on the thirty-fifth floor, just below the pyramid, is known as the Chinese Room for its dark carved wood ceiling and elaborately carved black furniture. The ceiling and the furniture were gifts from the Empress of China, a happy customer of Smith's. It may not have been a tacky Chinese restaurant, but the Chinese Room was stunning.

"One of the best Chinese restaurants in the city has a catering contract with the Smith Tower, and you can bring your own booze,"

Caroline said. "A small stage can go there for whatever Chinese performers you want to hire, and we can set up tables over here."

"We'll take it," Terry said. "Book it." Terry had been to a handful of the Chinese restaurants on Caroline's list, and all the banquet rooms were, he said, dark, dingy, and dirty. The Chinese Room was spotless and sparkling.

"There are some things you might want to think about first," Caroline said. "You can only have it until eleven P.M., which means you can't have an all-night affair. We might want to think about having a dinner up here and an after-party someplace else. And you can only have a hundred guests."

Caroline showed Terry around the bar area while I took another stroll around the balcony. Soon we were headed back down to the street in one of the Smith Tower's brass elevators, the last in the city to be manned by uniformed elevator operators.

"I've lived in Seattle for fourteen years and I never knew this was up here," I said to Caroline. "How did you find it?"

"This is where I got married," she said.

Caroline, slim and blond, in faded blue jeans and a red T-shirt, looked to be about twenty-six years old, which struck me as terribly young to be married in the Chinese Room—and she wasn't wearing a wedding ring, which struck me as terribly odd for someone who had been married in the Chinese Room.

"So . . . you're married?" I said.

"Not anymore," Caroline replied with a shrug.

"Widowed?"

"Please," she laughed. "I'm divorced."

"How long were you married?" I asked.

"Long enough to have a baby before discovering that my husband was addicted to coke," she sighed.

By now we were out on the street in front of the Smith Tower.

"I think we should think about it," I said. "Maybe we should look at a few other places."

Terry looked over at me and mouthed the words "drop it," then he turned to Caroline.

"Book it," he said. "It's perfect."

Terry knew what I was thinking. To me, the fact that our divorced wedding planner married a coke addict in the Chinese Room at the top of Smith Tower was the Mother of all Jinxes.

"Why would you want to put together a party here?" I asked. Terry put one hand over his eyes. "Isn't it a painful place for you to visit?"

"Doesn't bother me," Caroline said, smiling.

"You know, I think it might be bad luck for us—" I began to say.

"Forgive him," Terry said to Caroline, cutting me off. "He's a Catholic freak."

"Bad luck to have your party here because I got married here?" Caroline asked me.

"Yes," I mumbled, looking down at my shoes.

"I don't believe in that kind of stuff," Caroline said. "I believe in personal responsibility. Nothing can fuck you guys up but you guys. It's a beautiful space. Thousands of people have gotten married here, and not all of them have gotten divorced. Don't be such a pussy."

After Caroline booked the Chinese Room, she and Terry began meeting once a week to iron out all the details. There wasn't much left for me to do—besides pay for everything and show up on the night of the party. I had just two jobs: I had to write the text for the party invitations and come up with fortunes for the special-order fortune cookies Terry wanted.

We wanted the invitations to communicate to people that this party was a big deal, something we wanted them to take seriously.

We wanted people to feel honored to be invited, but we didn't want to promise them a *wedding*, as a marriage wasn't in the offing at this point. "Make them look like the kind of invitations a couple sends out only once in their lives, and people will treat them that way," my mother advised us in an e-mail. "Have them professionally printed, and include RSVP cards." Caroline found a printer and we picked an image that we wanted on the card—something secretly scandalous—but I couldn't come up with the text for the invitation. I hemmed and hawed about it for weeks until Caroline finally tracked me down in a café near my office. She sat down at my table and ordered me to stop whatever I was doing and write the text for the invitations.

"I will," I said, "on one condition."

"Shoot," she said.

"Tell me about your marriage."

Caroline laughed.

"It's a pretty boring story," she said, "but if that's what it takes to get the wording out of you, I'll bare my soul."

Caroline was an extraordinarily youthful looking thirty-four, not twenty-six. She met her ex-husband when they were both working in a coffee shop in their late twenties. They were romantic and foolish, she says, and decided to get married after they had been dating for a year.

"We said, 'Hey, we're in love! Let's get married!' We had the perfect relationship and then we had the perfect wedding, the perfect reception, and what I thought was the perfect marriage. But the entire time he was secretly doing coke. I should have known there was something wrong on our wedding night. We couldn't really do anything because he had a bloody nose."

Caroline's marriage lasted five years. She doesn't think it would have made it past three if she hadn't gotten pregnant with her daugh-

ter. What finally ended her marriage, "was a cocaine overdose followed by a Jerry Springer episode in our living room," she said, "and
we were done."

We sat in silence for a moment.

"You know what the worst part is of getting divorced?" she said.
"Feeling like another statistic, just another failed marriage."

Caroline sipped her coffee.

"If he had overdosed and died," I said, "your marriage would
have been a success. But because you divorced—"

"—it's a failure. I know. It's ridiculous. 'Oh, if only my ex-
husband had OD'd, then I wouldn't be such a failure!' Believe me,
that ran through my head when I was spending thousands of dollars
to get a divorce."

Would she ever get married again?

"No. It's so fucking easy to get married and so fucking hard to
get divorced. And it sucks because Ross," the man Caroline is with
now, "is exactly the man I should have married in the first place. I
wish I could face doing it again, because I'd love to marry him. But
then, not now. I don't think I could go through it again."

"So you probably don't think we should get married, huh?"

"I think people should wait," Caroline said. "I don't understand
what the rush is. People shouldn't rush into this shit. But you guys
have been together for ten years. You love each other. Terry's not a
coke addict. If anyone should get married, you guys should."

"Is your ex still a coke addict?" I asked.

"No, clean and sober—he has to be in order to see his daughter."
Caroline sighed and shook her head. "He was a bad husband but he
is a good dad."

Caroline took a magazine out of her bag.

"I'm going to sit here and read while you write the text for your
invitations. You're not leaving this café until it's done."

With Caroline sitting across from me, I started to bang out something I thought might work . . .

MR. DANIEL K. SAVAGE AND MR. TERRENCE A. MILLER

Request the honor of your presence at,
Well, not at the marriage of

———

MR. DANIEL K. SAVAGE
TO
MR. TERRENCE A. MILLER

———

Since they can't get married.
Gay marriage is illegal where they live.
Even if they could, they're not sure they would.
So while this may look like a wedding invitation,
It's actually an invitation to a party—are parties still legal?—
To celebrate Mr. Savage and Mr. Miller's Tenth Anniversary.

Saturday, the twenty-sixth of February, Two thousand and five,
At Six o'clock in the evening
At the Chinese Room, Smith Tower
506 Second Avenue, Seattle, Washington.

Dinner Will Be Served. Open Bar.
Reception to Follow at Re-bar.
No gifts, no toasts.

"That's perfect," Caroline said. "Just the right tone. People will get it. All I need from you now is fortunes for the cookies. By Monday, please."

*   *   *

Caroline came over to run through the final plan for the party with us. The invites were out, the RSVPs were coming in. There were going to be two parties, one at the Chinese Room, one at Re-bar, the nightclub where Terry and I met ten years ago. Nightclubs are like marriages—few last ten years. Re-bar was special. Other Seattle clubs came and went, but Re-bar hung in there, year after year.

Caroline had come over with menus for us to look over. I noticed that none of them included cake, something I had made it clear to Terry that I wanted.

"I thought we were going to have a cake," I said, looking up from the menus.

"We decided against cake," Terry said. He nodded his head toward Caroline. The two of them—that was the "we" he was a referring to.

"I want a cake," I said. Then I turned to Caroline. "We're having a cake."

"A cake says 'wedding,'" Terry said. "And I don't think this is going to be a wedding reception."

"Then we can have an anniversary cake that looks like a wedding cake," I said. "There has to be a cake. I want cake. I require cake."

"You do cross a line when you have a cake at a thing like this," Caroline said. "A cake will make your anniversary party look like it's really a wedding reception. You put a cake in that room and it's going to look like you two got married. Is that what you want?"

"No, it isn't," Terry said.

I put my foot down. I don't really like Chinese food much, and I certainly don't like traditional Chinese music. A few days before the cake showdown, Terry informed me that a band, IQU, would be performing at the party at Re-bar, as well as Seattle's best drag performer, Dina Martina, and Seattle hottest young DJ, DJ Fucking in the Streets. Terry was getting everything he wanted. We were even getting a $500 "double happiness" ice sculpture. I would be god-damned if we weren't going to have a fucking cake. In fact, I told Caroline, I wanted her to order TWO cakes—one for the party at the Chinese Room, the other for the party at Re-bar.

"Terry?" Caroline said.

"Whatever he wants," Terry said, rolling his eyes. "Get him as many cakes as he wants."

—11—
Five Cakes

Green Cake

When I was thirteen, my next-door neighbor, a middle-aged single parent living in a tiny, one-bedroom apartment with her four-year-old son, got married. When I asked her if she was going to have a reception, she said that marriage was no big deal, just a piece of paper. They'd both been married before and she didn't see any point in making a fuss. I decided that she had to be lying and I blamed her new husband. I'd never really liked him. He stank of cigarettes and beer and wore a mustache. He was the one who didn't want a fuss, not her.

I left her apartment and went home to bake a wedding cake—from scratch. If her awful husband wasn't going to make a fuss on their wedding day, I thought to myself, then I would. I had been on a baking kick since hitting puberty a year or two before and I was actually getting pretty good at sifting flour and greasing pans. Why baking? Why not baking? My friends-who-were-boys had abandoned me when we hit puberty because they could sense that my desire to wrestle or play cowboys and Indians had taken a prurient turn. I couldn't hang out with girls because that would give me away for sure. So I hung out at the house, reading and listening to eight-track tapes. My mother had inherited all of her mother's cookbooks and baking tins, and one day when I was bored I baked a cake. For two years, between the ages of twelve and fourteen, whenever I wasn't masturbating to thoughts of Leif Garrett or Shawn Cassidy, I was in the kitchen baking and eating and getting fat.

My thing for cake pre-dated my thing for Leif Garrett by almost a decade. My parents were the first in their circle of friends to get married and start a family. They wanted to have a social life, however, so they made their apartment available for birthday parties, New Year's Eve parties, and no-reason-at-all parties. Large sheet cakes were featured at many of these parties. There was usually half a sheet cake left the next morning. Unfortunately, the half that was left had become a huge, frosted ashtray at some point the previous night. Always an early riser, I would go straight to the cake on the dining table and carefully eat my way around the cigarette butts sticking out like birthday candles. While my parents and siblings slept, I would cut thin slices of from the edges of the cake, each more wonderfully stale and crunchy than the last, and eat myself into a sugar-fueled frenzy.

By the time I started baking my own cakes, the parties were a thing of the past. My parents' friends had all moved to the suburbs or divorced—or both. To re-create the delicious, stale cake of my childhood, I would cut the cakes I baked into slices and leave them out on the counter to dry overnight.

On my neighbor's wedding day, I whipped up a batch of a yellow cake batter, poured it into three different-sized round cake tins, and then ran to the Woolworth's a block away while they baked. You could still run to a Woolworth's in 1977, and they had everything. We used to buy school supplies, pet parakeets, and birthday presents for our mother at Woolworth's, and in the card aisle I found toppers.

The bride and groom were glued to a round plastic platform and standing under a plastic trellis.

I knew that white dresses were meant for first-time brides, for virgin brides, and that when a widow or a divorced woman remarried, she was supposed to wear something in a pastel, something in, say, a soft green or pink or yellow. Like I said, I was a gay thirteen-year-old boy. Since a white wedding cake wasn't appropriate to the occasion, I put a few drops of green food coloring into the frosting. I wanted a nice, soft, pastel green, but wound up with a bowl full of deep, dark-green buttercream frosting. After setting aside enough to frost over the plastic bride's little white dress, I assembled my cake.

I thought the cake looked amazing—it had three tiers!—and hurried over to my neighbor's back door, completely unaware of the emotional minefield I was about to go stomping through. It must have seemed so cheap, so tawdry, so pathetic, this little gay boy standing at the back door with a sad, dark-green wedding cake. My neighbor invited me in and set the cake on her kitchen counter. After telling me how lovely the cake was, she got out a knife and some plates so she could cut us both a piece. I sat at her kitchen table babbling about the recipe I used, how I got the bride and groom at Woolworth's, why I decided to use green frosting, and how I even thought to save some green frosting so I could frost over the bride's white dress, since it wasn't her first marriage and all, and brides don't wear white after they've been married once already.

She had a knife in her hands, and she probably would have been within her rights to stab me with it. Instead she set the knife down, put one hand on the counter, the other over her eyes, and began to sob.

Peach Cake

Two summers later, my Aunt Linda got married at big, fancy hotel in downtown Chicago.

Linda's wedding was remarkable for two reasons: First, she's the only one of my father's siblings still married to her first spouse, her husband Frank. Second, Linda's towering peach-colored wedding cake.

The wedding cake was pastel even though it was Linda's first and—fingers crossed—only wedding. She was the last of my father's five sisters to marry, and her parents went all-out. There were hundreds of guests at the reception, an open bar, mountains of shrimp, and that huge peach-colored wedding cake on a table in the center of the dance floor.

I had stopped baking the previous fall and had started the long process of fleeing home. Instead of spending all my time at home making cakes and cookies, a pastime I realized was making me fat, I bought myself a bicycle and rode it all over town. In a few months I was a skinny, tall, tan fifteen-year-old who was spending entirely too much time slowly riding his bike back and forth though Chicago's gay neighborhoods.

The estrangement I felt from my friends had spread to my family. I was acutely aware of my homosexuality and on guard at all times, terrified that my siblings or parents might discover my secret. Instead of mingling with my relatives during the wedding, I paced up and down the halls of the hotel. I wound up in a gift shop in the basement where I spotted something almost too good to be true: Gay porn. It was 1979, and gift shops that had long stocked *Penthouse* and *Playboy* were making room for *Playgirl* and *Blueboy*. After making sure that no one to whom I was related was in the gift shop, I snuck a peek at a *Blueboy*.

I headed back up to Linda and Frank's wedding reception with my corduroy jacket folded over one arm, covering my crotch, hoping no one noticed the lump in my pants. Things were winding down, and I waited impatiently for the huge peach-colored cake to be cut. I wasn't baking anymore, but I still loved cake, even if it wasn't stale. When Linda and Frank finally cut the cake I was crushed to discover that it was filled with sliced peaches and lemon curd. It wasn't really cake at all—it was an enormous fruit pudding with a sponge cake veneer! And the frosting didn't taste like it had any sugar in it at all; it tasted like an inch of peach-colored butter. Linda's cake was a huge disappointment to me.

Years later I would learn that it was not only a huge disappointment to me, but to Linda as well. She had asked the baker to make her a chocolate cake with white icing and specifically indicated that she did not want any fruit in her cake. When she saw the peach-colored, peach-filled monstrosity at her wedding reception, she advised her father not to pay for the cake.

Kink Cake

Being a sex advice columnist—particularly one who believes that people should enjoy their kinks—gives you a license to be nosy about other people's sexual interests. Take, for instance, the cake fetishist I met after giving a talk at a large university in the Midwest.

Before I get to the cake fetishist, though, a word for all the advocates of abstinence education out there: Thanks, gang. The brand of sex education you're pushing—so little useful information, so much misinformation—means I'll never be out of a job. I get questions every day from teenagers who think they can't get pregnant the first time they have sex, that you're still a virgin if you "only" have anal sex (in which case, Terry can wear white if we decide to get married), and that you can contract AIDS just by walking into a Banana Republic. Since eighteen-year-old high school seniors don't magically become informed, sophisticated eighteen-year-old college freshmen the day their parents drop them off at the dorms, universities pay me thousands of dollars to come in and undo some of the damage done by abstinence education. It's a nice little sideline, and one I'm grateful for. I'm tempted to name our second home Abstinence Manor.

When I do a speaking gig at a college, I take questions two ways. Students can raise their hands and ask questions in front of their friends and classmates, or they can write their questions down on a 3" by 5" card before the talk starts. Predictably, live questions tend to be about politics and the anonymous cards tend to be about sex. At one particularly memorable gig, I got a question about how one reveals a secret kink to a non-kinky partner. The person who wrote the question didn't mention what his or her kink was.

"If your mystery kink is extremely revolting or extremely rare," I said, offering up my boilerplate response to the what-do-I-do-about-my-kink question, "you might want to use the Internet to seek out like-minded pervs. But if it's something mild, something on the order of a foot fetish or a thing for being spanked, share the info with your sex partners. But you need to present it to them like it's no big deal. If you don't present it as if it's a problem, your partner is less likely to regard it as one. Present it as a perk, as if it were something that made you an even more fun, more interesting sex partner than they already know you to be."

After the talk I noticed a good-looking guy lurking in the back of the auditorium. I could tell he wanted to ask me about something, but by the time I answered the questions of the other students who hung out after the talk, the good-looking lurker was gone. At this particular university, speakers are put up at a small on-campus hotel right off the quad, something the lurker apparently knew, because he was standing in the lobby when I got back to the hotel. He walked up and introduced himself.

"I'm the one who asked the questing about being kinky," he said.

The advice I gave wasn't helpful, he went on, because his kink was both extremely rare and extremely mild.

"So what's the kink?" I asked.

He blushed and said he didn't want to say. I offered to give him some more advice, but he would have to tell me what kink it was we were talking about, otherwise he was wasting my time and his. He still couldn't bring himself to tell me, so I started rattling off kinks in a loud voice: feet, diapers, amputees, incest, piss, scat, BBWs, pegging, balloons, smokers, bondage, S&M. . . .

No, no—it wasn't anything like that. He wasn't into anything *extreme*, he emphasized again. His fetish was actually kind of sweet. And it wasn't *what* his fetish was that was problematic, but that he'd never, ever heard of anyone else who shared his fetish. After making me promise not to tell anyone he knew (I didn't know anyone he knew, I pointed out), he confessed: He had a thing for birthday cakes. Specifically, he got off on having birthday cakes smashed in his face.

I know what you're thinking: He was pulling my leg. I assure you, dear reader, he wasn't—and we'll get to exactly how I verified that in a moment. But I didn't doubt his fetish because it was actually a combo of two other well-known-if-rare fetishes: There are people who get off on having pies smashed in their faces (it's a humiliation/humor thing, perhaps the result of exposure to Three Stooges routines as a child), and there are people into "wet and messy" sex, or rolling around in baked beans, mud, condiments—whatever—and getting all sloppy, filthy, and harmlessly dirty during sex. Since I was familiar with both fetishes, although not intimately so, it didn't strike me as impossible that I was standing in a hotel lobby having a conversation with a straight boy who fantasized about pretty girls smashing birthday cakes in his face.

After asking him if I could take some notes, I began to lob questions at him. How long had he been into this? "Forever." Had anyone ever hit him in the face with a cake as a child? "Not that I remember." Did he have any special cake preferences? "Layer, not sheet. They're thicker, so it takes longer for your face to go all the way through." How old was he the first time he smashed a cake into his own face? "Thirteen." How old was he the first time someone else smashed a cake into his face?

He let out a little sigh.

"No one else has ever done it to me," he said.

My heart broke when he told me that the one and only time he told a girlfriend about his fetish, she promptly dumped him. Since then he'd been too afraid to tell anyone else.

"That girl was an idiot," I said. "You're gorgeous—I'd smash a cake in your face in heartbeat."

With God as my witness, I swear it wasn't an *offer*. I meant it as a joke and a compliment. I wasn't making a pass at the handsome cake fetishist. He was straight, I was gay, it was late, I'm not generally attracted to straight guys, and besides, it wasn't like I had a birthday cake up in my room. But his eyes lit up like a kid's on Christmas morning when I said I'd smash a cake in his face, and I was unprepared for what he said next.

"Do you mean it?" he said. "Would you?"

"Sure I would, I guess. I mean, why not?" I stammered. He looked so fragile! Like he would shatter if I refused! "But we don't have a cake. And I'm not exactly a pretty girl and I have an early flight—"

"I don't care that you're not a girl," he said. "I'll go get a cake. If you're serious. If you're not just making fun of me."

What could I do? What would you do? What would Jesus do?

Half an hour later he was back at my hotel with not one, but two store-bought layer cakes. After an awkward few moments spent making small talk, I asked him if he still wanted to go through with this. I wanted to make sure that he wouldn't regret squandering his cake-smashed-in-face virginity on a gay man. He reassured me that he wanted to do it. He got undressed and knelt in the bathtub. I remained fully clothed; this was about his needs, not mine—and besides, the sight of this boy naked was reward enough for me. The girlfriend who dumped him was a fool, I told him, as I lifted the lid off the cake.

"Now close your eyes and pretend I'm Hilary Swank," I said.

Wedding Cake

Oh, shit. There's something I forgot to mention that seems kind of relevant to this narrative: I've already been married. I had a wedding, I exchanged vows, I slid a ring on someone's finger, we had a wedding reception—I've starred in the whole marital floor show once before. I can't believe that we're two-hundred-odd pages into a book about marriage and it didn't even occur to me to mention my first marriage. And it wasn't a "marriage," a-marriage-in-quotes marriage, not a big, fake Bob-and-Rod gay "wedding," but a proper legal marriage, complete with a legally valid marriage license, a preacher, and a white wedding cake. I don't know why it slipped my mind—no, wait. I do know why it slipped my mind: Because I married a girl.

Shortly after gay couples began to marry in San Francisco and

Portland, one of *The Stranger*'s staff writers, Amy Jenniges, decided
to take her girlfriend Sonia down to the King County building in
Seattle to apply for a marriage license. I tagged along. We knew they
would be refused a license, as same-sex marriage was illegal in Washington, but Amy wanted to make a point. She was frustrated with the
complete lack of movement on the gay marriage issue in Seattle,
which has a huge gay population. She was particularly upset with
Seattle's elected officials, men and women who turn up at gay events
in search of votes and campaign contributions. County clerks in Oregon and New Mexico, and mayors in San Francisco and New Paltz,
New York, were sticking their necks out in support of gay marriage,
but there was silence from Seattle's political leaders. As Amy put it:
What the fuck?

When Amy and Sonia asked the clerk in room 403 of King
County Administration Building for a marriage license, the poor
woman turned white. She called over her manager, a nice older man,
who explained that Amy and Sonia couldn't have a marriage license.
So I asked if Amy and I could have one—even though I'm a gay man,
I explained, who lives with his boyfriend and Amy's a lesbian who
lives with her girlfriend. We made it clear that we didn't love each
other, didn't plan on having kids together, and would go on sleeping
with our same-sex partners. Could we get a marriage license?

"Sure," the man said. "If you've got fifty-four dollars."

Ten minutes later I had a marriage license—not to marry Terry,
but to marry Amy. Ah, the irony. The sacred institution of marriage
has to be protected from the homos at all costs, but any fag willing
to marry a dyke could get a marriage license for fifty-four dollars. Gay
men and lesbians could get married in Washington not only with the
state's blessing, but also with the blessing of the religious right.
How's that? Because one of us is a man and one of us is a woman.
Who cares that one of us is a gay man and one of us is a lesbian

woman? The ex-gay "movement" is all about pairing up fags and dykes and marrying them off.

One of the strangest arguments advanced by opponents of same-sex marriage is that gays and lesbians are not discriminated against. We enjoy the same rights that all heterosexuals do: Anytime we like, we're free to marry a member of the opposite sex.

As a correspondent at FreeRepublic.com, a radical right website, put it: "Not a single law in this country prohibits homosexuals from marrying. They are free to marry members of the opposite sex. Yet this isn't good enough for homosexual activists."

After we got our marriage license, Amy and I thought, shit, if the religious right can get behind loveless, sham, adulterous-by-design marriages, so could we. We decided to go ahead and get married. We figured we had the license, so why not call attention to the ridiculousness of the ban on gay marriage by marrying each other? So we booked a nightclub, hired a minister, and ordered a cake, and made the whole thing a benefit for Lambda Legal, a national gay rights group.

Then the shit hit the fan.

"OFFICIALS WORRIED GAY EDITOR WOULD BEAT THEM TO COURT," read the headline in the *Seattle Times* the morning after we got our marriage license. "Blame it on Dan Savage," the story began. "It was Savage, editor of *The Stranger*, a Seattle weekly newspaper, who pushed local gay-rights groups and King County Executive Ron Sims to challenge the state law prohibiting gay marriage yesterday. [After Savage showed up at the King County building, same-sex marriage] advocates and Sims were worried Savage would file a lawsuit challenging the state law before their own hand-picked gay couples did, thereby undermining an effort to use the most sympathetic local gays to test the legal waters."

A local leader of a gay-rights group was quoted in the story. In his opinion, Terry and I didn't qualify as "sympathetic local gays." What kind of gay couples were they looking for? "Ideally, those people would be stable, longtime gay couples, preferably with children," he said. The implication? Terry and I were an unstable, short-term gay couple, and D.J. was a hologram. This leader of a gay-rights group went on to speculate that I was planning to file a lawsuit for the publicity, without pausing to give a thought to the harm I could do to the gay-rights movement.

Two little ironies: First, I wasn't planning to file a lawsuit—I couldn't. I hadn't been denied anything at the King County building. I had my marriage license; what was I going to sue about? If the leader of the gay-rights group who insulted my family had bothered to pick up his phone and call, he would've known that. The second irony was the group he headed up: the local office of Lambda Legal, the very organization Amy and I were planning to raise money for at our wedding.

Two weeks after leaders of the gay-rights movement slimed my relationship in Washington state's largest newspaper, I stood up in front of a standing-room-only crowd and exchanged vows with Amy. We slid Ring Pops onto each other's fingers as three hundred people hooted and cheered. A lanky boy in a white Speedo and angel wings hovered over us pretending to be a cherub as a motley troupe of actors pretending to be ring girls, maids of honor, and groomsmen crowded around us. A large man in drag pretending to be the mother of the bride stood next to Amy pretending to cry. When the minister asked if anyone knew of a reason why Amy and I shouldn't be joined together in the state of holy matrimony, the crowd chanted, "They're queer! They're queer! They're queer!" It was a travesty, a farce, a sham—except for one teeny, tiny detail: It was all perfectly legal. We had lawfully obtained a marriage license and Amy and I were actually getting married—well, almost actually getting married. Having a marriage license doesn't mean you're married; not even exchanging vows does the trick anymore. There's one more step. You have to go sign a pile of documents given to you by the county along with your marriage license and mail them back. Only after your forms arrive safely at the county building are you legally married.

We didn't return our forms to the county. The state of Washington and the religious right may be willing to sign off on a loveless sham of a marriage between two homosexuals. Amy and I, however, couldn't do it. After we exchanged vows, after the minister pronounced us man and wife, after one chaste kiss, after the crowd threw rice at us, Amy and I tore up our marriage license and the forms we were supposed to send to the county. While I'm not sure if I want to get married, I am sure that I don't want to marry Amy.

When it was all over, we cut our cake. It was a towering chocolate cake with white icing, with a bride and groom perched on top. It was the cake my Aunt Linda wanted at her wedding. The topper looked like the one I bought at Woolworth's twenty-five years ago for my next-door neighbor. And after we cut the cake, Amy and I each smashed a piece into the other's face, an experience I enjoyed a whole lot less than that boy in the bathtub might have.

My Cake

Terry didn't really give a shit about the cake—he doesn't share my passion for cake, or my long history with sugar frosting, and this is the first he'd heard of that boy with the cake fetish—so he left ordering the cake up to me and Caroline. He did have one requirement: The cake at the Chinese Room had to be Chinese, just like the décor, the food, and the entertainment. Now, as anyone who has ever attempted to order dessert in an Asian restaurant knows, the Chinese, Japanese, Koreans, and Vietnamese aren't known for their desserts. With the exception of green tea ice cream in Japanese restaurants, most Asian restaurants don't offer dessert, which is probably one of the reasons I never developed a taste for Chinese food. Knowing there isn't any dessert on the menu creates a powerful subconscious desire on my part to eat elsewhere.

Caroline found us a place that can do anything—anything—with cake, Mike's Amazing Cakes. She suggested that Terry could have his red and black tacky Chinese decorations, and eat them, too. She sat down with Mike and sketched out a three-tiered white chocolate cake with dark red frosting, gold and black bands around the outside, and tiny Chinese lanterns hanging under the top tier. For the Re-bar party, we went to a big Italian bakery and ordered a sprawling, multi-leveled pastel monstrosity, complete with plastic bridges to satellite tiers, and enough frosting flowers to build a float in the Rose Bowl Parade.

Total cost for our two amazing cakes? One thousand dollars and change.

"Christ almighty," I said to Caroline as we pulled out of the Italian bakery's parking lot, "this getting married shit is expensive!"

"You bet it is," she said, "but we're on budget."

"Budget?" I thought to myself. "We have a budget?"

"What is our budget?" I asked Caroline.

"Terry didn't tell you?" she said. "He told me he ran it past you."

"No, he didn't," I said. "I mean, I know we're going to be spending some money on this, but I don't really have a handle on how much. So how much are we spending?"

"We're going to come in under twenty thousand," Caroline said. "That's what I promised Terry."

It's a good thing I wasn't driving—it's a good thing I can't drive—because I would've crashed the car.

"It's not cheap, doing this," Caroline said, in an attempt to calm me down. "If you were just having an anniversary party, that would be one thing. But you're having an anniversary party that's pretending to be a wedding reception, and that's when it gets expensive. We just spent a grand on cakes. Then there's the catering, liquor, decorations—"

"Holy shit," I muttered.

"Look on the bright side," Caroline said. "You don't have to buy a dress. That's going to save you five grand right off the bat."

—12—
Four Fights

The Money

"So tell me about the top-secret budget."

We'd just gotten D.J. off to bed, and Terry and I were sitting on the sofa, having a beer, and watching *South Park*—the usual gay lifestyle stuff. We would have gotten around to sodomy, too, if I hadn't brought up the budget.

"It's reasonable," Terry said. "Nothing's going on the credit card."

"We're spending every cent we have in the bank," I said. "How is that reasonable? What if, say, Caroline showed me a line item on the budget for five hundred dollars' worth of souvenir chopsticks and I couldn't work for six months because I had a fucking stroke. How would we eat?"

Caroline had shown me a line item for $500 worth of chopsticks, and I almost did have a stroke, so it wasn't an entirely hypothetical scenario.

"Caroline tells me you spent a thousand dollars on a cake," Terry said.

"Two cakes."

"Oh, well, two cakes, that's fine then. Five hundred dollars on a cake is reasonable, but five hundred dollars on gifts for our guests is out of bounds. Or is it only okay when *you* blow money on something stupid?"

I sat in silence. Getting two cakes was pretty stupid, but it was too late to do anything about it.

"This is a once-in-a-lifetime thing," Terry said. "This is the only party like this we're ever going to have, the only time we're ever going to celebrate our great big gay love. I think we should go all-out."

"There's 'all-out,' and there's 'all-out' of your mind."

At this point, the conversation degenerated into our usual fight about money—one we should burn onto a CD along with the fight about music in the car, so we can just press play and save ourselves the trouble of stating and restating our positions, which never change and can be summed up like this:

DAN: Money has become an abstraction to you, something that magically appears in our bank account, and you spend it without thinking.

TERRY: If I don't spend your money, who will? Now go get me another beer, bitch.

I'm probably not doing Terry's position justice—he'll have to write his own book if he wants to see his point of view accurately portrayed.

No matter how many times we have the money fight, I don't think I'll ever be able to wrap my mind around his attitude. Long ago he broke me of thinking of the money I bring in as *my* money, despite all the checks that arrive made out to me. We're in this together and he's a great parent and he takes such good care of me and D.J.

that I feel he's entitled to regard the money as his, too. We're a team. I couldn't work as much as I do if he weren't doing my laundry and cooking my dinner. I like coming home to clean clothes and a full refrigerator, and Terry enjoyed not having to worry about money while he got his pottery career off the ground. Still, when the money pours out as fast as it comes in, I get nervous.

I can't help it. My parents were chronically broke when I was growing up—that's what you get when you have four kids in braces and Catholic schools on a Chicago cop's salary—and money issues still make me tense even though, knock on wood, we've got plenty of it for now. There's one thing I don't get tense about anymore, though, and it's what we call the "GD" issue. I was already making a semi-decent living answering questions about sex practices so esoteric I never got around to trying them. And what was Terry doing when we met? He was a twenty-three-year-old pothead who worked in a video store, the ur-slacker job, and went to raves with e-popping friends. He had long hair, no apparent ambitions, and possessed what was then, and remains today, the hottest ass our species has ever produced.

Okay, the "GD" issue: About two years after Terry moved in, just as we were about to adopt a kid, a concerned friend pulled me aside and poured a little poison in my ear. He thought I was making a mistake starting a family with Terry. "How do you know your cute little boyfriend isn't just a great big golddigger?" The poison worked. A month later in Las Vegas, Terry was losing money at the craps tables at the Venetian. "Oh well," he announced. "It's only money!" I didn't say anything then, but my friend's crack ate at me all night. The following morning at the pool, I told Terry that what he said at the craps table bothered me.

"It's not 'only money,' " I said. "Sometimes I worry that you're a golddigger."

We were at the pool and Terry had been swimming laps. He gave me a long, sad look, then got up and walked to the bar at the other end of the patio. He was only wearing a Speedo, and all eyes, including mine, followed him as he walked to the bar. There was a large group of gay men at the far end of the patio, talking, smoking, and tanning, and they went silent as Terry approached. After he passed them, one of the men in the group got up and followed Terry to the bar to introduce himself, then offered to buy Terry a drink. Terry smiled and gestured toward me. After he passed by the group of gay men on his way back, another one of the men put his hand over his heart and pretended to have a heart attack.

When Terry returned to me, he sat down on the chaise lounge next to mine and handed me a beer.

"If I were a golddigger, honey," he said slowly, tilting his head toward the gay men at the other end of the patio, "I could get a guy with a lot more gold."

The Music

Caroline burst into my office with some CDs. "You have to listen to this," she said, slipping one into my computer.

It was a traditional Chinese performer playing a traditional Chinese instrument as she sang a traditional Chinese folk song. This was the act that Terry wanted Caroline to book for the Chinese Room. If she couldn't get this performer, Terry had selected two other performers. She had their CDs, too.

"But this woman is the 'best,' as hard as that might be to believe," Caroline said.

Now before I say something offensive, let me get this on the record: I'm sure that, to Chinese ears—not Chinese-American ears, but to the Chinese ears of Chinese people born and raised in China—

the traditional Chinese folk song threatening to melt my hard drive was melodic, lovely, and deeply moving. But to my Irish-American ears, it sounded like a live cat in a George Foreman Grill.

"The Chinese thing is cute and funny," Caroline said, "and all the cute, funny touches are part of what's making your party so much fun to work on, you know? But I think there's a limit to how far you guys should carry this concept."

Caroline had already tried to talk Terry out of traditional Chinese music, but he was dead-set on having it, she said, and she wanted me to intervene. We were at AP minus three weeks—that's "anniversary party minus three weeks"—and we were running out of time. If we wanted to book some other kind of performer, we needed to get on the stick. I thought of my brother Eddie and the fact that three or four more decades would have to pass before he lived down the smudging ritual at his wedding. Then I told Caroline to hire a nice man to sit in the corner and play the piano—something dignified, something that might be pleasing to western ears.

"What are we going to tell Terry?" she asked.

"We're not going to tell Terry anything," I said. "At least not until it's too late to do anything about it. Just like me and the budget."

Two weeks later, Terry called Caroline specifically to check on the music. Caroline told him she had booked someone to play the piano, a lounge artist. I okayed it, she told him.

"I thought he ran it past you," Caroline lied.

Terry was pretty upset when I got home.

"I'm not angry that you booked some lame piano player," Terry said, clearly angrier than he had been in a long, long time. "I'm angry that you hid it from me."

"You picked a DJ, a live band, and a drag queen to perform at the after party," I said, "all without consulting with me." But I liked the drag queen, I thought the DJ was hot, and the band did an amazing version of Minnie Riperton's "Loving You" on the theremin, Terry pointed out, so it wasn't as if he needed to consult with me. "Yeah," I said, "but you didn't consult me just the same—and let's not forget the budget I never saw."

Then I played my trump card.

"Chinese folk music would have been our 'smudging ceremony.' Do you really want to listen to my family bitch about the Chinese performers at our party for the rest of your life?" I said. "Because I wouldn't have taken the fall for it. I would have laid it all at your feet."

"It's not the same thing!" Terry shouted.

"It's exactly the same thing!" I said, also shouting. We were now indistinguishable from the fighting couple on Bravo's *Gay Weddings*. "Eddie isn't Native American, we're not Chinese American. There's a point at which a cute, humorous theme becomes a hard-to-take-seriously pain in everyone's ass. At Eddie's wedding, it was the burning sage. At our party, it would've been those 'traditional Chinese folk songs.' Did you listen to those CDs? It would've ruined the night for everyone involved!"

Terry stalked off—something he only does when he knows I'm right. I didn't even get to tell him that the piano player we hired knew the entire score of Rodgers and Hammerstein's *Flower Drum Song*, a musical set in San Francisco's Chinatown. He would get his tacky Chinese tunes in the end.

The Mural

"What's with the invitations?"

My mother was on the phone. I didn't know what she was talking about: The invitations had gone out weeks ago, and we were already getting RSVP cards from Chicago, San Diego, Spokane, New York City, Washington, D.C., and Portland, Oregon. What was she upset about? As it turns out, Mom didn't mean "where are the invitations," but what was up with the image we used on the invitations. On the front of the card was an oil painting of three horned Viking helmets resting on tall, spindly hat stands. There was a rough black border and what appeared to be several holes drilled clean through the painting.

"I tell everyone that you're having a Chinese-themed party and then these strange Viking helmets come in the mail," Mom said. "Are you planning to spring something on everyone? Are Viking helmets some sort of gay code?"

"Viking helmets are not gay code, Mom," I said. "Viking ranges, yes. Viking helmets, no."

"So what should I tell people they mean?"

"Tell them it's none of their business," I said. "I can't believe anyone even gives a shit."

"Daniel," Mom said. "Your ignorance of wedding traditions is showing." She began to speak slowly, as if she were talking to a non-native English speaker. "When a couple puts a picture on their wedding invitations, their guests naturally assume it has some special meaning to the couple. It has to have some significance, otherwise they wouldn't have used it, correct? Often the meaning is obvious: hearts and flowers, golden rings, a snapshot of the couple. But three Viking helmets? That's not easy for people to figure out on their own. It makes them wonder what the hell is going on. And people naturally want to know what it means because it might give them some idea of what to expect at the party to which they've been invited."

"I see," I said. "Well, we're all going to get in long boats and row across Puget Sound and attack a naval shipyard in Bremerton. First we rape and pillage, then we cut the cake."

There was a pause.

"It's not some sort of a poke at me, is it?" Mom said.

"A poke at you?"

"Yes, a poke at me! Your pushy mother dragging you two by your hair to the altar, like a marauding Viking or something."

"Mother, please."

Billy's vasectomy was a critique of her parenting and now our Viking invites were, too. Do all mothers read critiques of their parenting skills into random shit that has nothing whatsoever to do with them? Or is this a super power that only my mother possesses?

"Well?"

"Well, what?"

"Well are you going to tell me what the Viking helmets are about or not?"

Speaking in italics is exhausting, so I decided to spill.

"Remember how I met Terry, Mom?" I asked. "Drunk, stoned, in a bar, wound up making out in the men's room?"

"Yes, I remember," she said. "I like to pretend it was all very wholesome, but I know it wasn't."

Before we proceed, I would like to mention that my mother is not a prude. She's always had a sense of humor about sex—and about bathrooms. Once a friend gave her a large plaster statue of Mary as a gift. With her arms spread and her eyes downcast, this particular Mary was meant to sit on a high shelf, or in a niche in a church, looking down at the faithful. My mother put it on the tank of the toilet in our bathroom. Sitting atop the tank, Mary's downcast eyes appeared to be looking straight at your crotch as you faced the toilet. My mother told her sons that we had better start putting the toilet seat up before we peed because the Mother of God was watching us. Now, back to those Viking helmets:

"That picture was on the wall in the bathroom of the bar," I said. "It was above the long trough urinal. It's just a sneaky reference to the night we met, Mom, not some bizarre critique of your parenting skills."

What Mom didn't know was that the Viking helmets were no longer hanging above the urinal in the men's room at Re-bar. They were in our living room. After it became clear that something lasting and wholesome had come out of our sleazy hookup, Terry and I asked the owner of Re-bar, Steve Wells, if we could have the painting. He was happy for us to have it, but getting to yes was the easy part. The hard part was getting it home. A terrific Seattle artist named Parris painted the Viking helmets directly on to the wallboard above the urinal. We had to hire a carpenter to cut around the edges of the painting—that's why the edges of the painting are ragged— and carefully remove the 6' by 4' piece of wallboard. The holes in the painting are from the spots where the wallboard had been nailed to the two-by-fours in the bathroom walls. Once we got the Viking helmets out of Re-bar, we had it framed, and now it's on our living room wall—all two hundred pounds of it.

Sometimes, late at night when I can't sleep, I sit in our living room and look at the Viking helmets and picture all the men who looked up at them over all the years they hung above the urinal at Re-bar. So many men, so many dicks in so many hands, so much piss going down the drain—and one night, Terry and I made out in front of them. It was a sleazy meeting, but so what? A lot of good, decent people in stable, long-term relationships met under deeply sleazy circumstances. I know happy couples that met in rehab or doing sex work or slaving away in the Clinton White House. A few years ago, I attended a big, traditional wedding at which I was one of a handful of guests who knew that the twenty-something, blue-blooded bride met her thirty-something, old-money groom at the domination studio where she worked in New York City. She was a professional dominatrix, he was a client. One day they ran into each other in a bar. He looked nervous, she says, so she sent him a drink. They soon discovered they had more in common than a sincere belief in the superiority of females. The story of their meeting is so sweet it's really a shame they can't share it with their loved ones.

Couples that met sleazy not only have nothing to be ashamed of, in my opinion, they have a duty to share their stories with the world. People need to know that a sleazy meeting doesn't rule out the possibility of a lasting, loving relationship. Terry and I didn't consummate our relationship in Re-bar's bathroom that night, but we came close. And that's okay. We can't all meet cute. It seemed fitting that we use an image on our invitation that had a sleazy provenance since our relationship did, too. A decade's worth of Seattle punks, hipsters, drag queens, thugs, and drug dealers relieved themselves in front of that painting. Nirvana's record-release party for *Nevermind* was held at Re-bar, so it's possible that Kurt Cobain took a leak in front of those Viking helmets. Now all of my siblings and my parents and our friends and my great-aunts had all seen it, and that's sleazy and perverse and beautiful and touching.

After I finished with my speech, my mother sighed.

"I'll let everyone know what the Viking helmets are about," she said, "but not Aunt Katie. We'll just tell Aunt Katie you have a thing for helmets with horns."

Mom had one last question before we got off the phone.

"People want to know what kind of attire you would like them wear."

"Whatever they would wear to a wedding reception," I said.

"What are *you* planning to wear?" she asked, the italics slowly slipping back into her voice.

"What I always wear to weddings," I said.

I could hear that faint cracking sound again, the sound of a Diet Coke freezing solid in my mother's hand.

"Daniel."

"Mother."

"Promise me you're not wearing what you would normally wear to a wedding reception."

I'm infamous for turning up at wedding receptions, funerals, christenings, retirement parties, and other formal and semiformal family events in jeans and a T-shirt. If I'm feeling dressy, I may wear a baseball hat. I'm almost forty and I don't own a suit, and I would sooner wear a bra than a tie. I'm just not comfortable in "nice" clothes, I look ridiculous in them, and I can't handle shopping for them. After two decades of showing up at other people's special occasions looking like the dishwasher, I had no intention of showing up at my special occasion in a suit.

"It would be retroactively disrespectful to all those couples, birthday boys and girls, newborn babies, retirees, and dearly departed whose special events I showed up at in jeans and a T-shirt," I said to my mother. "I mean, what would it say if I showed up at my own party in a suit? 'To your special event I wore jeans and a T-shirt, but to my special event I wore a suit.' It would be so disrespectful!"

"Then how can you ask other people to dress up?"

"I'm only asking people to do what I'm doing: Wear what you would normally wear to a party like this, which is just what I'm planning to do," I said. "So tell everyone to wear what they would wear to a wedding. I'm not dressing down for our party, so why should they?"

"I shudder to think what you would consider 'dressing down,' Daniel."

The Meltdown

"So are we getting married or what?"

I'd been surfing the Web while Terry got D.J. in and out of the shower and ready for bed. When I took over to read D.J. a bedtime story, Terry checked out my browser history—technically a violation of my privacy, but I used to do the same to him all the time. I stopped after I realized that the all the porn I was downloading featured pictures of guys who looked a lot like Terry, while all the porn Terry was downloading was pictures of guys who looked nothing at all like me. Looking at his browsing history was shredding my self-esteem, so I stopped. But when he looked at my history that night, he didn't find the usual mix of porn and news, but links to websites about how to get married in Canada.

"I don't know," I said. "I was just thinking that, you know, with everyone coming to town, and with our tenth anniversary party looking so much like a wedding reception—it certainly is costing as much as one—that we might want to, you know, slip up to Canada and get married and get it over with. Just do the deed."

"Is that what you want to do?" he said. "You want to get married?"

"I don't know," I said. "Do you want to get married?"

"No, I don't," Terry said, "not at this moment."

"I was thinking that maybe we should do it, you know, for D.J., like Mom says."

"For D.J.? He doesn't want us to get married," Terry said.

"He doesn't want us to get married for all the wrong reasons," I said. "It might be a good way to break him of his 'boy stuff/girl stuff' hang-ups."

"Or it might scar him for life," Terry said. "I thought we had agreed that we weren't doing this."

"I know," I said. "I just think people with kids should get married, I guess. Call me old fashioned."

"Have you been talking to your mother?"

I shrugged. Busted.

"I tell you what," Terry said. "We can get married if we get the tattoos."

The "Property of . . ." tattoos were still very much on the table. They tended to come up whenever we had sex, as we both found the ownership thing disturbingly erotic. (And if you think this is over-sharing, you should see the two sentences Terry made me cut from this paragraph.) But time was getting short. If we were going to get "Property of . . ." tattoos, Terry wanted to get them at least a week before the party. He wanted to be able to show them off in place of the wedding rings that, regardless of whether we got married, we would *not* be wearing. The tattoos would need time for to heal.

While I had been looking into quickie weddings in Vancouver, Terry had taken the initiative on the tattoo front. He went so far as to get a friend to work up a design, just in case we decided to go for it. When he held up an acetate of the one that would go on my arm— "Property of Terry Miller since 1995"—we had to stop what we were doing and go and have sex.

After we were done reaffirming our partnership, the tattoos suddenly didn't seem like a great idea anymore. That was the problem with them, at least as far as I was concerned: Talking about "Property of . . ." tattoos was fun and sexy and it turned me on and I was sorely tempted, but the thought of having "Property of Terry Miller" permanently tattooed on my body didn't seem quite as sexy after we had sex. I saw the tattoos as sex toys, and anyone who uses sex toys will tell you that the sight of sex toys isn't so sexy immediately after sex. When you're done, you just want to put them away. But we wouldn't be able to put the tattoos away after sex. We'd be stuck with them.

My fear of getting the tattoo was compounded pretty much every time I left the house. Everywhere you go in Seattle you see the remains of unfortunate tattoos. Sitting at a table in a bar writing a column, looking up into the gap between a middle-aged woman's low-rise jeans and her high-rise top, I could see an unfortunate tribal tattoo. Two big, black swoops came together in a point that directed your eyes down her ass crack. The tattoo, like the woman wearing it, was probably hot once upon a time. Now it only served to call attention to how much time had passed since then.

There is one person in Seattle who makes me want to get tattoos, though—lots and lots of tattoos. About four years ago, a good-looking guy started waiting tables at one of our favorite restaurants. We have a sentimental attachment to the place; it was where Terry and I decided to adopt D.J. When the good-looking guy started, he had only a few tattoos, and over the years we've watched as new tattoos gradually creep out from under his tight black T-shirts, slowly spreading down his arms and up his neck.

My crush on the tattooed rocker boy (TRB) is out of character. I'm not into rocker boys as a general rule, but TRB's appeal is such that he transcends his sex-object genre. It helps that he's my favorite type of waiter: completely silent. In the five years he's been waiting on us, he hasn't said more than a dozen words to me. He comes up to the table and takes out his pad. He writes down your order. He brings your food. He takes your plates away. He makes your change.

There's no hostility in his silence, just a comfortable, reassuring economy. Do waiters really need to say "Can I take your order?" "How's your food?" or "Come again"? Don't we all know the restaurant drill? Why should TRB waste his breath on stock waiter/customer inanities? I know he's there to take my order, he knows I'm there to give it.

I went to TRB's restaurant the morning after Terry and I first argued, then screwed, then argued some more about getting tattoos. When TRB came to silently take my order, I noticed a new tattoo on his neck. It was a phrase, written in a large semi-circle under his Adam's apple. Each letter was crisp and clean and the semi-circle a perfect arc. Whoever did that tattoo, I thought, would be able to do the tattoos Terry and I had been talking about getting.

I opened my mouth to speak. I wanted to ask TRB about his new tattoo, the one that started below the large red skull under his right ear and stretched almost all the way to the dark blue scorpion under his left ear. But all that would come out of my mouth was "Two eggs over easy, bacon, toast, no potatoes, blackcurrant tea," then he turned and left.

Good-looking guys have that effect on me. I'm afraid of them, a phobia that has its roots in the all-boys Catholic high school I attended, a school that was every inch as homophobic as it was homoerotic. How else to explain the two "Disciplinarians," young priests whose full-time jobs consisted of spanking naughty teenage boys? Or that seniors took their swim class in the nude? Or all the kneeling we were forced to do? The homoeroticism, however, was covert, while the homophobia was overt—and violent. Anyone who was perceived as gay could count on having the crap beaten out of him on a daily basis. God help the boy who got an erection in the showers. Since being good looking was considered slightly faggy, the good-looking straight boys compensated by being even more violently homophobic. A moment's carelessness around one of the good-looking boys—absentmindedly staring at a corduroy-covered butt, getting caught making eye contact with an upperclassman, the dreaded erection-in-the-shower—could get you killed. To this day I still find it hard to talk to good-looking guys. (Looking isn't a problem, however, as TRB can attest.) Beautiful men that I have to interact with socially often get the impression that I don't like them, misreading my silence as hostility. But I'm frowning, looking at the ground, and mumbling because I'm afraid they'll beat the shit out of me.

That's why I couldn't bring myself to ask TRB about his tattoos that morning. He brought me my eggs in silence, took my plate away in silence, and made my change in silence. But a few hours later on the same day, I saw TRB walking down the street. It was less intimidating seeing him on the street; maybe it was the fact that I wasn't seated, my head at the level of his crotch, looking up at him. When I pointed to the tattoo on his neck, TRB was only too delighted to give me the name of his tattoo artist.

"I'm on my way to have a drink with him," TRB said. "You can tag along if you want to meet him."

Was TRB actually inviting me to join him (and his tattoo artist) for a drink? It was like being asked to prom by the best-looking boy in school—better, actually, since I could have a beer. I called Terry on his cell and asked him to meet us down at Linda's, a hipster bar popular with straight rocker boys, with the designs for our potential tattoos.

"Are you guys nuts?"

Ego, TRB's tattoo artist, didn't like the design. Ego was Terry's age, with thinning red hair, and he was wearing a tank top in Seattle in February in order to show off the tattoos that covered his arms and shoulders. And to be fair to our friend who designed the tattoos, Ego liked the *design* just fine. It was the content he took issue with.

"I don't do names," he said, shaking his head.

My eyes darted to TRB's throat.

"That's a phrase, not a name," Ego said, gesturing toward TRB's new tattoo. "You know what we call names? The kiss of death. People come in and they say, 'Oh, we're so in love, we're so in love!' Six months later we're covering up their tattoos and half the time they're mad at us for doing the tattoo in the first place."

"We're not going to break up," Terry said. "We've been together for ten years. We have a kid. You don't have to worry about us."

Ego looked at Terry, then at me.

"If you're one hundred percent certain and you're dead set on having your names on each other, I'll do it," he said, handing Terry his card. It had a skull on it. "But I'm going to give you a hard time about it. And if you break up, don't come back to my shop looking for a cover-up tattoo."

"We'll make an appointment," Terry said to Ego, then turning to me he said, "I have to go pick up D.J." We got up to leave, and I shook Ego's hand and thanked TRB for his help.

TRB nodded, not saying a word.

When we got home the mail had arrived. Along with *The New Yorker* and the *New Republic* there was an envelope with "The Mad Clipper" in the spot where the return address should have been. There were three clips—one from the *Chicago Tribune* about strategies for married couples that want to stay thin; one from the *Chicago Sun-Times* about the art and science of tattoo removal; and one from a celebrity gossip magazine about temporary henna tattoos.

"What about henna?" I asked Terry, handing him the clipping. "It fades away in three or four months. It would be like having a tattoo but not having to live with it forever."

Terry glared at me.

"Okay," he said, "we can get henna tattoos—but only if we can get the kind of marriage that fades away in three or four months, too."

"I'm sorry," I said, "I just think henna might be a good compromise."

"So temporary tattoos for me and death-do-us-part for you?"

"Well—"

"At this point I don't care what we do," Terry said. "Tattoos, yes or no? Marriage, yes or no? I can't take this endless back-and-forth anymore. It's driving me nuts. Let's just make a decision already and live with it."

—13—

Three Second Opinions

Terry wouldn't marry me if I didn't get a tattoo. I wouldn't get a tattoo if Terry didn't marry me. It was a deadlock.

We needed some advice.

The question most frequently asked of professional advice columnists after "What's the strangest question you've ever gotten?" is, "Who do you go to when you need advice?" I usually go to my mother, but she had a conflict of interest, to put it mildly, and I knew I couldn't rely on her for impartial advice on this matter. So I decided to assemble a jury of my peers, a three-columnist panel of other professional advice columnists.

There aren't many professional advice columnists out there—and by "professional advice columnists," I mean individuals who make a living writing an advice column, not individuals who write an advice column as a sideline. Ann Landers was a professional advice columnist. Billy Graham, who writes an advice column when he's not counseling presidents or leading America's never-ending religious revival, is not.

Although most advice columnists urge their readers to make nice with other people, we seem to find it difficult to make nice with each

other. Ann Landers didn't speak to her twin sister, Abigail V
Buren, for decades after Abigail started a rival advice column. Wh
the *Chicago Tribune* hired Amy Dickinson to write an advice colum
and promoted her as "the new Ann Landers," Landers' daught
Margo Howard, who writes the syndicated advice column "D
Prudence," was none too pleased. I myself have feuded publicly wi
two rival advice columnists who write for weekly publications.

The field is too competitive for all of us to get along. There a
only so many papers out there. It's also hard to see someone els
column in a paper without thinking, "Why aren't they running m
column?" and it's hard to read someone else's advice without thin
ing, "I could've done better!"

While I can't help but view people writing advice columns f
other weekly papers as a threat, I can afford to be generous when
comes to people writing for daily papers. My advice column, "Sava
Love," doesn't run in any daily papers—and it never, ever will. I'
too fond of the word "fuck" for America's "family newspapers," a
I don't think infidelity is a hanging offense, which further disqua
fies me. The downside is that I will probably never be in more pape
than I am now; "Savage Love" has conquered America's alternati
weeklies. The upside is that I can appreciate mainstream advi
columns because none of the papers that run Amy Dickinson's co
umn or Margo Howard's would ever run mine.

Daily-paper advice columnists aren't my competition, they're n
colleagues, and so I turned to them in my hour of need. I wrote u
my problem in the form of a letter to an advice columnist and sent
to three of the best in the biz today: Margo "Dear Prudence
Howard, Amy "Ask Amy" Dickinson, and Carolyn "Tell Me Abou
It" Hax. All three women get more mail than they can possibly re
spond to, and I had to pull some strings to get my letter to the to
of their in-boxes.

I'm a thirty-nine-year-old gay man facing a couple of difficult choices. I've been with my thirty-four-year-old boyfriend for ten years, and we have a six-year-old son. My mother would like my boyfriend and me to get married. She believes we should make a formal commitment, and I think she's tired of us calling each other "boyfriends" after all these years. The problem is that my boyfriend and I aren't sure we want to get married. I'm afraid of jinxing our relationship—so far, so good, why mess with it? We don't live in a state where gay marriage is legal, so it's not like we would receive any of the benefits of marriage. My boyfriend says he "doesn't want to act like straight people," which annoys my mother, since we're parents, and she thinks that's pretty straight of us.

Oh, and our son? He's against it, too. Our son says "boys don't marry boys," if you can believe that. Our son! Where did we go wrong?

My boyfriend and I have talked about getting matching tattoos that say "Property of . . .", with my name on his arm and his name on mine. Would that be a better idea? Or should we just get married?

Wondering in Washington

Dear Wondering,

I'm curious about why your mother thinks you should tie the knot—whether it is for religious reasons or perhaps because she has a mint green chiffon "Mother of the Bride" number burning a hole in her clothes closet. If that's the case, please encourage her to let it out already so that it might roam free.

Your mother is the only person who seems to want this. That means she's doing her job as a mom—bless her. When your son gets older and is in a committed relationship of many years, you'll see—you may want this for him as well. Who knows—you may have a little chiffon number you'll want to pull out for the occasion.

I'm of the "if it ain't broke, don't fix it" school of rela-

tionships. It would be great if you lived in a state that sanctioned same-sex marriage so that you could see up close what the rest of us see—marriage doesn't fix anything, but it does seem to change things between people.

I'm not loving the tattoo idea; tattoos seem to create bad relationship karma. I'm thinking of Angelina Jolie here. I believe she's had to have several removed.

I hope this helps. Throwing a huge "We're Not Married" party where guests can publicly acknowledge and toast you as a couple might help get some of this out of everybody's system. —Amy Dickinson

Dear Wondering:
I'm wondering if conviction has become as endangered as hetero marriage. As arguments for getting hitched, you've offered:

1. Pleasing your mother.
2. Cleaning up the semantics.

And against:

1. Superstition.
2. "Ew, that's so straight."

Your mother believes in something. I believe in something: that it's fine to get married just for the gifts. (Okay. I believe in letting people decide for themselves whether they ought to get married.) Your six-year-old, bless his contrarian heart, believes in something.

Do you believe in marriage, or don't you? Do your values demand it, or not? —Carolyn Hax

Dear Won:
Prudie is not a believer in marrying to please a parent.

Her own marriages—every single one—were a result of

her own choosing. In your case, you and the beloved sound hesitant to monkey with a relationship that works. Many straight couples have the same feeling. On the other hand, it is not uncommon for long-term couples to say they felt a renewed commitment once they *did* tie the knot. It is interesting—and telling—that your six-year-old does not want the marriage; you might not want to tamper with his retro-hetero inclination. (Then again, you might.)

Prudie would advise against formalizing your love with tattooers' ink. (It didn't work for Angelina Jolie.) If you choose not to marry—which sounds like your preference— perhaps allow your mother to have a celebration with a short commitment ceremony. Such an observance is not binding, certainly, and would give the old girl a chance to acknowledge "her kids." Just for the record, Prudie's cred regarding same-sex marriage is unassailable: She was the (world's oldest) flower girl for two gay gentlemen not too many months ago.

Lovinginly, Prudie —Margo Howard

Like all good advice columnists, Amy and Margo instinctively side with the author of the letter, me, in my dispute with my mother, boyfriend, and son. This is as it should be. So long as the person who asks the question doesn't come across as crazy or self-destructive, an advice columnist's job is usually to divine what it is the reader wants to do and advise him or her to do just that. A great deal of the mail advice columnists get is from people seeking permission to do what- ever it is they want to do or know they must, all of which could be filed under "Mother, May I?"

Carolyn, however, doesn't bite. Instead of telling us to do what we want, instead of offering us any advice at all, Carolyn puts a pair of questions to us. And while her words are less comforting, she does manage to get to a little closer to the heart of the matter: "Do you believe in marriage, or don't you? Do your values demand it, or not?"

If I were to answer those questions honestly I would have to say that, yes, I do believe in marriage. I do. The trouble is that I live some-place where most people don't believe in the kind of marriage I would have to enter into. So what difference does it make what I believe?

—14—

Two Moments of
Transcendent Bliss

We were at AP minus two weeks when D.J. woke up in the middle of the night with an earache. Since Terry's on call during the day, he believes all late-night parental duties are my responsibility. Earaches, colds, nightmares—whatever the middle-of-the-night crisis is, sitting up with D.J. is my job. In all honesty, I don't mind. I'm a light sleeper and half the time I'm up anyway. But don't tell Terry, since I milk the nights I sit up with D.J. for maximum advantage.

I got some Children's Tylenol into D.J., and we curled up together on the couch in the living room waiting for the medicine to do its job. It was three in the morning on a Sunday. We talked about skateboarding, we talked about school, we talked about the cosmic injustice that earaches represent. D.J. doesn't think it's fair that adults never, ever get earaches. Children, I pointed out, never, ever get audited, or indicted by the state of Iowa, or threatened with lawsuits, so it's kind of a wash.

Then we talked about sex.

"I want to be gay with Joshua when I grow up," D.J. suddenly said.

It was radical change of topic, but it wasn't a bolt from the blue.

D.J. had been asking questions lately about what exactly being "gay" meant. He knew he had gay parents, and that "gay marriage" was always in the news, and that if his parents married, it would be one of those gay marriages. Despite our best efforts to explain what gayness was without popping in an old Chi Chi LaRue video, D.J. was still a little fuzzy on the concept. Apparently he'd concluded that being gay meant living with your best friend.

It was one of those through-the-looking-glass moments unique to gay parents, like the moment we saw our names on our adopted child's birth certificate on the lines marked "mother" and "father." I didn't want to tell D.J. he *couldn't* be gay when he grew up, but I didn't believe he was going to be gay when he grew up. It would be misleading to present gayness and straightness to him as an "either/or" proposition. Telling him he would be one or the other, gay or straight, would give him the false impression that sexual orientation was a coin toss.

But the odds weren't fifty/fifty; the odds were so clearly stacked in favor of D.J. being straight that I almost told him he wouldn't be gay. He plays with trucks, he likes the Power Rangers, he threw a perfect spiral the first time he picked up a football. The kid is straight. But on the off chance that he wasn't going to be straight, I started naming all the couples we knew, gay and straight, and D.J. joined in. There were Eddie & Mikki, Billy & Kelly, Laura & Joe, Grandma & Gramps, Mark & Diane, Tim & Abby, Mike & John, Shirley & Rose, Brad & Rachel, Nancy & Barak, David & Jake, Amy & Sonia, Henry & Beth, Maureen & Ed . . .

"Most of the men we know are with . . . ?" I asked.

"Girls," D.J. said.

"That's because most men wind up falling in love with women when they grow up, and most women wind up falling in love with men. Those kind of men are called 'straight.' Men who fall in love with men, men like me and Daddy, are called 'gay.' "

"Am I going to be gay?"

"I don't know, D.J., but probably not," I said. "Most men aren't gay. You could be gay when you grow up, but it's much more likely that you're going to be straight like Uncle Billy or Uncle Eddie or Tim or Brad or Barak."

"But I want to be gay like you and Daddy."

Ah, I thought, somewhere a fundamentalist Christian's heart is breaking. This is precisely what they worry about, they insist, when they condemn gay parents. Our kids will want to be gay, they will emulate their parents, and adopt their sexuality. If you believe—against all the evidence—that sexuality is a matter of choice, it may be a rational fear. But sexuality isn't a matter of choice, it's an inborn trait, and D.J. could no more choose to be gay, like his parents, than I could choose to be straight, like mine.

"It's not a decision you get to make," I said. "It's not a decision I got to make. It's a decision your heart makes."

"When?"

"When you're older," I said. "One day your heart will let you know whether you're going to be the kind of man who falls in love with a woman or a man."

There was a long silence, and I thought D.J. had fallen asleep. He was curled up next to me, resting his head against my side, and I couldn't see his face. I stayed very still, giving him enough time to fall into a deep enough sleep that I could carry him back to bed without waking him up. I was also savoring the moment—not the conversation, which, in all honesty, had scared the shit out of me. It was the kind of Very Important Father Son Talk that you can't enjoy as it's happening because you're so worried that you'll say the wrong thing and Fuck Your Kid Up Forever. No, I was savoring two delicious, intoxicating sensations only parents ever experience: The scent and the weight of our children. It wasn't until D.J. came along that

I fully understood why parents with grown children ache for grand-children. Once your children are grown, having grandchildren is the only way to experience those twin sensations again; the rich, humid scent of your child, the way your child's hand feels resting in your own, the trusting, contented weight of your child sitting on your lap while you read or watch TV.

D.J.'s seventh birthday is coming up, and he's getting too big to sit on our laps anymore. Cuddling is becoming physically awkward, soon it will be emotionally awkward, and then it will stop. Soon D.J. will pull away from us physically, just as I pulled away from my par-ents. One day I lived for my mother's lap or my father's shoulders, and the next day physical intimacy with my parents was limited to brief hugs. When that happens to me and D.J., I expect I'll start pes-tering him to have children of his own so I can feel the weight of a child on my lap again. But for now, I'm going to enjoy what will probably be the last of these precious moments of transcendent bliss.

"Grandma says you're supposed to marry the person you love," D.J. suddenly said. He hadn't fallen asleep; he was just quietly working through something.

"That's right," I said. "Grandma does say that."

"But you love me and we're not going to get married."

"Grown-up love is a special kind of love," I said. "People don't fall in that special kind of love with their sisters, or their mothers, or their sons. There's something in your heart that makes you go out into the world and find someone new, someone you've never met be-fore, and you fall in love with that new person."

"Why?"

"Because that's how new families are made. Two people who aren't already related fall in love with each other and bring their fam-ilies together, and create new relatives."

"Like Grandma and Grammy?"

"That's right. Once my mother and Terry's mother didn't know each other, and now they're related to each other through our family. And one day you'll meet the person you want to make a new family with and that's the person you're supposed to marry."

"Why?"

"Because marriage is a promise that you make to that other person, a promise to stay in love with them forever, to be related forever. My mom will always be my mom, and she'll always be your grandma. You'll always be my son. But when you meet someone new and fall in love, there's a chance you could fall out of love with that person. Marriage is a promise you make to always try and stay in love with each other, so that you'll always be together."

"Did Henry's parents fall out of love?"

Henry was a friend of D.J.'s whose parents were in the middle of an ugly divorce.

"Yes, they did."

"So they broke their promise?"

"Yes, I guess they did."

D.J. got quiet again.

"Do you and Daddy want to get married?" D.J. said.

"Sometimes we do," I said. "But sometimes we don't. Grandma wants us to get married. You don't."

"I changed my mind."

"Why?"

"You and Dad have to stay together forever."

"We will," I said. "We love each other and always will."

D.J. sat up on the couch and looked me in the eye.

"I want you and Daddy to promise, to pinky promise, to seriously and forever promise, and no breaking your promise."

So it was the idea of a promise that moved D.J. into the pro-marriage camp. As soon as they learn to talk, children learn to keep score, and God help the parent who fails to bring home a promised toy when work takes him out of town for a week (there wasn't a gift shop at the fetish prison!), or fails to take his kid on a promised skateboard outing (rain is no excuse!). For children, promises are a deadly serious business because it's all they really have. They don't own anything, they don't control anything. The promises their parents make them are all they've got. And while no parent can keep every promise he makes—no child can either—your credibility as a parent rests on a promises-kept-to-promises-broken ranking that your child carries around in his head. Keep more than you break, and you're a parent in good standing. Break more than you keep and you're in trouble.

"So you want us to get married, then?"

"Yes."

There it was—an unexpected second moment of transcendent bliss. A bonus round, my reward for a sleepless night. My son was giving me permission to marry.

"I'll tell Terry," I said. "We'll see what Daddy says."

There was another long silence, and again I thought D.J. was finally falling asleep. I heard the Sunday *New York Times* hit the steps outside the house.

"If you get married, Daddy," D.J. said, sounding very sleepy, "will there be a guy who says 'do you take' blah blah blah?"

"Yes, there will."

"Will he say 'you may now kiss' blah blah blah?"

"Yes, he will."

"Then I don't want to come. But you should still get married. I want you and Terry to make the promise. But I'm not going to watch."

—15—

One Last Try

"I'm going to make a little speech," Mom said, "and the two of you are going to do the old lady the honor of listening."

"Judy—" Terry said.

"And the honor of shutting up."

We were at AP minus one week and had flown to Chicago for my stepfather Jerry's retirement party, leaving everything in Caroline's capable hands. Our anniversary-party-pretending-to-be-a-wedding-reception was coming along fine, Caroline said, all but ordering us to get out of town for the weekend. As soon we arrived at the party, my mother pulled us aside. She told D.J. to run off and play with Cody because there was something she wanted to discuss with his dads.

"Let me get this out of the way," Mom began. "Now: How is your relationship not a marriage?"

We knew it was a rhetorical question and kept our mouths shut.

"In my eyes, it is. It's everything a marriage is and should be. That's why I think you should get married. Your parents, Daniel, and your parents, Terry, didn't marry because we were heterosexual. We married because we were in love."

Mom looked around the banquet hall. Was that it? If so, it wasn't much of a speech as Mom's speeches go. I took a breath to speak, but before I could say a word, Mom held up her hand—she wasn't finished. Not hardly.

"It seems crazy to me that your father and I could have our relationship blessed legally and by the church and you guys can't. You're being robbed of something by the dummies who voted for George W. Bush. But you guys are robbing yourselves, too. You're robbing yourselves of publicly saying 'I care about this person as much as I care about myself,' and having everyone around you applaud that and promise to support you."

Another pause.

"Mom—"

"I'm not finished. You guys don't have to get married, of course. But you know what?"

We made "what?" faces, not daring to speak.

"Jerry and I didn't have to get married either. We both knew the downside," Mom said. "We were both divorced after long marriages, and despite the trauma, we both learned to trust again, and that was very difficult. It wasn't easy to say 'I trust you' after what we had been through, believe me. We really knew what it meant the second time around. It felt risky and we didn't want to look foolish. We had to trust each other and that was hard. And trust is what marriage really means. You and Terry trust each other. When I look at you I see two people who have chosen to be together, in good times and bad, to put up with each other and love each other in spite of their shortcomings. I see two people who love and respect each other, two people who care enough about each other to want to adopt and raise a child together. I see two people who should *want* to be married."

"Judy!"

My Aunt Linda called to my mother from the other side of the room. Her husband Frank was with her. My mother waved back.

"Do you want to know what I think your problem is?" my mother said, turning back to us.

We shook our heads, still too terrified to speak.

"Jerkos have told you both that you're not worthy of marriage. You could flip off the jerkos by doing the right thing and getting married anyway, but you're way too clever for that. So you've decided to flip them off by refusing to get married. You say it's 'acting like straight people,' you say it's a jinx. Well, I've got news for you, Daniel. Life is a big jinx, and we're all going to die. And you should stop worrying about acting like straight people, Terry, and start acting like the person I know that you are—a serious, grown-up, responsible person who should be mature enough to make a serious commitment to the person he chose to start a family with, just like his parents did.

"End of speech," Mom said, standing up. "I'm going to mingle. Thank you both for coming. It means an awful lot to Jerry that you're here."

"I'm sorry," I said to Terry, after my mother walked over to say hello to Linda. "Sometimes my mother is—"

"Right," Terry said. "Sometimes she's right."

—16—
Zero Chance

By the time we got home from Chicago, Terry had changed his mind again: My mother was wrong about marriage. I had to agree. The party was less than a week away—what were we supposed to do? Run out and hire some awful nondenominational preacher and have a big fake gay "wedding" in the Chinese Room? Or, on the eve of hosting a huge anniversary party, take off on a road trip up to Canada, where we could tie the knot legally, only to have our marriage license turn back into a pumpkin the second we drove back across the border?

So, no, we didn't wind up getting married. Why jump through that hoop? My friend Dave—the guy who once remarked, "Gay people getting married is like retarded people getting together and giving each other Ph.D.s. It doesn't make them smart, and it doesn't make us married."—may have succumbed, but not Terry and me. We're made of stronger stuff.

We went ahead with the party, though. Frankly, we were getting cold feet about that, too, but it was too late to do anything about it. Our families and friends were on their way and we'd already laid out a lot of money on cakes and the Chinese Room and ice sculptures.

So our family and friends gathered to help us celebrate our tenth anniversary, and the quiet dignity of our long-term, same-sex, imperfect-if-perfectly-serviceable relationship survived our long flirtation with the institution of marriage. I wore jeans and a button-down shirt, D.J. wore his baseball hat backwards, and no toasts were offered. We served our guests black-and-red cake, my brothers made a few jokes about the Year of the Cock, and everyone flew home the next day.

It sure was fun thinking about marriage, though. Maybe one day it will be legal for us to marry in the United States, and then we'll think about it some more. Hell, there might be another book in it. Until then, though, we're not going to risk acting too much like straight people. Why jinx things?

And we didn't get the tattoos either.

THE END.

Acknowledgments

I would like to thank my editor, Brian Tart, for his patience, judgment, and skill, and my literary agent, Elizabeth Wales, for her energy, persistence, and support. I would also like to thank Julie Doughty, an editor at Dutton, for jumping in at the eleventh hour.

Many thanks to Tim Keck, Brad Steinbacher, and the rest of the staff of at *The Stranger*, as well as the staffs of Ringler's and Powell's Books in Portland, Oregon, and Victrola Coffee Company, Fuel Coffee, Tully's at 19th and Aloha, and the Virginia Inn in Seattle, Washington. Also, thanks to Brook Adams for the legwork; Eli Sanders for reading and critiquing an early draft; and Kate Thompson for her brilliant design.

Finally I'd like to thank all the couples in my life—gay and straight, married and not—who've set such good examples for me and Terry over the years: Judy & Jerry, Bill & Jo, Claudia & Dennis, Tim & Abby, Bob & Kate, Brad & Rachel, Nancy & Barak, Billy & Kelly, Henry & Beth, Eddie & Mikki, Hita & Carl, Laura & Joe, Mike & John, Mark & Dianne, Maureen & Ed, Dave & Jake, and Amy & Sonia. I hope you all make it to Maloney's.

About the Author

Dan Savage is the author of *The Kid*, *Savage Love*, and *Skipping Towards Gomorrah*. He is also the author of the internationally syndicated advice column "Savage Love," and the editor of *The Stranger*, Seattle's largest alternative weekly newspaper. He lives in Seattle, Washington, with his son, D.J., a deaf, brain-damaged, one-eyed poodle named Stinker, and his boyfriend, Terry.

—17—
We Do

Just kidding.

We wound up getting married—I mean, please. Don't all comedies end with a marriage? Could a book with a picture of a wedding band on the cover possibly end without a wedding? And, hey, you were too smart to fall for that false ending anyway. You got to "The End," thought "no fucking way," and kept on turning the pages until you found the two hidden chapters at the end of this book. I couldn't fool you.

Or, hey, maybe I did fool you. Maybe you didn't keep on turning the pages. Maybe you read "The End," closed the book, and tossed it aside. Reading about my fear of jinxing things and Terry's fear of making an ass of himself and D.J.'s unwillingness to be in the room during the do-you-take-blah-blah-blahs could lead a reasonable person to conclude that we didn't get married. So maybe you're not going to see this chapter. Maybe no one is.

That would be too bad, because we did wind up getting married. We couldn't let D.J. down. He asked us to promise and we wanted to come through for him. We couldn't let my mom down. She wanted to see us married. Most important, we didn't want to let ourselves down. We wanted to marry, too, and I think we both wanted it all along. Despite playing hard to get during all of 2004, I think we both knew we would have to make honest men out of each other sooner or later. The closer we actually got to making a decision, though, the colder our feet became. Terry's feet froze solid after he watched Bravo's *Gay Weddings*; mine turned to ice half an hour after we arrived at the Seattle Wedding Expo. But sometime between picking out the cakes for our anniversary-party-pretending-to-be-a-wedding-reception and the first of several planeloads of relatives touching down at Seattle's airport, our feet began to thaw. We wanted marriage, but we wanted it on our own terms—no jinx, no spectacle—and perhaps subconsciously we both knew that putting off the decision until the last possible minute was the best way to avoid both.

So two days before the anniversary party, we hopped into the car and made for the border. About three hours into the trip, stuck in a slow-moving line of cars waiting to cross into Canada, I had an epiphany that seemed inappropriate to the occasion.

I suddenly realized why so many marriages fail.

Cultural conservatives have made a sport of correlating rising divorce rates with rising rates of anything else they disapprove of, from women working outside the home to gay liberation to all those cowardly hippies who didn't want to die in Vietnam. (Not to be confused with all those cowardly Republicans—George W. Bush, Dick Cheney, John Ashcroft, Bill Frist, Karl Rove, Newt Gingrich, etc.—who didn't want to die in Vietnam.) But divorce rates in the United States began to climb at the beginning of the twentieth century, long before the emergence of the counterculture and the civil rights movements conservatives despise. There is only one social phenomenon that spans the entire twentieth century, only one line on the chart that truly correlates with divorce rates.

Automobile ownership.

In 1880, no one in the United States owned a car, and only 1 out of every 21 marriages ended in divorce. By 1916, Americans owned 3.5 million cars, and 1 out of 9 marriages ended in divorce, the highest divorce rate in the world at that time. Today, Americans own 230 million cars, more cars per capita than any other nation, and 1 out of every 2 marriages end in divorce, still the highest divorce rate in the world. Coincidence? I don't think so.

Modern humans evolved, according to evolutionary scientists, on the savannahs of Africa. We loped around grassy plains in large, sprawling tribes, enjoying the fresh air, occasionally being picked off by bigger, faster, meaner mammals. One advantage our ancestors enjoyed was the ability to wander off to another part of the savannah when they were annoyed with each other. While there are gaps in the fossil record, as creationists constantly point out (are there no gaps in the Bible?), scientists can nevertheless say with a great degree of certainty that our ancestors did not evolve in tiny metal boxes roaring up and down the highway. Consequently *Homo sapiens* are not designed—we are not wired physically or emotionally—for spending long periods of time sitting bolt upright in tightly confined spaces, everyone facing forward, with no means of escape. The inability to wander off when you're in a car is why even the tiniest disagreement gets spun up into a major conflict. You can't escape. You're trapped.

All of this occurs to me—indeed, I wrote these words on my laptop—as I sat in the car with Terry and D.J., an Iron Maiden CD blasting on the car's stereo, as we sat in a slow-moving lane waiting to cross the border into Canada on a Thursday afternoon. I had a splitting headache; Terry was suffering from low blood sugar; and D.J., bored out of his gourd, was taking out his mounting frustrations on us. Our anniversary-party-pretending-to-be-a-wedding-reception was less than forty-eight hours away and we were starting to worry that our quick trip to Canada might not be so quick. What will we do if we can't make it back across the border in time for the party? And if we don't get out of this car soon, what will our guests think when we announce that we broke up the day before the big party?

After D.J. decided that he wanted his parents to marry, I got online and looked up a Canadian wedding planner I had spoken with months earlier.

The wedding planner quoted me a price of $750 Canadian the first time we spoke. For that price she would arrange a license, two witnesses, some appropriate music, and a Canadian marriage commissioner to perform the ceremony. But when I called after we got back home from Chicago on the Monday before the party—right after Mom's Oscar-winning speech—and asked if she could arrange a wedding for that Thursday, the only day we could make it up to Vancouver before the party, she said no. There was a wedding expo in Vancouver that week and she couldn't help us. She would be happy to make arrangements for our big gay wedding anytime the following week, she said, but the rest of this week was shot. When I explained to her why we *had* to get married before Friday, when our families would begin to arrive in Seattle for our anniversary, she said there was nothing she could do. Dejected, I was about to hang up when I heard her mutter, "Oh, fuck it." After making me promise never to reveal her name, she gave me another name.

"My colleagues in the industry would kill me if they heard me doing this," she said, "but listen: Google 'Karen Ell.' She's a marriage commissioner, a wonderful woman, and she can perform a ceremony for you. She'll let you know what else you'll need to do."

Two minutes later I was on the phone with Karen Ell's husband,

Bob. He told me that Karen would be happy to marry us, but that Thursday wasn't good. She was already doing two weddings that day: one in the afternoon, one in the evening. She did, however, have an hour open in the afternoon. If we could be at their condominium sometime between four and five, she would be more than happy to marry us. I told him we'd be there.

"Do you have a license?" Bob asked.

No, we don't. I said. Did he know where we could get one?

"There's a London Drugs a few blocks from our house," Bob said. "You can pick one up on the way over."

"You can get a marriage license at a drug store?" I asked incredulously, picturing a gumball machine by the door filled with plastic balls, marriage licenses folded up inside.

"Oh, sure," Bob said. "Bring $100 and valid ID. They'll give you some papers you'll have to give Karen. Then come on by and we'll get you two sorted out."

We were on our way out of Seattle the next morning when my cell phone rang. It was Karen calling to confirm our appointment. It was already ten A.M. and the drive to Vancouver normally takes three and a half hours. We were cutting it close, I told Karen, but we were definitely on our way.

"Terrific," Karen said. "Let's hope the lines aren't long at the border. We'll see you at four P.M. Just bring your license and your rings."

Rings.

"Oh fuck, Terry," I said, covering the tiny hole on the bottom of my cell phone with right pinkie finger. "We need rings!"

"You owe me a dollar!"

D.J. was in the backseat drinking an orange juice. In an effort to cut down on the amount of profanity that came pouring out of our mouths, Terry had empowered D.J. to demand a dollar from us anytime we swore. At the end of what would prove to be a disastrous wedding day, D.J. had enough money to buy himself his own car. He wasn't supposed to come along on the trip to Canada; D.J. wanted us to get married, but he made it clear that he didn't want to watch. We had arranged for him to spend the night at a friend's house, but his friend came down with the flu and the sleepover got canceled at the last minute. Which meant D.J. was going to have to watch us get married whether he liked it or not.

Rings, rings, rings: I don't know how we managed to forget rings. There were dozens of jewelers at the wedding expo and there were rings on the fingers of all our married friends. What part of "with this ring, I thee wed" didn't we understand? I suddenly felt so pathetic. Was there a bigger wedding-disaster cliché than the bumbling groom who misplaces the rings? I flashed back on all the weddings I'd been to at which the best man stood at the altar pretending he couldn't find the ring in his pocket.

Ugh—we were acting like straight people!

Terry pulled off the interstate and headed into downtown Seattle, toward the Pike Place Market. He knew a place we could get a pair of cheap rings quickly, and get them fitted, too. Ten minutes later we were peering into grimy display cases in a tiny store owned by an ancient Chinese couple that scrape together a living selling traditional Chinese jewelry to other ancient Chinese people. The House of Jade, however, does a nice little sideline in the kind of chunky, cheaply made silver jewelry that's popular with Seattle punks, hipsters, and musicians.

In an effort to get D.J. into the mood, I told him he could pick out our rings. Our little heavy metal fan pointed to two silver rings, each with a large skull in the middle. Terry threw his head back and laughed. Earlier that week I objected to an Iron Maiden lunch box D.J. wanted; I didn't think a lunch box covered in zombies and skeletons was appropriate for a first grader, and I didn't imagine it would go over very well at his teeth-achingly PC school. I was overruled, as I almost always am in matters of music and fashion, and Terry got D.J. his Iron Maiden lunch box, which turned out to be a hit with his teachers.

"I'm not going to wear a skull ring, Terry," I whispered.

"You only have to wear it for one day," Terry said, "so what difference does it make?"

"What about these rings?" I said, directing D.J.'s attention to some plain silver bands. "They might be better."

"Or how about these rings," Terry said, pointing out some silver rings with handcuffs on them.

D.J. looked up at me like I was retarded. I knew that becoming a parent meant that one day I would be viewed as a humiliating embarrassment by someone whose bills I paid (someone other than Terry, I should say). I went into parenthood fully aware that the day would come when my son would view me as a hopeless 'tard, only redeemed by the food and clothing and skateboards that my income allowed him to purchase. But I wasn't prepared for how soon my child would drop his voice two octaves and say, "Daaaaaaaaaaaaaaad" through clenched teeth. The first time I heard that sound, we were in a supermarket in Spokane, Washington. D.J. asked to be carried and I picked him up and put him on my hip. "Daaaaaaaaaaaaaad," he said. "I'm not a baby!" He wanted to be on my shoulders, like all the other big boys being carried by their fathers. D.J. was three.

"The other rings are stooooopid," D.J. elaborated. "Skulls are cool."

"But they're not appropriate," I said. "Wedding rings don't have skulls on them."

"Daaaaaaaaaaaaaaaaaaaaaaaaaaaaaaaaaaad."

The "a" was getting longer as D.J.'s impatience with my imbecility grew.

"You're going to promise to stay with Terry until you *die*. So when you look at your ring, you'll see a skull and you'll remember that you and Dad will be together until you're both dead and you're both skeletons and both your skulls are showing."

I got out my credit card.

Driving into Canada is usually easier than driving into the United States, but not on the day we wanted to get married. We hit the backup at 2:15 P.M., and an hour later, we were still more than a mile from the customs house.

"We should have fucking flown," Terry said, earning D.J. another dollar.

"Alright!" I shouted. "We should have flown. I'm sorry!"

"I can't believe this shit," Terry muttered.

"Two dollars!" D.J. shouted. "You owe me two more dollars, Daddy!"

"I DON'T HAVE ANY MORE SINGLES!" Terry shouted.

"Jesus Christ, Terry!" I shouted.

"Three dollars!" D.J. shouted.

"Okay, it's quiet time," Terry announced. His voice was low and threatening. "Everybody in this car shuts up until we're across the border."

We had been in the car for almost four hours. We left Seattle in such a hurry that we didn't think to bring anything to eat; we had expected to be in Vancouver early enough to grab a late lunch before our big gay wedding. We hadn't anticipated waiting in line at the border for more than two hours, and as we sat there, all three of us now suffering from a bad case of low blood sugar, nerves were fraying. At the rate we were going, we wouldn't make it to Vancouver in time to get married at all.

And Terry wanted to make sure I knew it was my fault.

He had wanted to fly—a flight to Vancouver only takes thirty minutes. In the time we'd already spent creeping along in line we could have flown to Vancouver, gotten married, and flown back to Seattle. But I refused to fly because, as Terry put it, "you're a silly, superstitious little old Catholic lady." My fear of flying doesn't usually stop me from flying—I fly frequently for work, I wanted to fly to Michigan—but I allow myself to stress out over every possible risk, from terrorists hijacking the plane to poorly maintained engines dropping off in flight to the filth that coats absolutely everything inside an airplane's cabin. (One study of airline cleanliness found fecal matter on *every single surface tested*; every seatback, doorknob, blanket, pillow, and overheard compartment latch had human excrement on it. Think about that the next time you unlatch your tray table or contemplate hitting on a cute flight attendant.) My greatest fear is winding up in the "irony graph" that begins every newspaper story written about an airline disaster. "If Joe Blow's meeting in Atlanta hadn't been canceled, the widgets salesman would not have arrived at the airport early enough to get a standby seat on the doomed American Airlines flight that crashed on takeoff yesterday . . ."; "If Susie Sunshine, a homemaker from Ohio, hadn't agreed to take a later flight in exchange for a $200 travel voucher, she would not have been on the doomed United Airlines flight that exploded over Omaha, Nebraska, yesterday afternoon. . . ."

I panic when I'm waiting to board a flight and they start looking for volunteers to take later flights. If I take the later flight and the plane crashes, I'll be in the irony graph for sure. But sometimes the irony graph is about the person who survives an airline disaster. "If

John Doe hadn't given up his seat on the overbooked—and doomed—Alaskan Airlines flight, he would have been among the 190 who perished yesterday. . . ."

So while I rarely want to drive anywhere with Terry and D.J., flying to Vancouver two days before all of our friends and our families were set to arrive in Seattle for our anniversary party was out of the question. It was too risky. We would wind up in The Mother of All Irony Graphs: "Dan Savage and his longtime companion, Terry Miller, wanted to surprise their families by getting married before their tenth anniversary party, so they decided to fly up to Vancouver the day before their guests were supposed to gather in a ballroom in Seattle. A joyous celebration became a somber gathering when the doomed Canadian Airlines jet crashed into a Tim Horton's donut shop on its approach to Vancouver International Airport, killing everyone on board and scattering crullers over three square miles of downtown Vancouver. . . ."

So it was my fault that we were trapped in the car, going nowhere fast, with nothing to eat or drink, crawling toward the Canadian border, the window of opportunity for our marriage slowly closing.

"You and your fucking 'irony graphs,' " Terry muttered under his breath.

"Four dollars," D.J. muttered from the backseat.

As we sat in the car, I allowed myself to hope that we would turn on the news when we got to Vancouver and learn that—alright!—a flight from Seattle to Vancouver had indeed crashed into a Tim Horton's. In my half-starved, semi-psychotic state, the deaths of a few dozen strangers didn't seem too high a price to pay for vindication.

Any same-sex couples contemplating adoption should pay particular attention to this aspect of our story.

When D.J. was born, we didn't know what to do about a last

name. Last names are a difficult enough business for nontraditional straight couples, much less a same-sex couple. We debated the merits of my last name vs. Terry's last name; a hyphenated last name vs. a new last name for all three of us. At the very last minute—we were at the hospital two days after he was born and literally about to sign the paperwork that would make our adoption official—we decided to give D.J. his mother's last name. "D.J." stands for Daryl Jude; Daryl was Terry's father's name, Jude is the male form of my mother's name. Giving D.J. his mother's last name, Pierce, meant D.J. had one name from my family, one from Terry's, and one from Melissa's.

That sweet gesture, however, has had major repercussions. It isn't easy for two men to board an airplane with a small child who doesn't share either of their last names, nor is it easy to get through customs at an international boundary as a family when each of your passports has a different last name. I've lost count of the number of conscientious airline employees and customs agents who've asked us if we were abducting D.J. (What do people who are actually abducting children say when they're asked that question? "Why yes, I am abducting this child—does it show?") When we travel now, we have to take D.J.'s passport, his original birth certificate, our adoption decree, and his post-adoption birth certificate that lists my name on the "Mother" line and Terry's on the "Father" line along with us.

We were about three cars from customs when Terry realized that the binder in which we keep all those documents wasn't in the car. It was on the kitchen table back at the house, he told me, and then put his head down on the steering wheel and moaned. It was my turn to make D.J. a few dollars richer. We had our passports, but there wasn't any way of proving that Mr. Savage and Mr. Miller were Mr. Pierce's parents and legal guardians. Driving up to the custom agent's glass booth at 3:40, we were certain we would be asked to turn around and go home.

"Are you getting married in British Columbia within the next ninety days?"

"We're hoping to get married within the next ten minutes," I said.

We were standing in front of a clerk at the dingy insurance services desk inside a cavernous London Drugs in Vancouver, B.C. By some miracle we had been waved through customs with hardly a glance at our passports. I was relieved for a moment, then annoyed. How could that customs agent know we weren't abducting D.J.?

It was 4:20 when we got to the drugstore where Karen and Bob told us we could get our marriage license. While Terry waited in line with D.J. at the government-run insurance counter in the back of the store, I ran to the pharmacist's counter and bought myself a bottle of Tylenol with codeine, which is available over the counter in Canada, a bottle of water, and a bag of trail mix. Terry and D.J. needed to eat something quick and I needed to get rid of my stress- and Iron Maiden–induced headache. Hustling back to the insurance counter, I popped four codeine tablets and ripped open the trail mix for D.J., who took one look and began to wail. I had mistakenly purchased a bag of trail mix that didn't have M&Ms. Terry, who also had a headache, refused to take any codeine, stating that all he really needed was the Coke I neglected to buy him. He didn't ask me to get him a Coke, I said, but that was no excuse. After ten years together, he felt I should know that a Coke is all he needs when he has a headache.

Squabbling, the three of us approached the counter to buy a marriage license.

I don't want to insult the fine men and women in the Canadian

Civil Service, and as grateful as we were to be in a country that would give us a marriage license, I have to ask: What sort of an IQ test does a person have to fail to get a job passing out marriage licenses in drug stores in Canada? Working on a computerized form, the tall, thin, mustachioed South Asian clerk carefully entered our names, dates of birth, locations of birth, and parents' names and locations of birth. Then he handed us a test printout that we had to check before the final, official marriage license could be printed. If there were any errors on the official license, it was invalid; if we didn't catch the errors before the official license was printed, we would have to pay another hundred dollars for a new license.

On the test printout, my first name, Terry's middle name, both our birthdates, and the place of my birth were incorrect. My first name was spelled "Dnniel," Terry's middle name was spelled "Rthur," and the place of my birth, Chicago, was spelled "Shigaga." As the seconds ticked away, the clerk slowly re-entered our information. D.J., meanwhile, began to cry. He wanted a bag of M&Ms to stir into his trail mix. When Terry said he was going to get a Coke for himself and some M&Ms for D.J., the clerk asked him to wait. For legal reasons, we both had to be in his sight while he filled out these forms. When he handed us the second test printout, our dates of birth were correct, as were the spellings of "Daniel" and "Arthur," but he was still having a little trouble with Chicago, which was now spelled "Chigaco." On his third attempt, Chicago was rendered "Chcago."

It was 4:40.

I spelled "Chicago" again, very slowly, leaning over the counter to watch as the clerk slowly tapped each key with his right index finger:

C.

H.

I.

C.

A.

C.

"No!" I said, a little too loudly. "G! The next letter is 'G.' Then 'O.' "

"Ah!" he said. "Chicago, Illinois! I have been!"

He printed out the final, official, completely correct copy of our marriage license, slid it into a large white envelope with some other documents, and handed it to me.

"That will be $100, sir," he said.

License now safely in hand, Terry told me to meet him and D.J. back at the car and they both ran off to buy some M&Ms and a Coke. I gave the clerk a credit card and quickly signed the receipt. But before I could go, the clerk had one last matter to attend to.

"May I be the first to congratulate you and Mr. Miller on the happy occasion of your wedding day," he said. "I am proud that you can do this in my country. My very best wishes to you both."

"Thank you," I said, genuinely touched. So what if this man couldn't type or spell; he was the nicest Canadian civil servant I'd ever met.

"I am a married man myself, sir," he said.

Using the same index finger that he couldn't use to spell "Chicago," he pointed out a framed photo on his desk of a woman in a sari and two small children with spiky black hair.

"Marriage," he said. "It is an honorable state."

Terry was on the phone with Karen, getting directions to her house from the London Drugs when I got back to the car. It was 4:45. I wanted to tell him how sweet the clerk turned out to be, but Terry barked at me before I could say anything.

"We can do this right now," he said, "or we can do it in the morning before we drive home."

"What do you want to do?" I said.

"I don't care," he said.

D.J. was shoving fistfuls of M&Ms and trail mix into his mouth, and Terry was downing his Coke. My head didn't hurt anymore, but my stomach hurt; never take twice the recommended dose of codeine on an empty stomach.

"Let's do it in the morning," I said. "I don't think we're in any condition—"

"We'll be right over," Terry said into the phone.

"Honey?"

"Let's get this bullshit over with," Terry said, earning D.J. another dollar.

Canada can be a disorienting place. It looks like the United States, it feels like the United States, and everywhere you go outside of Quebec it sounds like the United States.

But it's not.

I've been on a lot of Canadian television programs—*Open Mike with Mike Bullard*, the *Vicki Gabereau Show*, *Canada AM*, *@ the End*—and when I ask Canadian television producers what their shows are like, so I can know what to expect and how to comport myself, their explanations invariably start with "Oh, it's the Canadian [fill in the blank]." Bullard's show, his producers told me, was the Canadian *Letterman*; *Canada AM* is the Canadian *Good Morning America*; Vicki Gabereau is the Canadian Oprah; *@ the End* was the Canadian *Politically Incorrect*. (I was on the Canadian and American versions of *Politically Incorrect*, and both have since been canceled—superstitious television producers take note!) Doing Mike Bullard's show was a lot like doing *Letterman*. Bullard's show was taped in a big theater in downtown Toronto that was converted into a TV studio for Bullard, just as the Ed Sullivan Theater was for Letterman. There's a band, a desk, and a couch, just like on Letterman, and Bullard's a dry, acerbic guy, just like Letterman.

Being an American on a national Canadian television show feels like being dropped into an alternate reality, a parallel North American universe, where you speak the language but you don't have all the cultural information you need to be a fully functioning member of society. You're being shown to your dressing room when suddenly someone who's strangely tan for Canada strides past you in the hall trailing a crowd of writers, make-up artists, assistants, and producers. The person you just walked past looks like a television celebrity, and it's plain that everyone is treating this person like a television celebrity, *but you don't have the faintest idea who he is.* Indeed, the first time I was on Mike Bullard's show, he came into the dressing room where I was getting into makeup and asked me a few questions about my column. I answered his questions politely, wondering why I was doing a second pre-interview with yet another producer. When the man left, I asked the makeup artist who that was.

"He's Mike Bullard!" she said, genuinely shocked. "He's the star of the show! He's famous!" Then she added, "Well, in Canada at any rate."

Being a gay American in Canada is a lot like being an American guest on a national Canadian television program. You're in an alternate reality, a parallel universe where everything looks familiar, but then something comes along and reminds you that you're not in the United States anymore. You catch a glimpse of the Queen of England on a ten-dollar bill or marry the man you love in a stranger's living room—and you think to yourself: Shit, I'm not at home, am I?

We got to Karen's condominium at 4:55 P.M. Karen, glamorously attired for the wedding she would be performing at 6 P.M., looked to be in her forties; her husband, Bob, also well dressed, appeared to be a bit older. He had thick white hair, a large mustache, and an ingratiating manner. Terry and I looked like hell; we looked like two guys who should be sweeping up after a wedding reception, not two guys who were getting married themselves. We were both in jeans and T-shirts, baseball hats on our heads, grubby jackets folded over our arms.

Terry and I went over the forms in the folder with Karen while Bob ran out to knock on doors and round up another witness. D.J., jazzed up on his M&M-heavy trail mix, couldn't sit still, so I put him up on my shoulders. Bob quickly returned with a smiling man in a red "Canada" sweatshirt, who shook our hands and, like the clerk at London Drugs, told us he was proud that we could do this in Canada.

We were all set to go.

Karen asked Terry and me to stand by the fireplace. Bob and their next-door neighbor took up positions opposite us, and I set D.J. down on the sofa. Before we could begin, D.J. slid off the sofa, onto the floor, and then under Karen's glass-topped coffee table on which were perched several fragile-looking objets d'art. I got down on the floor and pulled D.J. out from under the coffee table and placed him back on the sofa. We were about to begin a second time when D.J. got back down on the floor again. This time he slid under the sofa. I decided to leave him there.

"We are here today to celebrate the love and commitment that Dan and Terry have for each other and their son," Karen began, gesturing toward her sofa. Suddenly one of D.J.'s hands appeared above the top of the sofa, tucked inside a dirty sock that D.J. had removed while he was under the sofa. D.J. didn't want to watch us say I-take-you-blah-blah-blah or you-may-now-kiss-blah-blah-blah, he announced, but Mr. Ghost, his imaginary friend who sometimes takes the form of an improvised sock puppet, did. The sock puppet looked from Terry to me to Karen to Bob and the next-door neighbor. Karen paused, smiling, waiting to see what we wanted to do. Terry moved to get D.J. and return him to the sofa, but I put my hand on his shoulder.

"Let him watch from there," I said. "Karen's living room is safer with him behind the sofa."

"We know that marriage is not created by ceremonies and legal documents," Karen said, resuming the ceremony. "For true marriage occurs in the hearts and minds of two people who choose one another above all others. But from this day forward, Dan and Terry, you will not only be married in your hearts, but legally married, for this marriage is recognized as a legal union by the Province of British Columbia."

Here was our "we're not in the United States" moment, I thought, as Karen asked me to repeat after her. We were about to be legally married and there wasn't anything James Dobson or Gary Bauer could do about it.

"Repeat after me," Karen said, looking at me. "I solemnly declare that I do not know of any lawful impediment why I, Daniel Savage, may not be joined in matrimony to Terry Miller." After Terry made the same declaration, Karen asked us to join hands. I knew it was going to be a quickie ceremony; Karen had told me on the phone the day before that the whole thing would take less than ten minutes. I also knew that I didn't want to cry. I've only seen Terry cry three times in ten years (once on the anniversary of his father's death, at the hospital the day D.J. was born, and the day Stinker got hurt), but Terry has seen me cry on several dozen occasions. I'm the weepy one in the relationship, and I knew from past experience that Terry wouldn't let me live it down if I wept during our wedding ceremony.

So I had planned to brace myself, to get a grip, and do what I could to keep my eyes dry during the ceremony. But the rush to Vancouver, my headache, the wait at the drug store, and the fear that D.J. would lay waste to Karen and Bob's condo distracted me, and I was thoroughly vulnerable when Karen moved on to the next part of the ceremony.

"Dan do you take Terry to be your lawful wedded husband and life partner?"

Holy shit!

The "I dos"

Already?

Oh my God!

No way!

Before I could begin to form the words, before I could even take a breath, I choked up. Terry laughed. "I knew you wouldn't be able to get through this," he said, then mouthed the word "pussy."

"Shut up," I said, and then mouthed the word "asshole."

I looked over at Karen, willing my eyes to stay dry.

"I do. I take him," I said. Then I turned back to Terry and opened my dry eyes wide. "I take you. Who else would be fool enough?"

"Terry, do you take Dan to be your lawful wedded husband and life partner?"

"I do," Terry said, pretending to wipe away a tear. "Who else would be fool enough?"

"Dan," Karen said, "repeat after me: I call on those present to witness that I, Daniel, take you, Terry, to be my lawful wedded husband and partner in life. I pledge to share my life openly with you, to care for you, and encourage you through all the changes of our lives. I make this pledge to you as my friend and my companion and I will love you as long as we both live."

I tried, I really did, but by the time I got to "care for you" the tears were streaming down my face. When I tried to say "my companion" no sound came out, and after squeaking out a barely audible "as long as we both shall live," I had to take one of my hands out of Terry's and wipe my eyes.

Terry, repeating the same speech, not only stayed dry-eyed the whole time, but tacked a "ha-ha" on to the end.

"Is Daddy crying?" D.J. asked from behind the couch.

"Yes, he is," Terry said.

"Ha-ha!" D.J. repeated.

"You have chosen to exchange rings today," Karen continued. "These rings are perfect circles, symbolizing the unbroken unity of love." Perfect circles? We had shown Karen the rings before we got started, and explained why D.J. picked them out for us, but she chose not to mention the skulls or dwell on their morbid symbolism. "These rings represent that truth of life: As you give to each other, you receive from each other. As you give your love, understanding, and compassion to each other, it will be returned to you enhanced."

"Oh no," D.J. said from behind the couch, "kisses are coming!"

"D.J., hush," Terry said, gently. I thought I heard a catch in his voice. Was he choking up, too?

"Repeat after me, Dan," Karen said. "With this ring, I marry you."

"With this ring I marry you," I said, slipping a silver skull on the ring finger of Terry's left hand. I wasn't even trying to stop crying now.

"Repeat after me, Terry: With this ring, I marry you."

"With this ring, I marry you," Terry said, slipping a silver skull on the ring finger of my left hand. I swear I saw a tear in his eye but Terry insists that I saw the water in my own eyes superimposed over his.

"Dan and Terry, you have come together in marriage today before your witnesses and your son"—and a sock puppet—"pledging your love to each other. It gives me great pleasure to pronounce that you are husbands and life partners together from this very special day forward."

"No kissing! No kissing!" D.J. said from behind the couch, but it was too late.

And . . . scene.

After ten years, two homes, and one child, we were finally married. But what had we done, exactly?

According to the traditional wedding vows available online at www.bible.org, Terry and I had taken each other, "to have and to hold, from this day forward, for better, for worse, for richer, for poorer, in sickness and in health, to love and to cherish, 'til death do us part."

Note that these traditional vows, lifted from a Christian website no less, make no mention of children. Christian conservatives have lately insisted that marriage is about the having and raising of children. Since same-sex couples can't conceive, it's ridiculous to suggest that we should be able to marry. Oh, sure, some of us have kids, but allowing gays and lesbians with kids to marry would fatally undermine the institution of marriage and threaten heterosexual marriages by, er . . . well, no one can quite say. It just would.

But when you read the vows that heterosexuals exchange, it's apparent that marriage isn't about children. Once marriage evolved away from being a property transaction, it was redefined as all about love, baby, sweet love. Some people in love decide to have children, some don't, but either way, society benefits when two people in love make a formal commitment to care for each other. Society invests in couples—tax breaks, social advantages—in exchange for couples promising to tough out whatever bad times may come.

Denying same-sex couples the right to marry amounts to a refusal to recognize that gays and lesbians are capable of love. It also communicates to gays and lesbians that we are better off single than coupled.

Both are lies.

In a church in Iowa during a presidential election year, I listened as conservative leader Gary Bauer told the congregation that homosexuals were "seeking our approval for their lifestyle," and demanded that same-sex relationships be seen as the "moral equivalent of heterosexual marriage." Well, yes. I do believe that my relationship is the moral equivalent of a heterosexual marriage. But we are not seeking anyone's approval, much less waiting for it. When Terry and I promised to love and cherish each other, we were promising to do something that we had already been doing for years. I can't quite put my finger on when we stopped being boyfriends and started to regard caring for each other as our mutual responsibility, but we did it without the benefits of marriage or the approval of people who regard even the most destructive heterosexual relationship as morally superior to the most functional gay relationship.

So what had we done in Karen's living room? Not much, really. If marriage was a promise to care for another person, Terry and I had been married for a long time. When he calls, I drop everything. When I'm sick, he takes care of me. I don't see how our commitment to each other threatens traditional marriage, but if it does, well, then traditional marriage will just have to tough it out.

Besides our wedding, which was profound in its own weird way, our very special day was distinguished by stress, hunger, lines, and numbing headaches. Any hopes that the ten minutes we spent in Karen's condominium with her charming husband and smiling neighbor, or the good wishes of the man who sold us our marriage license, had broken our spell of bad luck were shattered when we arrived at our hotel and discovered that our "deluxe suite" was small and dirty. There was a decent sushi place across the street, but our little wedding banquet was ruined by the man at the next table who shouted at his wife and two daughters—in Russian—the entire time we were in the restaurant. We took D.J. swimming in the hotel pool later in the evening, but there was a crowd of twenty-something boys in the Jacuzzi talking animatedly about the prostitutes they'd banged on a recent trip to Bangkok, so we left.

It was nearly nine o'clock when Terry suggested that we go out for cake. The first all-cupcakes bakery in North America was in Vancouver—Cupcakes, on Denman Street—and we had stumbled into it the day it opened in 2002. I'd made a point of avoiding the place ever since—that's how good the cupcakes are. But it was our wedding day and, calories be damned, we were going to have some cake. Cupcakes was a short walk from our hotel, and we got there a few minutes before they closed and ordered three chocolate cupcakes with white frosting.

"What's the occasion?" the girl behind the counter asked D.J. as she boxed up our cupcakes. "Is it your birthday, little guy?"

D.J. didn't respond; he turned and buried his face in the side of my leg. It's his shy routine. I expect that, like cuddling, soon I'll miss the times when D.J. pressed his forehead into my leg to avoid a stranger's questions.

"He's shy," I explained to the girl behind the counter.

"Really?" she said. "Well, cupcakes are a cure for shyness."

There are no tables inside Cupcakes, so we took our cupcakes outside and sat at one of the two little café tables set up in front of the store. We had just taken our cupcakes out of the box when two groups of teenagers walking down the sidewalk collided right in front of our table—literally. A shoving match broke out among four boys.

Terry lifted D.J. up and out of his chair as one boy stumbled backward into our table, knocking it over, our cupcakes landing frosting-side-down on the sidewalk.

A question hung in the air as we stood there looking at the cupcakes: Who would burst into tears first? Me or D.J.? The sight of three cupcakes upside-down the sidewalk was almost too much for me to bear, but D.J.'s tears came faster. Terry was our hero, dashing back into Cupcakes just before they locked the doors, and buying the last three cupcakes in the place.

"This day has been absolutely cursed," Terry said, coming out of the bakery. "Christ, we can't catch a break today!"

"Let's just go back to the hotel and chill," I said. "Let's just go lie around our room and wait out the rest of this day."

Looking out the window of the cab as we headed back to the hotel, I remembered what the wedding planner told me on the phone: ". . . my colleagues would kill me if they heard me doing this." Now I knew why she was risking her life. She was going to charge us $750 for the license, the services of a marriage commissioner, and two witnesses. Acting as our own marriage planners (with Karen and Bob's help), we got a marriage license for $100, a marriage commissioner for $80 (Karen's fee), and two witnesses gratis. We saved $570, almost enough to cover our hotel room, sushi, cupcakes, and the cab ride.

What a wedding planner sells, of course, is expertise, and we wouldn't have been able to marry in time for our party if the wedding planner hadn't shared Karen's name with us. Still, 416% seems like an awfully steep markup, expertise or no expertise. To protect profit margins like that, I don't doubt for a moment that goons from the marital-industrial complex would rub out any wedding planners who told people how to get married on the cheap.

Besides the wedding ceremony (and the money we saved on it), the highlight of the trip was spending our wedding night in our small, dirty suite. We couldn't consummate our marriage, not with D.J. along, although I don't think we would have had the energy even if we were alone. Instead the three of us sat in the king-sized bed and ate our cupcakes while we watched *SpongeBob SquarePants,* of all things, on television. Soon D.J. was asleep, curled up between me and Terry, the cupcake crumbs on his pillow forming a pointillist halo around his head. After Terry dropped off a few minutes later, I got up and turned off the TV, tossed our cupcake wrappers in the trash, and got back in bed.

I couldn't sleep. I lay there, holding my left hand in front of my face, looking at my wedding ring in the dark. With my left thumb I turned the skull ring round and round on my finger. I've never been able to wear jewelry. I got my left ear pierced when I first came out and wore a garnet stud for a few months before a friend told me I looked ridiculous. My objection to jewelry isn't aesthetic, nor is it about gender; it's not like my objection to two men ballroom dancing. I actually like jewelry on men. Terry was wearing gold hoops in both ears and a Puka shell necklace on the night we met. I just don't like jewelry on me. There's something about the way rings or necklaces or watches feel against the skin on my fingers, neck, or wrist that annoys me. But for some reason I couldn't bring myself to take the skull ring off. With everything else that had gone wrong that day, we didn't need any more bad luck, so I would have to sleep with my wedding ring on.

I was about to roll over when I noticed that Terry was awake, propped up on an elbow, watching me turn my wedding ring round and round on my finger. Terry made a fist with his left hand and held it out, above our sleeping son, his silver skull glinting in the dark. I made a fist with my left hand and we knocked our knuckles together, our silver skulls clacking as they smacked into each other.

"Powers of gay marriage activate," Terry said, smiling sleepily.

The next day the lines to get into the United States were short, our first bit of good luck in the last twenty-four hours. Soon after arriving at the border, we got the green light and drove up to a customs agent's booth.

Terry rolled down his window and handed the customs agent, a bearded, middle-aged white man, our passports.

"And how are you three . . ." the agent paused and leaned down to peer at D.J., ". . . acquainted?"

"We're his parents," Terry said.

The agent's eyes darted from Terry's face to mine.

"I see," he said.

Then made an audible grunt—more like a tiny, disgusted snort—and turned to run our passport numbers through his computer. He sighed loudly as he waited for something to pop up on his screen. He was no fan of same-sex relationships, to say nothing of families headed by same-sex couples, and he was doing all he could to make sure we knew it—all three of us, D.J. included.

"How long were you in Canada?" he asked, turning back to us.

"Just overnight," Terry said.

"And were you visiting Canada for business or pleasure?" he asked.

"Pleasure," Terry said.

"Pleasure?" the border guard repeated, a smirk slashing across his face. "Did you purchase anything on your pleasure trip?"

"No," Terry said.

I felt very conspicuous sitting there. And vulnerable. I wondered if we could get in trouble for failing to declare the $100 marriage license we purchased in Canada, to say nothing of the bottle of codeine in my bag. We also had no way of proving we were D.J. Pierce's parents. If we told him we got married, I doubted very much he would congratulate us, or show us a picture of himself with his wife and kids. He could, however, choose to fuck with us. He could have our car searched, just for the hell of it, or order us to pull over and make us wait for an hour or two. Our marriage felt like so much B.C. bud we were attempting to smuggle into the United States.

"Have a nice day," the agent said abruptly, giving us one last dirty look as he handed Terry our passports and waved us into the country. Our country, at least for now.

"Why didn't you tell him?" D.J. asked when we drove off.

"Because he works for George Bush," Terry said, "and we don't trust people who work for George Bush."

D.J. turned in his seat, trying to get a better look back at a man who works for George W. Bush, but the customs house was quickly receding. D.J. rolled down his window.

"George Bush is a weasel!" he shouted.

When we stepped off the elevator into the Chinese Room at 6:30 P.M. the following day we were quickly enveloped by friends and family. I assumed we would just slip quietly into the room and mingle with our guests, but there was a stampede to the front of the ballroom the moment we got off the elevator. As D.J. ran off to play with his cousins, Terry and I greeted the crush of guests pressing in around us. It was less mingling and more mangling.

Eventually we split up and began working opposite sides of the room. I said hello to Terry's mother and stepfather, and his aunt, uncle, and cousins. I saw Terry saying hello to my parents, step-parents, siblings, and an aunt and uncle from Tucson. Friends of the family had flown in for the party, people who watched me grow up, along with Peter, my first serious boyfriend, and Donna, my best friend from high school. Add all of our friends from Seattle and Vashon Island and it was quite a crowd. Terry and I didn't do much for the first hour but say hello, kiss people, and accept hugs—and that's not easy for me. I don't like to be hugged, but what was I supposed to tell people who've been hugging me since I was an infant? They traveled halfway across the continent for our anniversary party—how could I refuse to hug them?

We worked our way around opposite edges of the Chinese Room, eventually backing into each other in the middle of the ballroom. We had been so busy greeting people that neither of us had a drink, something my eagle-eyed sister spotted from across the room. She came up and asked us if she could get us something and a minute later she was back with two glasses of wine.

Our wedding reception was not as grand as my grandparents', perhaps a little grander than my parents', but doubtless the first in either of our families' histories to feature a wedding cake topped by two golden cocks—roosters, thank you very much, not phalli—instead of a bride and groom. And it was definitely the first big wedding reception in either family's history where the guests didn't know they were at a wedding reception. We had decided to keep our marriage in Vancouver a secret.

We told D.J. that we didn't want to tell anyone at the party about the wedding because they would feel bad about not bringing us wedding gifts, and, being six, he fell for it. The ability to mollify your child with a harmless but effective lie is something else I'm going miss as D.J. grows older. I did actually feel funny about making an announcement because we had specifically invited our friends and family to an anniversary-party-pretending-to-be-a-wedding-reception, not an actual wedding reception. I was content to let our party be a wedding-reception-pretending-to-be-an-anniversary-party-pretending-to-be-a-wedding-reception, the Victor/Victoria of wedding receptions.

And I wasn't sure I wanted to be congratulated for marrying Terry when our marriage had been seized at the border on the way back home yesterday. We may be married in Canada, but our party was in Seattle, and we're citizens of the United States—second-class citizens, but still citizens. Calling our party a wedding reception would have been dishonest. It felt better to celebrate what we had, the thing that no one could take away from us—the last ten years—than to celebrate something that had been taken from us the moment we crossed back into the United States.

So we decided to let our families and friends celebrate our ten years together. It was the party they were invited to. It was all we could legally celebrate.

Terry and I stepped out onto the terrace that stretches all the way around the Chinese Room after everyone sat down to dinner. We weren't missed. Since it wasn't a wedding reception, there wasn't a head table. It was beautiful night, clear and still, unseasonably warm and dry for February in Seattle. City lights were twinkling all around us, ferries making their way back and forth across Puget Sound, a hint of red behind the tops of the Olympic Mountains to the west.

We stood and watched through the windows as our worlds collided at the round tables set up in the Chinese Room. Our friends were sitting with our relatives; my dad and stepmother were chatting with Terry's mother and stepfather; my brothers were laughing at a story being told by David, our friend with a playroom/dungeon in his basement. D.J. sat next to Cody, teaching him how to use chopsticks.

Because it was so much brighter in the Chinese Room than it was on the balcony, we could see in but our guests couldn't see out. "Crazy," I said, nodding toward the crowd. I watched the Chinese waiters carry out trays of Chinese food, past the bowls of fortune cookies set out on side tables, as our guests picked up the black and red lacquered chopsticks at their place settings. I wondered what the cooks, bartenders, and waiters thought. Setting up a Chinese banquet in the Chinese room, they probably assumed the guests at the anniversary party they were working would be Chinese. Then at six o'clock the room filled up almost entirely with white people. And when the time came to cut the cake—the black-and-red cake with little Chinese lanterns hanging underneath the top tier and two golden cocks sitting on top—two men in jeans and button-down shirts would step forward to do the honors.

Terry put his arm around my waist and we moved away from the windows. We leaned against a column, and looked out at the city.

After a short silence, Terry put his hands on my shoulders and looked at me with his big, blue eyes.

"I marry you," he said.

"I marry you," I replied.

My mom came out and joined us on the balcony a few moments later, D.J. and Cody trailing along behind her.

"There you are!" she said. "Come inside! You need to cut the cake."

"I thought we'd wait a few minutes—"

"I'm sorry, my dears, but you have guests with small children and it's getting late and they can't leave until after you two cut the cake!"

"There's something we should probably tell you first," I said. "We—"

"Got married," my mother said, cutting me off with a wave of her hand. "I know. Stop tormenting the children and go cut the cake."

"How did you know?" I said.

"Did you tell Grandma, D.J.?" Terry asked.

"Daaaaaaaaaaaaaad," D.J. said. "No!"

"Your son is good at keeping secrets for a six-year-old," Mom said. "Your passports were on the counter in your kitchen, you're both wearing rings . . ." Mom said. "I'm an old lady but I'm not a senile old lady."

"I want cake!" Cody said, tugging at his grandmother's skirt.

"Inside, you two," Mom said. "Your guests are waiting."

After all this buildup, to say nothing of the considerable expense, I'm sad to report that our cake was a disappointment. It looked beautiful, but the cake itself was dry and the food coloring used to dye the frosting black and red turned everyone's tongues an alarming shade of purple. The fortune cookies, however, were a hit. I had chosen five quotes for our fortune cookies. There were two anti-gay fortunes:

> If a man also lie with mankind, as he lieth with a woman, both of them have committed an abomination.
> —THE OLD TESTAMENT

> If gays are granted rights, next we'll have to grant them to people who sleep with St. Bernards.
> —ANITA BRYANT

Two pro-gay fortunes:

> The important thing is not the object of love, but the emotion itself.
> —GORE VIDAL

Homosexuality is god's way of insuring that the truly gifted aren't burdened with children.

—SAM AUSTIN

And one neutral fortune:

Don't marry the person you think you can live with; marry only the individual you think you can't live without.

—DR. JAMES C. DOBSON

When I handed some fortune cookies to my dad, I told him they were designed with him in mind. They were, to borrow a phrase, "fair and balanced," fortune cookies by Fox News. My favorite was the neutral one. James Dobson is the prominent anti-gay conservative leader I mentioned earlier. While I can't generally abide anything that comes out of James Dobson's mouth, his quote amused me. "Don't marry the *person* you think you can live with," Dobson says, "marry only the *individual* you think you can't live without." Dobson isn't usually so vague about gender when discussing marriage. He almost sounds like a women's studies professor.

A friend who wanted to introduce me to her new boyfriend pulled me away from my father. When I turned back around, my dad was entertaining a small group of our gay friends with a story from my childhood. As I listened to him, I was thinking about what Andrew Sullivan had to say about the politics of repression. Social conservatives "want to create a shadow class of people operating somehow in a cultural and social limbo," the lives of gay people devalued, our relationships denigrated. "That strategy may have worked as long as gay people cooperated—by staying in the closet, keeping their heads down, playing the euphemism game—but the cooperation is over."

It was clear at our party that it isn't only gay people who refuse to cooperate anymore. The gay people in our lives who gathered at the Chinese Room and later that night at Re-bar—our gay friends, two of my exes, my gay co-workers—were outnumbered five to one by the straight people who came to celebrate our anniversary. Our straight friends and family members don't want us living in cultural and social limbo anymore either, even the Bush voters among them, and they refuse to cooperate with the Dobsons and Bauers and Falwells.

—18—

Loose Ends

The plan was to exchange vows, slip the rings on each other's fingers, and wear them for the day. Then we were going to take the rings off, and put them away. They would be keepsakes, mementos of that crazy day we got married up in Canada. They certainly weren't meant to be rings we wore every day. They were *skull* rings, for crying out loud. Not even Marilyn Manson would wear them every day.

But we found we couldn't take them off. After saying our "I dos"—the same words our parents had said to each other, the same words our grandparents had said to each other—neither of us had the heart to remove our rings. Terry would ask me when I was going to take mine off, and I would ask him when he was going to take his off. It was like a game of chicken. Who would remove his wedding ring first?

Days quickly turned into weeks, and weeks turned into months. The rings stayed on. Okay, I thought, maybe something had changed. It wasn't just my fear of jinxing things that kept a cheap and ugly skull ring on my finger, although that was a consideration. Something else was at work. When we put on those rings we made the same commitment my grandparents made and, however imperfectly, managed to keep. It was the same commitment my parents had made, a commitment I believe they kept, even if they didn't make it to the finish line at Maloney's Funeral Home. The rings D.J. had picked out for us symbolized our commitment, the promise we made each other, and if we hadn't exactly been transformed, they certainly had. They meant something now, somehow.

With any luck, however, we won't be wearing skull rings when we cross the finish line. Three months after we got married, I was back in Chicago for Memorial Day weekend. Walking down Michigan Avenue, I passed a C. D. Peacock's, the jewelry store where my grandparents' wedding bands and wedding cake toppers came from. I thought C. D. Peacock's had gone out of business, but I was wrong. They had closed their original shop, the one in the Palmer House Hotel, but there were still four other Peacock's in the Chicago area. A month later when we were passing through Chicago on our way to Saugatuck, Terry and I stopped at C. D. Peacock's and bought some real wedding bands—platinum, not silver, this time, and no skulls.

When we got home we tucked our serious wedding bands away in the dark green box with my grandmother's porcelain cake toppers. We keep the box behind some books on the shelves in our living room. If the commitment we've made to each other is ever recognized in the United States, or if we do decide to move to Canada, we'll take our platinum bands out of that box and put them on. Until then, we're going to keep wearing our skull rings, the rings D.J. picked out for us, the rings neither of us have the heart to remove.

Oh, and we got our tattoos, too. They're pretty hot. But don't tell my mom.

About the Author

Dan Savage is the author of *The Kid*, *Savage Love*, and *Skipping Towards Gomorrah*. He is also the author of the internationally syndicated advice column "Savage Love," and the editor of *The Stranger*, Seattle's largest alternative weekly newspaper. He lives in Seattle, Washington, with his son, D.J., a deaf, brain-damaged, one-eyed poodle named Stinker, and his husband, Terry.